Author information

Claire Bateson MBA, BA (Hons) is a Fellow of the *ifs* *School of Finance* and a chief examiner and moderator. Having worked in the financial services industry for over 20 years, Claire now runs her own consultancy, Cobalt Advantage Ltd, providing specialist training solutions and management development.

Institute of Financial Services™

Certificate in Retail Banking Conduct of Business

Claire Bateson

The Institute of Financial Services is a division of the **ifs** *School of Finance*, a registered charity, incorporated by Royal Charter.

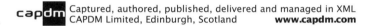 Captured, authored, published, delivered and managed in XML
CAPDM Limited, Edinburgh, Scotland   **www.capdm.com**

Contents

Module overview

There are two questions that need to be addressed before commencing with the study text:

◆ What is a retail customer?

◆ What is retail banking?

Financial service organisations tend to have differing views on the answers to these questions, so let us first see what definitions are available to us.

In the Banking Conduct of Business Sourcebook (BCOBS), the Financial Services Authority (FSA) defines a **retail banking customer** as:

◆ a consumer;

◆ a micro-enterprise, ie one that:

   — employs fewer than ten persons;

   — has a turnover or an annual balance sheet that does not exceed €2m;

   — may include self-employed persons, family businesses, partnerships, and associations regularly engaged in economic activity — the latter may include clubs and societies;

◆ a charity with an annual income of less than £1m; or

◆ a trustee of a trust that has a net asset value of less than £1m.

Logically it would follow that retail banking is the provision of banking facilities to these types of customer and the appropriate products and services that they use. This will be through a variety of **delivery channels**: branch, telephone, Internet and mobile technology.

However, some financial services providers do not include micro-enterprises — nor, possibly, charities' or trustees' accounts — within their retail business. Instead, these accounts are managed by the **corporate arm** of the organisation, perhaps because it is not a large part of their business and they prefer to keep the staff expertise within one area.

Some providers will include smaller enterprises, charities and trustees (say, with a turnover under £1m) within the retail bank but they will not be managed by the same group of staff as the 'consumer' group. There is a rationale for doing this, as it can be argued that the requirements of these smaller businesses are similar to the requirements of the 'personal' consumer group. It is also possible for employees to move between roles as their careers progress, taking valuable experience with them.

A further reason for using the £1m cut-off is that other organisations within the financial services sector use this limit. An example is the **Financial Ombudsman Service**, which customers can contact if they are unhappy with the outcome of a complaint they have made to their provider.

So, for the purposes of this text we will be covering **financial services organisations that provide banking or building society services** to:

◆ personal consumers;

◆ micro-enterprises that:

    — employ fewer than ten persons;

    — have a turnover or an annual balance sheet that does not exceed €2m;

    — may include self-employed persons, family businesses, partnerships, associations, clubs and societies;

◆ charities with an annual income of less than £1m; and

◆ trustees of a trust that has a net asset value of less than £1m.

We will make the distinction between **private limited companies** and **public limited companies** for completeness, even though the latter are outside the scope of our definition above. The main focus of the text will, however, be on the **personal consumers**, as for many retail banking organisations this will form the larger part of their business.

The changing face of UK financial regulation

The Conservative–Liberal Democrat coalition government is introducing fundamental change to the system of financial regulation in the UK. The headline points are as follows.

◆ The 'tripartite' system of regulation, introduced by the Labour government in 1997, comprising the Bank of England, the Financial Services Authority and the Treasury, is being discontinued.

◆ A new independent Financial Policy Committee (FPC) will be established at the Bank of England to anticipate and prevent macro (ie large-scale) issues that could threaten the economy or financial markets. The FPC will be accountable to Parliament. An interim FPC was created in February 2011 in order to carry out preparatory work for the establishment of the permanent body; it has also begun the work of identifying and monitoring specific risks and recommending corrective action.

◆ The Prudential Regulation Authority (PRA), a subsidiary of the Bank of England, will be responsible for microprudential regulation of firms that carry significant risks on their balance sheets, ie deposit-takers, insurers and some investment firms.

◆ The Financial Conduct Authority (FCA) will be responsible for conduct of business regulation across the financial services sector. (This authority had the provisional title of the Consumer Protection and Markets Authority until February 2011.)

◆ The PRA and the FCA will jointly take over the FSA's former responsibilities in relation to the Financial Services Compensation Scheme. The FCA will assume the FSA's former responsibilities in relation to the Financial Ombudsman Service (FOS) and the Money Advice Service (previously known, until April 2011, as the Consumer Financial Education Body). The Money Advice Service will play a key role in improving financial capability.

At the time of writing (March 2011), the government continues to consult on and develop its proposals. A draft Bill is scheduled for publication in spring 2011; the aim is to enact legislation to bring the new structures into operation by the end of 2012.

> **Notes for students**
>
> Please note that all Institute of Financial Services' assessments in the area of regulation are based on fact and standing legislation. Students will not, therefore, be assessed on aspects of regulation that are not confirmed by underpinning legislation. The Institute will publish updates to its learning materials for key regulatory issues and will advise students, in a reasonable timeframe, of the dates when this content will be assessed.

Topic 1
Common types of retail customer

Learning objective

After studying this topic, students should be able to demonstrate an understanding of the common types of retail customer and the key differences between them.

Introduction

The customer is the starting point for retail financial services providers when they are considering generating income from sales and service (ie how they interact with customers, rather than what products they offer). In the UK, excluding deposits of foreign currencies, £1,968bn was deposited in banks and building societies in 2009 by UK residents (*source:* Office for National Statistics), so we can see that the customer is of prime importance to the UK banking sector and national income. This topic sets the scene for the remainder of the text and introduces a number of themes we will return to in later topics.

We need to remember that there are a variety of **retail customers**, both personal and business, and each type, as we shall see below, has a defined legal status. A distinct legal entity is known as a '**legal person**' and can enter into contracts or be sued in a court of law. It is important to remember that a 'legal person' can be an individual operating in a personal capacity, or a group of individuals acting in a formal capacity, such as trustees. It can also be an organisation such as a limited company, which is deemed to be a separate 'legal person' from the people who run it.

Whatever type of customer we are considering, most will have a bank account for the simple purpose of being able to deposit money they have received and withdraw it in settlement of bills. Holding a bank account gives access to a range of other services that will satisfy life-cycle needs, wants and aspirations, which we will look at further in section 2.2.

1.1 Personal banking

People need to be able to receive their **income**, whether this is in the form of wages, salary, benefits, pensions or investment income. They will also use different **payment systems**, whether this is cash, payment facilities available through a bank account, electronic payments or a payment card. Before looking at the various types of bank account, let us consider how people might use these payments systems.

People who use **cash** may, broadly, fall into four groups.

◆ **Opportunity-seekers**, who like to have cash in their pocket for emergencies or opportunities. These people may be good at negotiating a better price for 'cash' and prefer to use payment systems that do not require a bank account.

◆ **Older people,** who grew up at a time when financial products such as credit and debit cards did not exist and are in the habit of using cash. They probably keep a lot of cash in the house and use it for most, if not all, of their payments. Many do not trust or understand electronic payments.

◆ **People who do not have bank accounts** – there are at least 1.75m adults in the UK who do not have an account at a bank or building society. They are generally known as the **unbanked**. They tend to be people with no family history of using bank services and they are more likely to have a low income or be unemployed. Since they do not have a bank account, they have limited access to services such as cheques, direct debits or payment cards. They receive and pay all transactions in cash. Many people in this group now have to open bank accounts because it is government policy to pay benefits by electronic direct transfer.

◆ **Members of the 'black economy'**, ie people who are working illegally, not declaring their income for tax purposes, or trading in some illegal product. They are forced to use cash to avoid leaving records of their illegal transactions. They may also be people involved in **money laundering** who are trying to get 'illegal' money into the financial services system.

Activity

> Cash still remains popular and its use has not declined in the same way that cheque usage has. In 2009 the transaction volume for cash was £266bn, representing 23 per cent of all payments made by consumers (*source*: UK Payments Administration).
>
> What are the disadvantages of using cash?

Some people are excluded from mainstream financial provision and suffer from **financial exclusion**. They may not be able to access accounts offered by financial services providers because they:

◆ have a bad credit history (because they have defaulted on lending in the past);

◆ choose not to use a financial services provider – perhaps because they don't trust them; or

◆ do not understand the products and systems or their own needs for financial services.

Understanding financial needs and how to deal with them is called **financial literacy**. Financial exclusion and poor financial literacy are surprisingly widespread problems in the UK and we shall look at this in more detail in section 2.1. The government has brought in a number of initiatives to deal with these problems, such as:

◆ seeking commitments from the financial services industry that it will support **basic** banking services for the financially excluded, even though lower profits may be made on these accounts; and

◆ public consumer education, such as that provided by the Money Advice Service (formerly the Consumer Financial Education Body).

People open bank accounts for a variety of reasons.

◆ Some people like to feel **in control** of their money and to have records of their income and outgoings. Having a chequebook and receiving bank statements allows them to know exactly how much money they have at any point in time. They can check how much income they are receiving and how much they are spending, and as a result they may feel that they are less likely to buy something they cannot afford. They might not like to be in debt. Having a bank current account also opens up other services to them, such as direct debits to pay utility bills.

◆ People who want **convenience** can use automatic payments and let technology manage their money for them, for example by using standing orders and direct debits for bill payments. This form of payment is especially suitable for people with regular habits. It means that they do not have to remember to pay regular bills or transfer money into a savings account, as it is done for them. They can check the transactions afterwards on their bank statement. Many utility companies provide incentives for customers to use the direct debit system (which is less costly for the utility company) by giving discounts off quarterly bills.

◆ People who want to use **credit** can arrange an overdraft on their current account, or use a credit card to finance their purchases. They can repay what they owe when they can afford it. They can also arrange a loan or hire purchase and make their repayments by setting up a direct debit on their current account.

◆ Payment cards provide people with an **easy method of payment**. This is convenient, enables them to pay for larger items, and can be used abroad. Cards also give users a period of credit, which they can prolong if they cannot afford to repay when the statement arrives.

◆ Some people, such as those with a hectic lifestyle, those who live in isolated areas, or those who work shifts, find it difficult to visit a branch and prefer the convenience offered by **telephone and online banking**. They can check their balance, make transfers, pay bills, and set up standing orders over the phone, either by using the telephone keypad or by talking to a customer adviser. They may also want to access their account online and make payments this way. In the future, payments may be made using mobile phones in much the same way.

We can see that different **services** appeal to the different **needs and attitudes** of individuals: one size does not fit all. Different people choose different ways of making payments and this also applies to the other financial services they choose — for example, methods of saving and borrowing. This will affect whether they choose to have a bank account and what **add-on services** they will take after opening their account.

Activity

> How do you use your bank account?
>
> Which of the types of customer listed above are you?
>
> When considering the customer visiting the branch, perhaps opening an account for the first time, how would you assess which of these types of customer they are likely to be?
>
> List the factors a customer might consider when choosing a provider with which to open a bank account.

Banks will also **segment** or divide their customer offerings to appeal to individuals with similar attributes, in order to facilitate the delivery of services appropriate to that segment. We will look at this topic again in section 2.2.1. The following case study shows how one bank has addressed **customer segmentation** in rather an exclusive way.

> ### Case study – HSBC, Poole branch
>
> In April 2007 HSBC announced that, from June, *only* wealthy customers who qualified for the bank's 'Premier' service would receive service from branch staff at its Canford Cliffs branch in Poole, Dorset. The branch was located in the small seaside village of Canford Cliffs, which contains the Sandbanks enclave and marina, one of the most expensive areas of Britain.
>
> The qualifying criteria for an HSBC Premier account was to have either £50,000 in savings or investments, a £75,000 income with a £100,000 mortgage, or a £200,000 mortgage. The monthly fee was £19.95. The area was home to a number of wealthy residents and it was at these customers that HSBC was aiming its service.
>
> Many of the other banks offer a premier service that includes a relationship manager, some of whom are branch based, some available by telephone. Some banks offer services to high-net-worth customers through different brands. For example, Royal Bank of Scotland offers its service through the private bank Coutts & Co.
>
> HSBC has 48 other Premier branches around the country, but they are all situated within existing branches. Canford Cliffs was to be the only branch available exclusively to Premier customers.

We can see that by 'extreme' segmentation of this sort a provider excluded a large proportion of its customer base.

Activity

> How appropriate do you think this segmentation exercise was?
>
> Why do you think it is not cost effective to offer this type of service to every customer?

Having looked at some of the background relating to personal banking, we will go on to examine the various types of personal account that can be opened.

1.1.1 Sole accounts

A personal customer is an individual acting on their own behalf for their own benefit and purpose. An account opened by someone specifically for their own use is also known as a **sole account**. Bank accounts are open to anyone and everyone (albeit subject to conditions in some cases). Financial services providers actively encourage the opening of accounts for the very young to establish a connection with that person at an early age. Customers tend to be very loyal even though the choice of bank is enormous. The individual is responsible for the operation of the account and is solely responsible for any debts that may be incurred, or loans taken out.

A personal account should only be used in respect of personal finances. Where any funds in the account relate to a business, then the customer is not acting in their personal capacity, and they should be asked to open a separate business account. This is so that the bank can charge the correct tariff for the business account and the customer has access to the relevant services.

A personal customer's banking needs vary as they go through life; the products and facilities they need may change according to their age and circumstances (often described as their 'life stage', which will be covered in section 2.2).

Activity

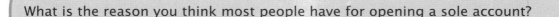

> What is the reason you think most people have for opening a sole account?

1.1.2 Joint accounts

A **joint account** is one that is opened in the name of two or more persons in their own capacity. Each account holder acts for themselves as well as acting for the other party or parties to the account. The most common example of this is where spouses or life-partners open an account together, perhaps for joint household expenditure.

Signing instructions are defined at the account opening stage, although they can be varied at any time. The bank receives instructions (a **mandate**) that set out who will have signing capacity on the account. All parties to the account will sign the mandate, and it will specify whether the signatories are one person only, any of the parties, all of the parties, or a set number of them, should there be more than two. For larger accounts the signatory may be one specific person, as well as any number of the others. It is possible for personal accounts to have more than two people responsible for the account. This may be where, for example, four students share a house and they want an account through which they can run the expenses of their house.

The account holders are **jointly and severally** liable for any debts incurred on the account. This means that if one of the account holders incurs a debt on the account, the other account holders will still be liable to repay it.

1.1.3 Accounts for minors

A **minor** is considered to be a person **under the age of 18**, ie who has not reached the 'age of majority' (power to vote in an election and be legally viewed as an adult). It is possible for a minor to open a bank account, and this is actively encouraged by the banks to ensure supplies of future customers. Often, a bank offers a range of accounts, designed for children of different ages.

Restrictions are imposed on the transactions that can be undertaken on a minor's account, and often the parents of the minor are asked to provide a guarantee to secure any potential debts.

The prime consideration is the minor's ability to enter into a contract that may lead to the account being overdrawn. Banking law is clear on the subject and relates mainly to what a minor can or cannot do. Minors are allowed to borrow for the purchase of 'necessities' (such as food or clothing), but not for 'luxury' items (such as an iPod). In practice, the accounts made available to minors do not usually allow overdrafts because, in the majority of cases, the debt would be unenforceable.

Some providers offer current accounts that offer cash card facilities at automatic teller machines (ATMs), but without the facility to issue cheques. The account is therefore maintained in credit, as the ATM will not pay out unless there are sufficient funds in the bank account. Cards can also be used to pay for goods and services at retail outlets, with confirmation at the point of sale that the account will not go overdrawn.

When a customer attains the age of majority, a bank can offer its full range of banking services and make use of new sales opportunities.

Activity

> For your bank, list the different types of personal account that are available and the type of customer at which each is aimed.
>
> Compare this with the personal accounts offered by a competitor financial services provider.

1.2 Business accounts

It is unlikely that there are many businesses that can run on a purely cash basis, so anyone starting a business will have to consider what they want from their provider. The main facilities will be a selection of the following, depending on the business and the markets in which it operates.

◆ **Money transmission services** – a business needs a method of paying wages and salaries, and for larger payrolls it is more efficient to use electronic means that will deposit funds directly to employees' bank accounts. Some businesses also like to be able to make payments directly to suppliers through the electronic clearing system, and in the same way businesses may receive payments by direct credit. Cheques and cash, however, need to be paid in at a bank's premises.

◆ **Working capital** – businesses need day-to-day funds to bridge the gap between money due from customers and payments to be made to suppliers and employees. Some businesses will take this in the form of overdraft facilities from their bank, in the same way that a personal customer uses an overdraft for day-to-day personal expenditure.

◆ **Capital investment** – if a business wants to grow, it sometimes needs to make an investment in resources such as plant, machinery, equipment or more employees. It may approach its bank for the funds to do this on a longer-term loan basis.

◆ **Protection from risk** – businesses can be subject to a number of risks and banks can provide insurance to cover these. For example, there may be a risk to premises from fire, flood or theft, which, if they occurred, could cause significant interruption to the business.

◆ **Foreign business services** – this may be as simple as sending money to suppliers overseas but could include foreign export services such as letters of credit for overseas trade.

◆ **Treasury services**– some businesses are so large that they have to manage large sums of money on a daily basis. Treasury services can provide transaction, investment and information services for chief financial officers or treasurers.

◆ **Business advice** – most businesses will have a named relationship manager who can give advice and help to the people who run the business.

Activity

What services do businesses visiting a branch use most frequently?

Which services are less frequently used?

1.2.1 Types of business

One term that is often found within business is **'SME'**. This stands for **small to medium-sized enterprises** and refers to companies whose headcount of employees or turnover falls below certain limits. Generally speaking, in the UK companies with fewer than 50 employees are classed as 'small' and those with fewer than 250 are classed as 'medium'.

In most economies, smaller enterprises are much greater in number than larger ones. In the European Union, SMEs comprise approximately 99 per cent of all business organisations and employ between them about 65m people. In many sectors, SMEs are also responsible for driving innovation and competition.

Another term that will be seen is **micro-enterprise**. This can be a sole proprietor, partnership or limited company that employs fewer than ten people and with turnover of less than €2m. It is likely that many businesses of this type have accounts with retail banks.

Activity

> List the reasons why banks provide relationship managers for business accounts but not for most personal accounts.

The legal form that a business takes — the rules that govern the way it is owned and run — have an impact on its legal status and on the types of financial product that are suitable for it. We will now look at the different types of business from a 'legal persons' perspective.

1.2.2 Sole proprietors

A **sole proprietor** (sometimes known as a **sole trader**) is an individual acting in a business capacity. This person may be starting up in business and opening a business account for the first time. As that person's business expands, they may take on a partner and want to convert that business into a partnership, or even a limited company. The type of account they require will change as well.

A sole proprietor has an account that is similar to a personal account, as the person conducting the account is solely liable for any debts or loans incurred. It differs from a personal account in that the source of funds is from a business. Typical sole proprietor's accounts might include the local plumber or electrician, as well as local corner shops. It is advantageous from the proprietor's point of view to keep the personal and business finances separate. This ensures that when the end of the financial year comes it is easier to identify the transactions that relate to the business, thus allowing their accountant to make the necessary returns to HM Revenue and Customs for **tax purposes**.

It is often said that the only difference between a business account and a personal account is that a business account attracts **bank charges** and the personal account does not. Similarly, a business loan is essentially no different from a personal loan. While some banks may argue over the subtleties between the two, when they are lending to a sole trader they are lending to an individual. If they had to recover money because of a bad debt they can only approach the individual, because the individual *is* the business.

A sole proprietor may be an employer (for instance, a plumber may employ an apprentice), with some taking on a number of employees. This does not mean that employees become liable for any debts incurred, even if they are allowed to sign on the account, as these will remain the sole responsibility of the sole proprietor.

Their **additional needs** could be a business overdraft, business loans, credit cards and possibly some form of business protection. Banks assess **business lending** for a sole proprietor in a more detailed way than personal lending, as the success of the business to date and its likely performance in the future have to be taken into consideration, as well as the proprietor's personal creditworthiness.

A sole proprietor may want to **protect** their business in the event that they are unable to work and generate income. For instance, if they are unable to work they might have to pay someone to look after their shop or fulfil contracts on their behalf. An option would be to take out **insurance** for this situation. It would be taken out on the individual, although replacement income or a lump sum might be used to protect the business or the individual.

Anyone employing more than five people has to provide the opportunity for their employees to join a **stakeholder pension scheme**. The stakeholder pension market is one for which all banks will be keen to provide facilities. The **National Employment Savings Trust (NEST)** is a new low-cost pension scheme any employer can use from October 2012 in order to comply with new legal requirements. It is designed to address the needs of people who are largely new to pension saving.

Activity

> How does your organisation enable branch staff to tell the difference between a sole personal account and a sole proprietor's business account by looking at a statement or chequebook?

1.2.3 Partnerships

A **partnership** is an arrangement between people who are carrying on a business together for profit. A partnership is *not* a separate legal entity and the partners jointly own both the assets and the liabilities of the partnership. A partner has **unlimited liability** for the debts of the partnership, unless they are a limited liability partner – in this case their liability is usually limited to the amount of capital they have invested.

Partnerships should have a written agreement that sets out in detail the relationship between the partners, including the proportions in which they share the partnership's profits and what will happen when a partner leaves, retires or dies. The mandate is similar to that of a joint account as it can have a variety of different signing arrangements. The bank has a duty to conform strictly to these arrangements.

Partnerships can come in a variety of sizes, from two members to five hundred or more. The larger partnerships (with more than, say, thirty partners) are traditionally solicitors, accountants and estate agencies, although nowadays there is a tendency for these to be established as **limited liability partnerships (LLPs)** (see section 1.2.4). The very large partnerships (with, say, over a hundred partners) have different needs from the smaller ones, and it is common to see them banking centrally through a **corporate relationship manager**, although maintaining 'satellite accounts' at local branches. The central function will hold and maintain mandates for all of the satellites, passing them out to individual branches.

Solicitors and accountants are legally required to maintain **separate accounts** for business expenses and clients' money. It is common to see these designated as 'client account' and 'office account'.

Activity

> Why do you think it is important to keep clients' money separate from the money used in the running of the business?

For the types of small partnership accounts held in the retail bank network, needs will be similar to those of the sole trader, but because a few other parties are involved, the question of **business protection** becomes very important. If one partner dies, the survivor(s) may be left with a problem; the deceased's family will want their share of the business (ie the capital the deceased partner has invested) – either in cash, or as an ongoing concern. It is unlikely that the surviving partner(s) will have the cash to buy out the beneficiaries, and may not want them as business partners.

Partnership protection is **life assurance**, taken out by each partner in trust for the others. In the event of one partner's death, the surviving partner(s) will receive the lump sum via the trust, and can either buy out their partner's share, or use the cash as they wish. For a small partnership of two, being able to do this may be very important. However, for a long-established law firm with 500 partners, it may not be as critical to the business. There may be some agreement whereby, when an individual attains 'partner' status, the firm puts them onto a central register through an insurance company and insures the individual in a manner that ensures the capital taken out of the firm on death is replaced.

Larger partnerships may also provide **pension schemes** for the partners, as well as providing a **stakeholder pension scheme** if the partnership employs more than five people and does not have any other pension arrangements for them. The **NEST** scheme (see section 1.2) will be available from October 2012.

1.2.4 Limited liability partnerships

Since 2001, it has been possible to run a business as a **limited liability partnership (LLP)**. This means that partners have a **limited personal liability** if the business should collapse: their liability is limited to the amount that they have invested in the partnership, together with any personal guarantees they have given, for example to a bank that has made a loan to the business.

As with companies, limited liability partnerships have to be **registered** with Companies House; they are clearly more like companies than are standard partnerships but the taxation of LLPs is not the corporation tax regime that applies to companies. LLPs are **taxed** in the same way as other partnerships: each partner is taxed on a self-employed basis, with their individual share of the profits being treated as their own personal income and subject to income tax.

LLPs will require the traditional business account/loans alongside the need to protect the business against the risks of losing senior members of the partnership. Pension facilities can also be required, as outlined above.

1.2.5 Private limited companies (Ltd)

Companies are **legal entities**, quite separate from their shareholders or their individual employees. Shareholders of a limited company cannot be held personally responsible for the debts of the company, the limit of their **liability** being the amount that they have invested in company shares. This is the most they could lose if the company were to become insolvent with large debts and had to be wound up. In return for their investment, they are paid a **dividend** based on the **profits** of the company and according to how many shares they hold.

One of the main **benefits** of this type of limited company, and the public limited company that we shall cover in the next section, is that the **personnel can**

change, they can come and go, but the company itself remains as a legal entity and unchanged. Just because, say, the chief executive officer retires, it does not mean that the company ceases to be. It is also important when considering continuing banking facilities, especially lending, because the liability remains in the company's name rather than being the responsibility of the individuals involved. This means that the owners of the company can change, too, without having to renegotiate facilities.

However, a key feature of this type of company is that the **shares are not easily transferable**, as they are not listed on the stock exchange. This means the values may be difficult to assess, because if the holder wanted to sell them they would not have access to a ready market for them. Traditionally, many of these types of business have been owned by several members of a family, who would not be attracted to selling the shares.

The nature of the company, and the rules about what it can and cannot do, are set out in its **memorandum and articles of association**. In relation to a company's ability to borrow money, for example, the **memorandum** normally includes the **power to borrow**, but may place limits or restrictions on that power in terms of amounts or purpose. This will be significant if the company wishes to take out a mortgage or other form of loan.

The actions of the company are, of course, carried out by the people employed by it. When making a contract with a company or lending money to a company, it is essential to check that the persons committing the company to a particular course of action are authorised and empowered to do so.

The **articles of association** detail the working rules such as the powers, duties and appointment of directors; the transfer of shares and rights of shareholders; and the general conduct of the company at meetings.

A **certificate of incorporation** evidences the company's formation, and details about the company are held on the central registry at **Companies House**. This states the shareholding and shareholders, as well as listing the names and addresses of the directors and company secretary. Generally, a minimum of two people — usually a director and a company secretary — are required to run a company because one person is not permitted to act as both director and company secretary. However, the Companies Act 2006 amended the rules to allow private limited companies to exist with just one director so long as the company's articles did not expressly require a secretary. If one is required, then the sole director can appoint a corporate firm of company secretaries who will act for them when formalities have to be completed.

Historically, it has been necessary for the company's bank to have a copy of the memorandum and articles of association and to take copies at the time the account is opened. Lenders had to check if the company was authorised to undertake its current business (by checking the objects clause); that it could borrow money; and that the directors were authorised to allow the company to borrow to that amount. This changed in the Companies Act 1989 as it stated:

> 'a party to a transaction with a company is not bound to enquire as to whether it is permitted by the company's memorandum or as to any limitation on the powers of the board of directors to bind the company or authorise others to do so.'

Although most banks are happy to rely on this, some still insist on a resolution by the company when borrowing money, confirming that it is acting under the correct authorities.

A **mandate** for a company will not give a bank recourse to recover any money from those individuals who may have acted on behalf of the company. This is different from checking that the company has the power to borrow money, or that the directors are not allowing it to borrow over its pre-set limits.

The needs of a company are similar to those of a partnership, although if **protection** is taken out this will be done by the company to protect itself against something happening to one of its directors. This type of insurance is known as **key person insurance**. Larger limited companies may wish to make **other benefits** available to their staff and may need to offer **stakeholder pension** or **NEST** arrangements (see section 1.2.2)and **health insurance**.

Activity

> Obtain a mandate used for limited companies. How does it differ from those used for partnerships?

1.2.6 Public limited companies (plcs)

Public limited companies (plcs) are, as their name suggests, able to sell their shares to the public via a stock exchange. The Companies Act specifies that the share capital of a plc should be a minimum of £50,000. We all recognise the larger plcs — household names such as Vodafone, Barclays Bank, or Tesco — with share capital in the billions of pounds. Most plcs, however, are far, far smaller in terms of capitalisation, employees and profits. Their origins normally lie in a successful limited company that has reinvested its profits and achieved long-term growth. Generally the size of a plc will not be immediately obvious unless it is a recognised name, but an examination of the audited accounts will make it very clear.

A plc obtains a **trading certificate**, rather than the certificate of incorporation that is required for a limited company.

The term '**flotation**' normally means obtaining a **listing** on the stock market. Typically a company floats first on the **Alternative Investment Market (AIM)**, which started in 1995, as a stepping stone to a full listing on the **London Stock Exchange**. It does this by meeting some standard requirements and being able to state that appropriate measures are both in place and have been completed. These measures are slightly less than those required by companies that apply for a full listing on the stock market. 'Going public', 'going for a listing', or 'floating' does not guarantee that the company will continue to be successful, although it does help to have a history of well-maintained growth and regular profits. The 1990s saw the 'dotcom' boom in which many newly created plcs of little substance floated, only to crash a relatively short time later.

The plc can sell its shares to members of the public (which a private limited company is barred from doing). A **board of directors** runs a plc. The members of the board (who will probably be shareholders as well) are appointed by **shareholders** at the annual general meetings. The directors are responsible for the overall strategy and direction of the company; in most cases, the day-to-day matters may be in the hands of the **chief executive officer** (commonly known as the CEO) and other employed managers.

In the UK's largest plcs, **institutional investors**, rather than individuals, often hold the majority of the share capital. These institutional investors (fund managers from large pension funds and investment houses) will often own sufficient shares to have a board member by right and that individual will represent the interests of the institutional investor. It is highly unlikely that the CEO of a major plc will also be the majority shareholder.

Activity

> In your organisation, who manages the relationship with these large accounts?
>
> Why is it likely that specialist knowledge and expertise is required?

1.3 Other non-personal customers

There are a variety of other accounts that are designated 'other non-personal' accounts: that is, they are neither personal accounts nor business accounts. Examples might include the local Women's Institute, football team, youth centre or hospice charity. Their requirements differ depending on the specific type of 'legal persons' involved and the purpose of their role. It is likely that the accounts will maintain good credit balances and the people running them will also have other accounts with the provider. In general this means that they are good customers and well worth looking after.

The first two instances we shall look at involve individuals entrusted with looking after funds for the benefit of others, where the person giving the money no longer has any control over it.

1.3.1 Trustees

A **trust** (also known as a **settlement**) is a method by which the owner of an asset (the **settlor**) can distribute or use that asset for the benefit of another person or persons (the **beneficiaries**) without allowing them control over the asset while it remains in trust. Depending on the nature of the trust, the beneficiaries may eventually become the absolute owners of the asset. Trusts were typically set up to allow parents (or grandparents) to **pass assets on** to children, particularly in the event of the settlor's death while the children were relatively young. There also used to be some **tax advantages** to setting up a trust but the rules on this have been tightened in recent times.

The settlor is the person who creates the trust and originally owned the assets placed in the trust (the **trust property**). Once it is placed in trust, the asset is no longer owned by the settlor. A trust can either arise from the death of the settlor, having been created under the terms of a will, or from a wish by the settlor to establish a trust while they are living. In this case, once the trust is created, the settlor will have no rights to the property after that date (although a settlor may be a trustee).

The beneficiaries are the people or organisations that will benefit from the trust property. They may be named specifically or be referred to as a group, for example 'all my children'.

The **trustees** are the people, appointed by the settlor, who will take **legal ownership** of the trust property and administer the property under the terms of the **trust deed**. The trustees, who can include the settlor, are named in the trust deed. Trustees must be aged 18 or over and of sound mind. If a trustee dies, the remaining trustees, or their personal representatives, can appoint a new trustee.

◆ Trustees must act in accordance with the terms of the trust deed. If the trust deed gives them discretion to exercise their powers (for example, discretion over which beneficiaries shall receive the trust benefits), the **agreement** of *all* the trustees is required before a course of action can be taken.

◆ Trustees must act in the **best interests** of the beneficiaries, balancing fairly the rights of different beneficiaries if these should conflict. For example, some trusts provide income to certain beneficiaries and, later, distribution of capital to other beneficiaries; the chosen investment must preserve a fair balance between income levels and capital guarantee/capital growth.

In addition, under the Trustee Act 2000, trustees who exercise investment powers are required to:

◆ be aware of the need for suitability and diversification of assets;

◆ obtain and consider proper advice when making or reviewing investments;

◆ keep investments under review.

It will be the trustees who require **banking facilities** in order to make payments to the beneficiaries. They may also require access to **money market interest rates** if they have large amounts of cash within the trust, and they may require access to **investment services**. Should the trustees wish to **borrow** from their banker they will be **personally liable** for the debt. They have no power to charge assets of the trust unless they are authorised to do so under the terms of the trust.

1.3.2 Personal representatives

People who carry out the procedures necessary to distribute the **estate** (the assets less the liabilities) of someone who has died are known as the deceased person's **personal representatives**. Whether they are **executors** or **administrators** depends on whether the person who has died has made a will or not.

An **executor** is appointed when a **valid will** is held. For a will to be valid it must be:

◆ completed by a person over the age of 18;

◆ completed in writing; and

◆ properly executed.

The executor(s) apply for a **grant of probate**, which will allow them to distribute the estate of the deceased person (referred to as the '**testator**') in accordance with their wishes. The grant of probate gives the executors **legal authority** to act on behalf of the testator.

However, while it may be the deceased person's wish that a son, daughter or long-time family friend is appointed an executor, this does not mean that they have to take up the role. It is not uncommon for these people to waive the right and appoint solicitors to act for them. The role is time-consuming and can be onerous at a stressful time for those closest to the deceased. In many ways, appointing solicitors can be a good thing, as the estate is dealt with by professionals well versed in the requirements and impartial in decision-making.

If there is **no will** (or the will is invalid), a **grant of letters of administration** is issued to an appropriate person(s), who is known as the **administrator**. Once again, this may be a surviving spouse, son, daughter, or a member of the family, although it may be easier to appoint a professional to deal with the estate. Unlike a will, which gives the testator the opportunity of expressing their wishes as to how the estate is divided, a person dying without a will (**intestate**) does not have that luxury. Their estate is dealt with under the **laws of intestacy**, and divided accordingly.

◆ **If the deceased leaves a spouse but no children**: the spouse gets the first £450,000, plus half the remainder; the balance goes to the deceased's parents, or if they are dead, to the deceased's brothers and sisters.

◆ **If there is a spouse and children**: the spouse gets the first £250,000 − half of the balance goes to the children; the other half of the balance goes into a trust from which the spouse receives an income for life, but the capital goes to the children when the spouse dies.

◆ **If there are children, but no spouse**: the estate is shared equally among the children.

◆ **If there is no spouse or children**: the estate goes to the deceased's parents or, if they are dead, to the deceased's brothers and sisters.

With rising house prices, estates of relatively high values have become more commonplace. Anybody dying intestate in these circumstances could cause a great many of problems for the surviving relatives, and should the issue arise in open conversation with a customer they should be encouraged to make a will.

Executors and administrators can open an **account**, and this can be opened as a sole account or jointly. The mandate can be completed so that they may act together, or in a sole capacity. From a practical point of view, there is an issue with executors and administrators. When do they have the authority to open the account? As explained previously, they are appointed by grant of probate or letters of administration, although in law they cannot be called or act as executors or administrators until probate is granted, or the letters are issued. To have probate or letters issued there may have to be a **payment of inheritance tax**. So how can they pay fees and taxes if they cannot open an account into which to pay assets? Banks take a practical view in these circumstances, usually accepting a certified copy of the will as evidence of the requirements. However, where a person has died intestate, banks may be reluctant to help unless a known solicitor is acting for the administrators.

The bank may also help with a loan to pay inheritance tax (known as a **probate loan**). The personal representatives are **personally liable** for any borrowing and cannot give assets from the deceased's estate as security before probate or letters have been obtained. The lender would have to be satisfied of the integrity of the personal representatives, that the amount of inheritance tax is reasonable and that the advance can be repaid quickly from the realisation of assets held.

Activity

Research what process has to be followed when relatives inform the bank that one of its customers has died.

1.3.3 Charities

A charity is a **non-profit-making** organisation established to provide assistance to those in need. The largest are well-known names – Oxfam, the Red Cross, St John's Ambulance and Macmillan Cancer Relief, for instance. These larger charities have needs similar to those of a medium-sized company. On the other hand, there are many small charities established to help local causes or small groups.

Organisations must register with the **Charity Commission** in order to obtain **charitable status**. The Charity Commission exists to give the public confidence in the integrity of charities in the UK. It is a UK government organisation responsible to the courts for its decisions, and to the Home Secretary for the way it manages its resources.

A small charity may be run by just a few people, who are all volunteers, but charities can be huge organisations with large numbers of employees. Whatever their size, they will require the standard **business banking accounts**, and the larger charities will need more sophisticated services to enable them to **distribute funds**, whether in the UK or abroad. They will also have a number of **satellite offices** throughout the UK that will require banking services.

1.3.4 Clubs, associations and societies

A club, association or society is a gathering of people with a common goal and it can take a variety of forms and sizes. It could be a women's group gathering each Wednesday for a cup of coffee; a bikers' club meeting every Sunday for a ride in the country; a social club, or a sports club.

The larger clubs are run by committee, with rules, regulations and appointed representatives, although the smaller ones may be just one or two people organising a regular get together. Some clubs may be **companies limited by guarantee** and can be quite large – for example, the British Sub Aqua Club, the governing body for scuba diving in the UK, has a turnover of £3m.

However, in general, clubs, associations and societies are **not separate legal entities**, and cannot be sued for their debts. Individual members of the club, association or society are not personally responsible for any debts of the officers running the organisation. If the bank is lending to the organisation then it must ensure that somebody with the capacity to repay assumes **full liability**. The main needs are basic **business banking services**, with current and deposit accounts. The larger clubs may need more sophisticated services such as general **insurance** and **money management business services**.

Review questions

The following review questions are designed so that you can check your understanding of this topic.

The answers to the questions are provided at the end of these learning materials.

1. Why do customers prefer to have bank accounts rather than deal in cash?

2. What is the purpose of 'segmenting' the customer base?

3. Who is responsible for the debt on a personal joint account?

4. What are the potential problems with regard to lending to a minor?

5. What are the main facilities required from a business account?

6. What is the purpose of forming a limited liability partnership?

7. What are the differences between a private limited company and a public limited company?

8. Why might the holder of a large financial asset decide to put it into trust?

9. What are the dangers of not making a will?

10. List the banking facilities required by a large charity with a chain of retail outlets.

Topic 2

The range of customer backgrounds, needs, wants and aspirations

Learning objectives

After studying this topic, students should be able to demonstrate an understanding of the range of customer backgrounds, needs, wants and aspirations.

Introduction

In the last topic we considered the different types of customer and the various 'legal persons' that exist. We started to explore the needs of each of these entities and how financial services products can fulfil them.

We will now look at various aspects of personal finance, starting with **financial capability**. Now that more people are required to open bank accounts and use financial services, it has become obvious that some people lack the capability to deal with them and, as a result, make inappropriate choices. We will see how the government is trying to help those people and make the industry more accessible to all.

We will then consider how people pass through a '**life cycle**' and, depending on a variety of factors, will need different products and services during that journey. Moreover, not only do they have **needs** for particular services, they may also have **wants** – life goals that may affect their choices.

An individual's **attitude to risk** will also affect their choices. Attitudes will depend on past life experiences and a number of other influences, all of which will affect the types of financial services that they buy.

Finally, we shall consider briefly the **cultural and ethnic issues** that exist within the UK. These will impact on the financial services offered to customers, how they are offered and how they are received by customers.

2.1 Financial capability

Financial capability means being able to:

◆ manage your money;

◆ keep track of your finances;

◆ plan ahead;

◆ make informed decisions about financial products; and

◆ stay up to date about financial matters.

Financial capability is a broad concept, encompassing people's knowledge and skills to understand their own financial circumstances, along with the motivation to take action. Financially capable consumers find and use information, know when to seek advice and can understand and act on this advice. This leads to **greater participation** in the financial services market, driving competition and choice.

2.1.1 The scale of the challenge

The following extract from a speech by Ed Balls MP, then Economic Secretary to the Treasury, is indicative of the need to improve financial capability in the UK population.

'The scale of the challenge that we face is formidable. I am sure you have all seen the FSA's excellent baseline survey.

Some of the statistics bear repeating. Forty per cent of people sometimes or always run out of money at the end of the week or month. Ten per cent say they make no provision for planned expenditure, for example quarterly or annual bills. Some findings were even more worrying: 70 per cent had made no personal provision to cover an unexpected drop in income and over 90 per cent of individuals who had recently purchased stocks and shares perceived them to be 'no risk' or 'low-to-moderate risk' purchases.

Not all groups are equally capable (or incapable). The survey found that 18–30 year olds were the least capable in most areas, which is particularly worrying as we ask our young people to take on a lot of responsibility. While today's over 70s have also been highlighted as a vulnerable group, performing below average in terms of capacity for choosing financial products and for staying informed about financial matters.'

Source: Speech by Economic Secretary to the Treasury Ed Balls MP, at the Financial Capability Conference, 18 October 2006

As a result of this research the Labour government set out its long-term approach to financial capability in **Financial Capability: the Government's Long-Term Approach** (published 15 January 2007). The report set out the government's long-term aspirations to ensure that:

◆ all adults in the UK have access to high-quality generic financial advice to help them engage with their financial affairs and make effective decisions about their money;

◆ all children and young people have access to a planned and coherent programme of personal finance education, so that they leave school with the skills and confidence to manage their money well; and

◆ a range of government programmes is focused on improving financial capability, particularly to help those who are most vulnerable to the consequences of poor financial decisions.

The Consumer Financial Education Body (CFEB; renamed the Money Advice Service in April 2011) was launched in June 2010. It was tasked with leading the National Strategy for Financial Capability and delivering a national money guidance service. It brings together interested parties, including industry, consumer bodies, voluntary organisations, government and the media, with the aim of improving knowledge and understanding of personal finance. Its vision is better informed and more confident citizens, able to take greater responsibility for their financial affairs and choose products and services that meet their needs (source: www.cfebuk.org.uk).

Having a strategy in place to improve financial capability was deemed necessary for the following reasons.

◆ More than ever before, people are being asked to take **responsibility** for managing their finances. They are living longer and being expected to make choices about **long-term provision**, such as mortgages and pensions, at a relatively early age.

◆ People can find this daunting and confusing, particularly if they are struggling to manage debt or meet other commitments. Consumers who are knowledgeable about what is available are able to **shop around** and will **demand better products and services** from providers.

◆ The number and **complexity of choices** to be made has increased dramatically over the last 25 years. The long-term nature of many products means that assumptions made at the time a product, for example a pension, is sold may not be realised at maturity. People do not get many chances to make a repeat purchase and learn as they go along.

◆ Competition, technological advances and product innovation mean that the **range** of financial services offered has increased and become much more complex. The ways of accessing financial services have also changed, adding to the range of options people need to make choices about.

◆ Individuals are being required to take on more responsibility for their financial decisions. As we have seen, many are not equipped with the skills or knowledge to do so, and some groups are particularly **vulnerable**.

The National Strategy for Financial Capability aims to remedy this with a five-year plan to increase financial capability education, information and advice reaching targeted groups of consumers of priority need. This will be complemented by a range of resources to help consumers make better decisions.

The following headlines from the news section of the FSA's website show the impact of low levels of financial capability.

Final Demand – Debt and Mental Health

'The FSA has funded a new resource for health and social care professionals in partnership with Rethink and the Royal College of Psychiatrists. The 'Final Demand' booklet cites a shocking new statistic, showing one in two adults with debts also has a mental health problem.'

Source: www.fsa.gov.uk, 30 April 2009

Financial Capability and Wellbeing – new research

Last week we [the FSA] published Occasional Paper 34, which indicates that an improvement in financial capability leads to an improvement in psychological wellbeing. The results of the research suggest that moving from low to average levels of financial capability:

◆ increases psychological wellbeing by 5.6 per cent;

◆ increases life satisfaction by 2.4 per cent; and

◆ decreases anxiety and depression by 15 per cent.

The 2.4 per cent increase in life satisfaction is 12 times bigger than the impact of earning an extra £1000 a year.'

The research indicates that there is a real need for better financial capability to improve the quality of life of individuals and society as a whole. The impact of poor financial capability is affecting people's health and therefore their ability to improve their situation by finding stable employment and ways of dealing with the situation. Source: www.fsa.gov.uk,18 May 2009

2.2   The personal life cycle

People's **financial requirements** change over the course of their lifetime. We will consider the average **life cycle** and the sorts of experience that are common to most people's lives. Everyone will not necessarily experience such life events in the same order or within the same time frame. Differences can arise due to circumstances such as:

◆ the country in which people live, and its cultures and customs;

◆ their wealth, health and family situations;

◆ unforeseen or unexpected events.

Some things (such as growing up and getting old) are more fixed than others (such as getting married or changing career) and some people may face more changes in their life than others.

A personal customer's financial needs vary according to where they are in life (often described as their **life stage**), as each stage may require different products and facilities.

Activity

> Match the life event to the age range at which people are most likely to experience it.
>
> | Life event | Age range |
> | --- | --- |
> | 1. Getting your first part-time job | a. Mid 60s+ |
> | 2. Leaving home to live with friends or go to university | b. 20s–40s |
> | 3. Children leave home | c. Early 20s |
> | 4. Starting a family | d. 18–20 |
> | 5. Needing to live on a pension | e. 50s–60s |
> | 6. Getting your first full-time job | f. 13–16 |

Table 2.1 shows the 'typical' stages of a life cycle. All of the age ranges given are approximate and, as we have said, may change between countries and cultures, and between different people in the same country or culture. For example, in some countries, formal schooling will start much later and may not extend beyond the age of 9 or 10. In some cultures, marriage and children are encouraged at an earlier age. People in the UK today are living longer than ever before. In 1950, a man aged 65 could expect to live on average to the age of 76; today, he can expect to live to 85 (source: http://www.dwp.gov.uk/policy/ageing-society/). However, in some countries, health and other problems may mean that **life expectancy** is much lower.

Table 2.1.   Typical stages during the life cycle

Life stage	Typical age range	Typical events
Birth and infanthood	0–2 yrs old	◆ Birth ◆ Learns to walk ◆ Learns to talk
Childhood – pre-school	2–5 yrs old	◆ Nursery and pre-school ◆ Makes friends ◆ Learns through play ◆ Develops communication skills
Childhood – school	5–12 yrs old	◆ Starts school ◆ Makes longer-term friends ◆ Learns skills such as reading and writing

Table 2.1. (cont.)   Typical stages during the life cycle

Teenager	13–19 years old	◆ Puberty and adolescence
		◆ School tests and examinations
		◆ Starts a part-time job
		◆ Goes to college or sixth form
		◆ Learns to drive
		◆ Relationships
		◆ May leave home
Young adult	18–25 yrs old	◆ Goes to university
		◆ Moves away from home
		◆ Qualifies
		◆ Starts a full-time job
Mature adult	26–40 yrs old	◆ Career promotions
		◆ Career changes
		◆ Marriage
		◆ Children
		◆ Buys property
		◆ Takes on a mortgage
		◆ Divorce
		◆ Redundancy
		◆ Starts a business
		◆ Illness
Middle age to late middle age	41–60 yrs old/55–65 yrs old	◆ Career promotions
		◆ Career changes
		◆ Children leave home
		◆ Divorce
		◆ Pays off mortgage
		◆ Redundancy
		◆ Illness
		◆ Early retirement
		◆ Retirement

Table 2.1. (cont.)   Typical stages during the life cycle

Old age	65 onwards	◆ Retirement
		◆ Becomes a grandparent
		◆ Loss of physical fitness
		◆ Poor health
		◆ Bereavement

Activity

> For each of the life stages make a list of the products that could be taken up by an individual or their parent or guardian.

2.2.1 Marketing and the life cycle

Life-cycle stages can be used in marketing to put people into **life-cycle categories** so that providers can target marketing and advertising accurately.

One current set of marketing categories includes those set out in Table 2.2.

Table 2.2.   Marketing categories

Marketing category	Category characteristics
Young children (0–5 years)	Parents of this category are targeted to do 'what is best' for the baby or toddler
'Tweens' (7–10 years)	Have no income of their own, but can use pester power to pursue products marketed to them. Typical products are toys and games, most heavily targeted as Christmas and other holidays approach
Proto-teens (11–14 years)	Income from pocket money and part-time work. Typical products that are targeted at this group are hair and body-related
Mid-teens (15–16 years)	Has more income. Typical products targeted are linked to more active social life
Old teens (17–18 years)	Seen as possible car drivers and property renters, but are frequently still at home, so benefit from continued financial support
College/ university students	More independent, but generally have a low income. Typical products targeted include take-away and fast food, music and travel deals
Trendy singles	Individuals often have good income, no dependants and few outgoings. They are targeted for fashion goods, expensive foods, cars, travel and entertainment

Table 2.2. (cont.)   Marketing categories

Nest invaders	Move back in with parents after time living away: maybe after university; maybe after a relationship breaks down. Have independent income, but are also backed by family spending power
Double income, no kids ('Dinkies')	Possibly married, have two good incomes, but have no dependants. They are targeted for products such as cars and long-haul holidays, eating out and credit cards
New parents	The income of a new parent is reduced, while outgoings are increased. Typical products targeted towards this category include 'family' cars and fixed-rate mortgages
Non-employed homemaker (with dependants aged under 12)	Traditionally, the homemaker is targeted, through daytime television, with leisure or entertainment products and 'bargains'
Employed homemaker (with dependants aged under 12)	Benefits from a reasonable income, but needs to pay more for childcare and transport. Financial products include life assurance to protect dependants, mortgages and pensions
Empty nesters	The dependants of this group of people have left home, so 'empty nesters' may decide to sell up and downsize their property. Utility bills and travel costs fall; they may take more holidays. Typical products targeted are leisure or comfort-related. Financial products include wills and investments
Grey market	The 'grey market' is seen as those who are retired but wealthy, with lots of disposable income. Typical products are, again, leisure or comfort-related

Segmenting the customer base into these life-cycle categories enables the marketing team to pinpoint the stage of the life cycle through which a person is currently passing. From information held about the customers, their account profiles and socio-demographic information, they will be able to **target** each segment with a range of products that are most likely to be suitable.

This information will include additional indicators such as:

◆ levels and patterns of spending;

◆ debt held and attitudes to debt;

◆ level of income;

◆ family size and structure;

◆ level of education;

◆ attitudes to risk (and to the future);

◆ propensity (tendency) to purchase;

◆ penetration of existing products sold.

Profiles can be created that can help providers to understand their customer base and target effort where it is most needed.

Activity

> How does an individual's attitude to debt affect the products a financial services provider can offer to them?

2.2.2 The financial consequences of lifestyle choices

Attitudes to debt, risk and patterns of spending are all factors in **lifestyle choices**. Making choices involves both monetary and non-monetary factors. In this section we will concentrate on the financial consequences of various lifestyle choices.

Consuming now and paying later: millions of people buy items now that they cannot actually afford by anticipating their future incomes and taking out a loan that they will pay back over the coming months or years. People who take out a personal loan or hire purchase, or who use their credit card extensively, should be aware of what might happen if they cannot make their repayments on time.

There is nothing wrong with using affordable credit. The one item that almost nobody can afford without borrowing is a house: the fact that so many people in the UK now own their homes is due to the huge expansion of the mortgage business, making it possible for them to finance such a large purchase. After the house come the furniture and fittings, the car, the foreign holiday, and the evening out at a restaurant.

At some point, it is advisable to draw the line and pay off the outstanding debts before making further commitments. Money borrowed today must be repaid tomorrow and cannot be spent on something else in the future. The economic crisis saw a fall in property prices and the availability of credit secured against homes dried up. The ability to pay off debts using equity in the home has reduced dramatically, leaving some people in a position of over-indebtedness and financial hardship.

Saving now for something bigger later: saving is often seen as a good thing that people do not do enough, rather like going on a diet or taking exercise. The money that most people save will be used to finance some expenditure they intend to make later. In the short term, they could be saving up for some piece of consumer expenditure, such as a holiday. In the medium term they may save up for a deposit on a house (which is a type of investment) and in the much longer term they save for their retirement. So saving is more or less the opposite of borrowing in that people spend less than they earn and wait until they have enough to pay for what they want.

Saving up for something instead of taking out a loan suits those who can be patient or who are unwilling to take on the risk of borrowing. However, even these people would borrow to buy a house: it is not feasible to put away the large amount of money needed to pay for the whole value of the house, and a family must live somewhere in the meantime. Borrowing money via a mortgage loan means that they will ultimately own their property, can live in it, and can benefit from any increase in its value that may take place.

Getting married or entering into a civil partnership: has an enormous financial implication. Different couples arrange their finances in different ways: some may pool all income and expenditure in a joint account, others may keep totally separate accounts and make individual contributions to common expenditure. Most probably make a compromise between these two extremes. Even so, each is dependent not only on themselves but also on the other person. Couples should discuss their finances and agree ground rules before they move in together or open joint accounts.

Activity

> One lifestyle choice is deciding whether to rent or buy a property. From a financial service provider's perspective, why are customers who choose to buy their house considered to be a better credit risk than those who rent, even though taking on a mortgage loan is in itself a risk?

2.3   Defining current financial circumstances

Financial choices are driven by life-cycle demands and lifestyle choices and these will impact on a customer's current financial circumstances. These choices are no different from other choices we have to make. However, we are all consumers who are surrounded by an extremely wide range of goods and services that compete for our limited incomes. In order to make choices between alternative products, people must decide on the needs and wants they are going to satisfy. Everyone needs food, drink and protection from the elements in the form of clothes and shelter.

Needs are defined as those things without which we would not survive. People also have **wants**, not necessarily essential items, but those that satisfy the ego in some way, such as a top-of-the-range car when the basic model would be equally good at transporting someone to work every day. People will buy products to satisfy both needs and wants. Very often people buy things they want but do not really need. So, one person may eat a basic diet and forego entertainment in order to put most of his resources into the biggest and most comfortable house he can afford, while someone else will rent a small flat and spend all her money on travelling around the world. No two people in the world buy exactly the same mixture of goods and services.

These life choices also affect the financial services that people buy. Financial services can be seen as **enabling** people to achieve their life choices. The young man with the big house probably has a large mortgage and related insurances but no savings, whereas the young woman travelling around the world has a credit card, travel insurance and perhaps a personal loan.

Aspirations also play a part in helping people to choose financial products. Aspirations are what people hope to achieve in the future and understanding these will help the customer to choose the most suitable financial product. Someone who regularly spends all their monthly income needs financial products that help them to finance consumption, such as credit cards and hire purchase, whereas someone who feels a strong need to save for their future and their eventual retirement needs long-term savings products and a pension scheme.

Activity

> Consider what other long-term aspirations people have.
>
> How can financial services providers enable people to achieve their long-term aspirations?

A good customer adviser will be able to ask relevant questions about the customer's circumstances, to enable them to understand the customer's life stage, needs, wants and aspirations. This will be something the adviser can do with both personal customers and business customers. **Businesses** will also have a life stage, depending on how long the business has been in existence and whether it is:

◆ growing and needing to increase its resources;

◆ in a period of maturity and perhaps looking for new products or markets; or

◆ going through a decline where, perhaps, the owners are thinking of retiring.

We will consider how an adviser collects this information from personal customers in later topics.

2.4   Attitudes to risk

Knowing their current needs, wants, and aspirations helps people to identify their **financial goals**. The next step is deciding how these financial goals will be met. When selecting financial products, they need to weigh up the **risk and reward** involved – the greater the potential reward, the greater the risk. It is the role of the financial planning adviser for regulated product sales (we will look at which products are regulated in section 5.3) to help customers identify their financial goals and select the right product according to the customer's **attitude to risk**.

All financial products involve some risk. If people save money in an ordinary savings account with a well-known bank, they will not earn a high rate of interest. However, traditionally, people felt that banks were a relatively safe place to put their money; it was unlikely that the bank would collapse. As we have seen in recent years with banks like Icesave, there *is* always a chance that a bank could fail (we will look at this issue in Topic 3).

Also, people's attitude to risk is not always directly related to the true impact of a risk on their lives. Some people are more timid than others – that is, they are more **risk-averse** – and some people will happily run quite dangerous risks because they are brave or foolhardy. Just as we saw with needs, wants and aspirations, everyone's attitude to risk is unique. Here are a few examples of where risk enters the financial planning picture.

◆ **Foreign holiday**: do people going on holiday abroad buy travel insurance, or do they save money by not buying it and take the risk that they might sustain loss or injury while they are away?

◆ **Savings**: people want to have savings but where do they put this money? Savings in a bank deposit account are safe but do not earn a high rate of interest; if people want the potential to earn more, they must buy riskier investments such as stocks and shares, and they could lose their money if the shares fall in value.

◆ **Starting a business**: some people will need a bank loan to do this. Suppose someone wants to start their own business but the bank will only lend them money if they put up their home as security for the loan. Their house may already be mortgaged with another lender. Are they willing to risk their house for the sake of a business that might not succeed?

◆ **Planning for retirement**: some people put money aside to cover their retirement, others risk arriving at pension age and managing as best they can then. If people do decide to put some money into a pension fund, are they willing to take the risk that the pension fund will not perform as expected when they reach retirement age? Pension funds do not always perform as expected. Equitable Life was a life assurance company that could not pay its customers what it had promised them, as the following case study shows.

Case study – FSA fines Barclays £7.7 million for investment advice failings and secures as much as £60 million in redress for customers

In January 2011 the Financial Services Authority (FSA) announced that it had fined Barclays Bank plc £7.7m for failures in relation to the sale of two funds. Barclays will contact customers and pay redress where appropriate.

Between July 2006 and November 2008 Barclays sold Aviva's Global Balanced Income Fund (the Balanced Fund) and Global Cautious Income Fund (the Cautious Fund) to 12,331 people with investments totalling £692m.

However, there were a number of serious failings in the way the funds were sold. These include failing to:

◆ ensure the funds were suitable for customers in view of their investment objectives, financial circumstances, investment knowledge and experience;

◆ ensure that training given to sales staff adequately explained the risks associated with the funds;

◆ ensure product brochures and other documents given to customers clearly explained the risks involved and could not mislead customers;

◆ have adequate procedures for monitoring sales processes and responding promptly when issues were identified.

The FSA's investigation revealed that, even though Barclays had itself identified potentially unsuitable sales as early as June 2008, it did not take appropriate and timely action. In fact, of the 12,000 or so investors, most of whom were retired or nearing retirement, 1,730 complained about the advice they were given to invest in the funds. This equates to approximately one in seven investors.

During the investigation Barclays continued to carry out a past business review to evaluate the suitability of the sales of both funds: 3,099 sales of the Cautious Fund (51 per cent of all sold) and 3,378 of the Balanced Fund (74 per cent of all sold) have been identified as requiring further consideration.

As a result Barclays has already paid approximately £17m in compensation and the FSA estimates up to £42m further could be paid to customers who received unsuitable advice.

Margaret Cole, the FSA's managing director of enforcement and financial crime, said:

'The FSA requires firms to have robust procedures in place to ensure any advice given to customers is suitable. Therefore, when recommending investment products, firms should take account of a customer's financial circumstances, their attitude to risk and what they hope to achieve by investing.

'On this occasion, however, Barclays failed to do this and thousands of investors, many of whom were seeking to invest their retirement savings, have suffered. To compound matters, Barclays failed to take effective action when it detected the failings at an early stage.

'Because of this, and given Barclays' position as one of the UK's major retail banks, we view these breaches as particularly serious and fully deserving of what is a very substantial fine.'

The fine is the highest fine imposed by the FSA for retail failings.

Source: www.fsa.gov.uk/pages/Library/Communication/PR/2011/006.shtml

We can see therefore that the consequences for an individual of taking a risk can be very great. All financial decisions involve some degree of risk and this applies to decisions taken by financial companies, as well as to those made by individuals. Just as consumers make risk judgements about which financial products to buy, so the company they buy from must decide how to manage the money that investors give them.

Professional dealers in financial markets try to minimise their risks by **hedging**. This means covering a risky deal with one that is less risky or that is likely to have the opposite result. For example, if an investment firm makes a deal in which it will gain if interest rates rise, it can also make another deal in which it will gain if interest rates fall. Most individuals do not own large enough sums of money to be able to do this.

If people want to save for their retirement, it is easier and potentially more rewarding to put all their savings into one large fund, rather than splitting it up into many different ones; yet, if that fund fails, they could lose everything. With shorter-term savings, they have to decide between the potential reward of a fund that is higher risk and the lower return of a safer fund. Some people 'hedge' in a small way, by putting a proportion of their savings into a riskier fund and the rest in a safer fund. They are making a decision to gamble with some of their savings in the hope of getting a better return, but they also know that they could lose some value.

Throughout life, we are vulnerable to various risks — that is, the possibility of things going wrong. Our attitude to risk changes throughout our lives: often, people want less risk as they get older; this is called being **risk averse**. Some people, however, get more relaxed with age, taking the view that they have seen and survived all kinds of supposedly disastrous events. If they have saved up plenty of money, they may feel financially secure enough to take bigger risks with part of their savings.

Your stage in the life cycle can affect your likely attitude to risk. Different stages also mean that particular risks will be higher or lower, and risk events may be more or less damaging. For example, if you lose all of your savings when you are in your late 20s, you do at least have the chance to rebuild them; someone in their 60s who loses all of their savings could be in a much worse position, having very little working time left during which to rebuild their savings to secure their old age.

2.5 Cultural and ethnic issues

We said at the beginning of this topic that cultural differences have an impact on life-cycle events and the ages at which people may enter the different stages. The UK is a **multicultural** country that has to accommodate the requirements of a **diverse population**.

Many different **languages** are spoken. For example, in Wales many people speak English and Welsh and most written media are in both languages. The UK is home to many **migrant workers** who want to send money home in a secure way and also wish to discuss their bank accounts in their own language, as we shall see in the next section.

The UK is part of the European Union (EU) and as such needs to ensure the free flow of funds around the EU. One of the reasons why the Payment Services Regulations (covered in detail in section 5.11) were brought in was to make information about such payments available and to enhance consumer protection. This should improve mobility of people between countries and drive competitiveness between providers.

For the Muslim population of the UK, their use of banking and other financial services is influenced by the teachings of Islam. **Islamic banking** or **Sharia banking** has expanded to meet their needs, as we will explore below.

From a provision of service perspective, financial services organisations need to recognise cultural and ethnic differences and accommodate them. Some areas of towns or cities have a high density of people from particular ethnic backgrounds, so it would make sense to staff local branches with some employees who have a command of the appropriate language and an understanding of the cultural background.

2.5.1 Language

In order to accommodate language differences in a very different way, NatWest introduced an account for Polish nationals as the following case study shows.

Case study – NatWest launches first dedicated Polish bank account in Britain

In January 2007 NatWest brought to market a brand new current account for Polish-speaking customers. The NatWest Welcome Account was designed specifically to meet the banking needs of Polish-speaking migrants who were new to the UK and it was the first bank account in which all services were in Polish, including telephone and Internet banking, as well as a dedicated telephony unit staffed by Polish speakers.

At the time there were approximately 300,000 Polish speakers working in the UK, and NatWest had conducted extensive research among existing Polish-speaking communities. It found that top of their wish list was the need to transfer money to family members in Poland in a cost-effective and secure way.

As a result of the research, NatWest created an account that was, in fact, two accounts in one. Not only did it provide Polish customers in Britain with a current account for their day-to-day needs but it also came with a money transfer account into which customers were able to transfer funds straight from their current account. This then allowed a family member or friend in Poland,

---

> nominated by the NatWest Welcome Account holder at account opening, to withdraw those funds from that account via a cash machine card, also provided by NatWest, from cash machines in Poland or anywhere in the world.

2.5.2 Sharia banking

Sharia-compliant, or **Islamic**, **finance** is one of the fastest-growing sectors in the financial services industry. Its growth and development have been rapid over the past ten years, during which Islamic products have appeared in over 75 countries worldwide. In order to obtain a better understanding of Islamic finance, let us first consider some of the foundations of Islam.

Islam is a religion that was founded over 1,400 years ago and was revealed to the Prophet Mohammed (PBUH)[1]. Although Islam is a religion, it is better described as a way of life or an entire code setting out how to conduct one's life, both spiritually and financially. Islam is derived from the **Holy Qu'ran**, which is recognised by Muslims to be the most sacrosanct text and the word of God. Examples of how to apply the principles laid down in the Qu'ran in a practical way were drawn from the **Sunnah** and **Hadith**. Sunnah means 'well-known path' and relates to acts and deeds of the Prophet (PBUH), and the Hadith gives the sayings of the Prophet (PBUH). Collectively the Qu'ran, Sunnah and Hadith are referred to as the **Sharia**.

While references may be made to 'Islamic law', there is no codified single Islamic law. A more accurate reference is to Sharia, which is a consolidation of sources of Islamic principles. However, there are a number of religious perspectives in Islam, in which the application and interpretation of Sharia may vary. These differing religious perspectives are referred to as 'schools of thought' and there are five predominant schools. The impact of these differences can be seen in Islamic financial transactions and creates some problems within the industry.

The core message of Islam is one of peace and the need to be fair and ethical in personal conduct and in dealings with others; certain acts that could be harmful are prohibited. Sharia banking is committed to promoting goals of **equity, moderation and social justice**. It is a system that revolves around **prudent lending**, the **reduction of risk** and the **sharing of profits**. There is an **absolute ban on speculation** and the short-selling of stocks. Debt is actively discouraged, and so dealings with any organisation where more than a third of the balance sheet is debt are forbidden. So too are investments in enterprises deemed unethical by Islamic scholars, such as casinos or weapons factories.

Each Islamic bank will appoint either a single scholar or a panel of three members to review and validate the products and services offered. These scholars are appropriately trained and versed in Islamic law or Sharia.

The feature that most strongly distinguishes Sharia banking from Western-style banking is the **prohibition of interest** – or making money out of money. This is based on the prohibition on **'Riba'**, which literally translated means 'excess'. In financial terms it means an excess over the principal amount, and the prohibition relates to both the giving and receiving of Riba. As it is not permissible for banks to charge interest on loans, a Sharia-compliant mortgage, for example, is usually structured so that the bank leases the property to the homeowner, who effectively pays rent until ownership is transferred.

Viewed from a conventional Western banking perspective, it could be argued that the payments made under a Shari'a mortgage seem remarkably similar to interest payments made under a conventional mortgage. Also, it costs homeowners more to set up and pay off an Islamic mortgage than a conventional product.

However, Islamic financiers stress the joint-ownership and profit-sharing aspects of the Sharia model. The relationship between bank and customer is based on **sharing risk and rewards** from the financing and investments made on the customer's behalf. The returns gained are based on the amount of profit realised from each transaction.

The Financial Services Authority has licensed five standalone Islamic banks – including the Islamic Bank of Britain, which reported a significant increase in the number of non-Muslim customers applying for accounts in the wake of the financial crisis. Numbers are growing because Islamic finance offers a 'safer option' for savers and investors, regardless of faith.

However, you don't have to go to a purely Islamic bank to open an Islamic bank account. So far, 20 major global banks have set up units to provide Sharia-compliant financial services. HSBC began offering Islamic products and services to its customers in 2003; Lloyds TSB followed in 2005.

The government has been actively encouraging the expansion of Sharia-compliant financial institutions for several years. When he was chancellor, Gordon Brown repeatedly urged the City of London to become the 'gateway to Islamic finance'. In November 2008, the government announced the launch of the first **Sharia-compliant pension funds**.

Activity

> List the ways in which your organisation aims to meet the needs of people of differing cultural and ethnic backgrounds.

Endnotes

1   PBUH means 'peace be upon him' and is used each time the Prophet Mohammed's (PBUH) name is mentioned, as a mark of respect.

Resources

www.hm-treasury.gov.uk

www.fsa.gov.uk/financial_capability

www.cfebuk.org.uk

Review questions

The following review questions are designed so that you can check your understanding of this topic.

The answers to the questions are provided at the end of these learning materials.

1. What does 'financial capability' mean?

2. Why is it necessary to improve levels of financial capability?

3. Which events tend to be fixed for most people within their personal life cycle?

4. Why is the life cycle important to the marketing of products and services?

5. Compare and contrast the lifestyle choice of 'consume now, pay later' with 'save now, buy later'. How do people develop these different attitudes?

6. How do 'wants' differ from 'needs'?

7. What might be the drawbacks of being too risk averse?

8. What do you consider to be the impact of cases like the failure of Barclays Bank to provide adequate advice to investors?

9. Why might some people be reluctant to take out financial products and services that are delivered in a language that is not their own?

10. Why do you think it is appropriate to consider different individuals' religious beliefs when offering banking services?

Topic 3
Consumer sources of guidance and information

Learning objective

After studying this topic, students should be able to demonstrate an understanding of relevant consumer sources of guidance and information.

Introduction

In the last topic we looked at the issues surrounding financial capability and how a large proportion of the population need help in improving this skill. People have to make some significant choices throughout their lives, some of which will involve the allocation of a large proportion of their incomes.

This topic focuses mainly on the **protection** that is available to consumers if something goes wrong that is outside their control, such as the collapse of their financial provider. We will also look at what happens if they have a **complaint** that their provider is unable to resolve to their satisfaction, or if the service they receive does not meet certain minimum standards. Consumers may also need advice and protection if they get into **financial difficulty**, irrespective of the cause. There are a number of bodies that can help in this instance and it is important that providers of credit understand what this help is and how it is delivered.

However, before considering these various aspects of protection it is first worth looking at the issue of consumer responsibility, which is where this topic starts.

3.1   Consumer responsibilities

There has been some debate in the financial services sector about customers taking more responsibility for their financial well-being and what the term **'consumer responsibility'** actually means. There are certain legal requirements relating to the law of contract (we cover this in more detail in Topic 6) that customers should follow. In outline these are:

◆ to act lawfully and in good faith;

◆ not to make misrepresentations or withhold material information;

◆ to abide by the terms of the contract;

◆ to take responsibility for their own decisions.

However, this final point is dependent upon the financial services provider giving information that is clear and not misleading. If this is the case, then it could be argued that the customer has the responsibility to make sure they understand what they are buying and tell the provider if this is not so. If they do not do this, then the provider will have to presume that the customer has understood. The complication comes when dealing with customers of **differing financial capability** and also depends on the **nature of the product or service** being offered. The more complex the product or service, the more difficult it is for the customer to understand, whatever their levels of capability.

The old principle of *caveat emptor* or '**let the buyer beware**' in relation to contracts has been eroding for well over a century through increasing amounts of protective consumer law but its lessening importance does not entirely remove the need for consumers to take **personal responsibility**. In addition, legal responsibilities have to be separated from moral duties, such as taking reasonable steps to make an informed choice, so the responsibilities of the consumer become somewhat difficult to define.

Responsibilities of consumers that are not covered by law could include:

◆ **taking responsibility** for management of their finances, so undertaking budgeting and understanding the difference between needs and wants, and linked to this is understanding the legal consequences of not repaying a debt;

◆ **gathering relevant information** about products to be able to make an informed choice. This could be as simple as reading all the information sent with a quote for a mortgage, for example, and asking questions about areas in which they feel uncertain.

In December 2008 the Financial Services Authority (FSA) published a discussion paper that asked what is the right balance of responsibility between consumers and firms in the sale of products, where that balance currently lies, and what can be done by both parties to help consumers look after their own interests. The FSA has no power to impose responsibilities on consumers, but in order to set the appropriate level of protection the Financial Services and Markets Act (FSMA) 2000 states that it must note the 'general principle that consumers should take responsibility for their decisions'.

However, some consumer bodies felt that the concentration by the FSA on consumer responsibility was unrealistic and unhelpful in discussions about how to create an effective and efficient retail market, placing unrealistic expectations on consumers. One reason for this is that the complexity of many financial products and the difficulty of finding an acceptable way to describe risk means that most consumers are ill-equipped to judge how a product will perform in future, and whether it meets their needs.

Activity

> What methods does your organisation use to explain the nature of risk to customers?

3.2 Consumer protection

We can see from the previous section that defining some aspects of consumer responsibilities is difficult. Equally, in certain instances consumers need protection from large organisations that could, because of their size and resources, treat customers quite unfairly. One of the stated objectives of the FSA is to 'secure an appropriate level of protection for consumers'. There is a limitation, in that the FSA emphasises that it cannot provide 100 per cent protection and protection depends upon a number of factors, such as:

◆ the economic climate;

◆ financial literacy of consumers; and

◆ speed of reforms.

Additionally, there are a number of areas where the FSA currently does not have direct control and we shall consider these in the remainder of this topic.

3.2.1 Financial Services Compensation Scheme

To improve **customer confidence** in the financial services industry, compensation arrangements for customers who have lost money through the insolvency of an authorised firm have been co-ordinated under a single scheme called the **Financial Services Compensation Scheme** (FSCS). It is made up of a number of sub-schemes relating to different default situations, as follows.

◆ **Default of an insurance company**: compensation is 90 per cent of the balance, with no upper limit. If the insurance is compulsory (such as employer's liability cover or some types of motor insurance), the figure is 100 per cent of the whole amount.

◆ **Loss due to insolvency** of a firm carrying out investment business regulated under FSMA 2000: 100 per cent of the claim, up to a maximum of £50,000.

◆ **Loss of deposited funds due to the default of a bank or building society**: 100 per cent of the first £85,000. The majority of cases are paid within seven days, with more complex cases taking up to 20 days.

◆ **Claims against firms involved in mortgage advice and arranging**: 100 per cent of the claim, up to a maximum of £50,000.

◆ **Claims against insurance intermediaries**: the amount that can be claimed will depend on the nature of the circumstances.

Claims cannot be made against the FSCS for other losses, such as losses due to negligence, poor advice or a fall in stock market values. In some cases, however, the customer may be able to sue for compensation through the civil courts.

The FSCS has played an important role in securing compensation for investors, not just in the UK but also abroad. The following case study also shows how important it was for the government to step in to bolster confidence in the financial services industry.

Case study – Compensation for Icesave customers: timeline

October 2008

'FSCS gears up to assist Icesave's UK branch customers'
In the light of the uncertainties in October 2008, the Financial Services Compensation Scheme (FSCS) geared up in case it needed to assist approximately 200,000 savers at Icesave. Icesave was the UK branch of Landsbanki Islands hf, a European Economic Area bank authorised by the financial services regulator in Iceland. The FSA in the UK reported that Icesave was expected to go into insolvency proceedings in Iceland and this would trigger an FSCS default.

Eligible savers with Icesave were protected by the Icelandic Depositors' and Investors' Guarantee Fund, up to a limit of the first 20,887 euros of their deposits. As an Icelandic bank, Icesave was not automatically a member of the FSCS, but it did opt to become a 'top-up' member. That meant that eligible retail savers with Icesave's UK branch, whose savings exceed the Icelandic limit, would benefit from top-up compensation from the FSCS covering the amount over the Icelandic limit up to the FSCS compensation limit for deposits of £50,000.

'Treasury announcement on Icesave'
HM Treasury confirmed that if Landsbanki were declared in default, the Government would make sure that no retail depositor would lose any money as a result of the closure of Icesave. The Treasury also confirmed that arrangements were being put in place to ensure that all ISA customers of Icesave would continue to benefit from the tax-free status of their accounts.

'FSCS proposals for accelerated payment process being considered in Iceland'
The FSCS, together with representatives of HM Treasury, the FSA and the Bank of England met with the Icelandic authorities to agree on the process for accelerating the process of compensation to depositors.

November 2008

'FSCS sends first email to over 200,000 UK Icesave customers'
The FSCS sent the first emails to UK customers of Icesave with information about how to claim back their savings. The FSCS then sent second emails to customers, in phases, with a view to starting compensation payments in the second week of November. The second email provided instructions on how depositors could log on to their existing Icesave accounts to complete a short electronic process allowing them to receive their compensation. Once UK depositors completed the process, their money was transferred to their nominated account within five working days. UK Icesave customers who opted not to use the accelerated payout process were still able to claim compensation using a paper-based application, although this took longer to process.

November 2008	*'Almost £1bn in Icesave payments processed'* FSCS had signed off almost a billion pounds in payments to UK Icesave customers since it started the electronic payment process. More than £133m was being held to maturity by Icesave customers in fixed-term accounts. When Icesave went into default on 8 October, many Icesave customers feared it would be many months before they got their money back. Six weeks later, FSCS offered more than 100,000 Icesave customers the opportunity to claim compensation online through an electronic process.
December 2008	*'FSCS urges Icesave customers to claim their compensation'* FSCS had contacted almost all 214,713 Icesave customers offering them compensation following the closure of the Internet bank. Of the 198,219 customers eligible to use the online system, more than 183,000 people had completed the process. Customers who were unable to claim online by the deadline of 30 December were still able to make a paper-based application.
April 2009	The FSA announced new limits that would come into force in January 2010, which would help consumers to understand and have confidence in the protection provided by the FSCS.

Source: www.fscs.org.uk.

Activity

> Review the FSCS website for information on the Single Customer View for Faster Payments.

3.2.2 Financial Ombudsman Service

The FSMA 2000 provides for a mechanism under which 'certain disputes may be resolved quickly and with the minimum of formality by an independent person'. The concept of an **ombudsman**, as a person or organisation providing an independent facility for the resolution of complaints and disputes relating to public bodies and commercial organisations, has been with us for many years. Indeed, in the past, a number of separate ombudsman bureaux operated in the financial services marketplace, each of them dealing with problems arising in a particular sector. However, such a fragmented system was neither helpful nor efficient, and an integrated body, the **Financial Ombudsman Service (FOS)**, was established in 2001.

The FOS deals with complaints and disputes arising from almost any aspect of financial services (although certain types of pension and aspects of pension arrangements are dealt with by the Pension Ombudsman). The FOS does not make the rules under which firms are authorised, nor can it give advice about financial matters or debt problems.

The FOS is able to deal with complaints brought by:

◆ private individuals;

◆ small businesses with turnover under €2m;

◆ charities with an annual income of less than £1m; and

◆ trustees of a trust with a net asset value of less than £1m.

It is funded by organisations that are members of the FOS and membership is compulsory for all organisations authorised under the FSMA 2000.

Complainants must first complain to the provider itself; the FOS will become involved only when a provider's **internal complaints procedures** have been exhausted without the customer obtaining satisfaction. Complaints to the FOS must be made within **six years** of the event that gives rise to the complaint, or within **three years** of the time when the complainant should have become aware that they had cause for complaint, whichever is the later. The FOS will not usually consider any complaint that is the subject of a court case.

The FOS can make awards of up to **£100,000**, plus the complainant's **reasonable costs**. Judgments are **binding on the firm** but not on the complainant, who is free to pursue the matter further in the courts if they wish. The award is not intended to punish the firm, but to put the complainant back into the **same financial position** in which they would have been had the event complained about not taken place.

In September 2010 the FSA announced that this limit would be raised to £150,000, and students should be aware of when this increase will be introduced.

The following key figures show the scope of the work at the FOS.

Key figures about the Financial Ombudsman Service:

◆ The total number of new cases was 163,012, up from 127,471 on the previous year.

◆ Cases relating to banking and credit accounted for 44 per cent of the total, while 42 per cent related to insurance and 14 per cent to investment and pensions (including mortgage endowments).

◆ Cases relating to financial hardship increased dramatically to 13,213.

◆ The FOS operated on a budget of £92.4m and a cost per case of £555.

Source: http://financial-ombudsman.org.uk. All figures relate to the year ended 31 March 2010.

Activity

Why do you think the number of complaints to the FOS is increasing?

Following the Hunt report in 2008, the FOS has become more transparent about its work, the types of complaint it receives and which organisations consumers have made complaints about. It publishes six-monthly complaints data relating to individual financial businesses – including banks, insurance companies and investment firms. This information can be viewed in detail on its website.

3.2.3 The Lending Standards Board

The Lending Standards Board (LSB) monitors and enforces lending and credit standards, including those governing the treatment of customers in financial difficulty. It operates independently of the industry and is governed by a board of directors, a majority of whom are independent 'public interest' directors.

The **Lending Code** is a voluntary code that covers all unsecured lending to retail customers – overdrafts, loans and credit cards. Secured lending to small businesses is also covered. Subscribers to the Code agree to act fairly and reasonably in all their dealings with customers by, as a minimum, meeting all the commitments and standards set out in the Code. The key commitments are shown below (*source:* www.lendingstandardsboard.org.uk).

◆ Subscribers will make sure that **advertising and promotional literature** is fair, clear and not misleading and that customers are given clear information about products and services.

◆ Customers will be given **clear information** about accounts and services, how they work, their terms and conditions and the interest rates that apply to them.

◆ **Regular statements** will be made available to customers (if appropriate). Customers will also be informed about changes to the interest rates, charges or terms and conditions.

◆ Subscribers will **lend money responsibly**.

◆ Subscribers will deal **quickly and sympathetically** with things that go wrong and act sympathetically and positively when considering a customer's financial difficulties.

◆ **Personal information** will be treated as private and confidential, and subscribers will provide secure and reliable banking and payment systems.

◆ Subscribers will make sure their **staff are trained** to put the Code into practice.

The scope of the Code relates to:

◆ communications and financial promotions;

◆ credit reference agencies;

◆ credit assessment;

◆ current account overdrafts;

◆ credit cards;

◆ loans;

◆ terms and conditions;

◆ financial difficulties;

◆ complaints;

◆ monitoring (of the Code within organisations).

The Lending Code and the Banking Conduct of Business Sourcebook (BCOBS) replaced the Banking Codes in November 2009. However, while BCOBS imposes regulatory requirements on providers – as part of a general shift by the FSA towards tighter regulation and enhanced protection for consumers – the Lending

Code remains voluntary. Some key stakeholders have expressed concern that the protection for borrowers will be eroded as a result.

A LSB Consumer Forum has been established to ensure full engagement with consumer and debt advice bodies. The Lending Code is reviewed on a regular basis, with the first full revision of the code coming into effect in March 2011.

3.2.4 Payment Services Directive

The European Union's Payment Services Directive (PSD) was implemented on 1 November 2009, making the FSA the UK's **'competent authority'**, responsible for regulation of the payment transactions of banks, building societies and other organisations that transfer money for clients.

Payment Service Regulations (PSRs) cover most payment services, including the provision and operation of 'payment accounts'. Payment accounts cover accounts on which payment transactions may be made and where access to funds is not restricted, for example, in fixed-term deposits. The regulations extend from information to be provided before a payment is made to the remedial action firms must take if a payment goes wrong.

The PSR conduct of business provisions only apply to payment services made in euro or sterling, so primarily to sterling and euro denominated accounts. The Financial Ombudsman Service will provide 'out-of-court' redress, the Office of Fair Trading (at the time of writing – March 2011) will be responsible for requirements relating to access to payment systems, and HM Revenue and Customs will be responsible for the anti-money-laundering supervision of businesses providing payment services.

The PSR affects firms providing payment services and their customers. These firms include:

◆ banks;

◆ building societies;

◆ e-money issuers;

◆ money remitters;

◆ non-bank payment card issuers; and

◆ non-bank merchant acquirers.

There is a new class of regulated firm known as payment institutions (PIs), which must either be authorised or registered by the FSA. Authorised PIs are subject to prudential requirements. Conduct of business requirements apply to all payment service providers, including banks, building societies, e-money issuers and the new PIs.

3.3 Sources of education and advice

We have looked at ways in which consumers can be compensated in the event of financial loss. However, in order that they can take responsibility for their financial affairs as we discussed at the beginning of this topic, they need access to information and advice. There are two further areas of concern for consumers in relation to the provision of financial services.

1. How will **information** taken from consumers be used and is it safe? For example there have been numerous instances of **identify fraud** from the misuse of credit cards and Internet-related issues such as **phishing**.

2. What happens if consumers get into **debt**? Suffering financial hardship is stressful enough for most people, as we saw in Topic 2, but few people would know what to do if they were required to negotiate with their creditors or make a court appearance.

Fortunately there are various sources of education and advice available and we will look at several of the most well-known ones here.

3.3.1 Information Commissioner's Office

As a great deal of information on customers is held by financial services organisations there is the potential for poor administration or even misuse. The **Information Commissioner's Office (ICO)** is the UK's independent public body set up to enforce and oversee :

◆ the **Data Protection Act**;

◆ the **Freedom of Information Act**;

◆ the Environmental Information Regulations; and

◆ the Privacy and Electronic Communications Regulations.

The basis of the Data Protection Act and the Data Protection Principles are covered in more detail in section 6.5.

The main function of the ICO is to:

◆ **educate and influence** by promoting good practice and give information and advice;

◆ **resolve problems** by dealing with eligible complaints from people who think their rights have been breached;

◆ **enforce** by using legal sanctions against those who ignore or refuse to accept their obligations.

The main activities of the ICO are to:

◆ maintain the public register of data controllers under the Data Protection Act;

◆ approve publication schemes adopted by public authorities under the Freedom of Information Act;

◆ provide a general enquiry service for individuals and organisations through a customer service helpline and publish guidance and information to encourage organisations to achieve good practice and to help individuals to understand their rights;

◆ rule on eligible complaints from people who think the Data Protection Act or Freedom of Information Act has been breached.

The ICO has the power to issue penalties of up to £500,000 on businesses or government departments found to be in breach of the Data Protection Act.

3.3.1.1 Complaint handling

The ICO undertakes independent investigations and rules on eligible complaints from people who:

◆ are unhappy with the way public authorities have handled **requests for information** under the Freedom of Information Act;

◆ think organisations or individuals have **breached** the Data Protection Act in the way they hold and handle personal information.

However, the ICO cannot:

◆ award compensation for any breach of the Data Protection Act or the Freedom of Information Act;

◆ apply for an injunction to prevent the disclosure of information;

◆ make one organisation pass on personal information to another;

◆ prevent one individual from keeping or using personal information about another individual for purely domestic reasons.

There have been several complaints to the ICO regarding the incorrect disposal of confidential waste outside bank branches. The following case study is a good example.

Case study – disposal of personal data leads to action by ICO

In 2006 a complaint was made to the ICO that items of personal data were recovered from refuse bins outside branches of a bank in Fareham, Manchester, Nottingham and Glasgow. The material comprised three documents relating to individual accounts (Fareham); fifteen documents including application forms and a letter to a customer (Nottingham); a private banking form, computerised printout and a pre-release funds checklist (Glasgow); and a photocopy of a customer's provisional driving licence (Manchester).

The ICO found that the data controller (the bank) had breached the seventh Data Protection Principle according to the Data Protection Act 1998. It required the data controller to review the data protection procedures in place for handling and disposal of confidential waste, which is personal as defined in the Act. It also required that the appropriate data protection training be given to all relevant employees regarding the secure disposal of personal data.

Activity

How should banks safeguard information they hold about consumers?

3.3.2 Money Advice Trust

The Money Advice Trust (MAT) is a charity formed in 1991 to increase the quality and availability of free, independent money advice in the UK. Historically the money advice sector has been highly fragmented so by working in partnership with all the leading money advice agencies, MAT is creating a national strategy to:

◆ increase the supply of advice in the most cost-effective way;

◆ make it easier for people to access money advice;

◆ improve the efficiency and effectiveness of advice;

◆ enhance the support available to money advisers;

◆ raise the money needed to achieve the above;

◆ promote the role and value of money advice.

MAT's key activities are to support the debt advice sector through:

◆ training for money advisers;

◆ specialist support;

◆ quality assurance development, for example the Money Advice Quality Model.

It also offers direct service provision by giving debt advice to the public through the National Debtline and Business Debtline, raising funds to do so from their funders, who are financial services organisations, government departments and utility providers.

Source: www.moneyadvicetrust.org

Activity

> Why are utility providers interested in debt counselling for customers?

3.3.2.1 The Common Financial Statement

The Money Advice Trust has been instrumental in developing a tool called the '**Common Financial Statement**' (CFS). Financial statements set out the income and **essential expenditure** of a person in debt and how much money is available to repay creditors. These factors have always been a key tool in the money advice process. Creditors need to know that when reduced debt repayments are offered, these are fair and reasonable. Money advisers need to know that their clients will receive consistent treatment from the people to whom they owe money. Historically, a lack of agreement among money advisers regarding a common format for financial statements has led to a lack of consistency and, in some instances, this has led to creditors being reluctant to accept offers of payment.

The CFS was born out of a commitment from its sponsors to create a **uniform approach** to how advisers prepare financial statements, in order to encourage consistent responses from creditors and therefore help consumers. Agreement on use of the CFS should mean that when someone is faced with a difficult financial situation, a **fair resolution** can be found **without undue delay**.

The key benefit of the CFS is that it standardises the way that money advisers and creditors communicate with each other about repayment offers. This standard format includes:

◆ a **standard budgeting format** for all money advice organisations;

◆ a set of pre-agreed levels for certain areas of **discretionary expenditure** – these levels are known as **trigger figures** (see below);

◆ a **commitment** from supporting creditors to CFS principles so that offers made by independent money advisers will be accepted as long as expenditure is within the trigger figures and the guidelines have been followed;

◆ an understanding that if trigger figures have been exceeded, an explanation of the reasons for this should be provided by advisers – this will enable creditors to consider **exceptional circumstances**;

◆ a **streamlined process** so that repayment offers can be dealt with more quickly;

◆ a **partnership approach** to avoid unnecessary disputes between money advisers and creditors.

The **trigger figures** help creditors and money advisers to identify levels of monthly expenditure that are deemed reasonable and will not require comment or explanation. There are trigger figures for **telephone, travel, housekeeping** and '**other**' costs. This means that if a financial statement includes items of expenditure that are either at or below the level of the appropriate trigger figure, money advisers can expect that their payment offers should be accepted without the need for further discussion.

Categories of **fixed expenditure** such as rent and mortgage payments do not have their own trigger figure because what people spend on these items varies widely from household to household. Also it is rarely possible to have any real control over these expenditure levels.

The CFS is the result of effective partnership working between creditors and the money advice sector. Due to the level of trust that now exists, creditors can be confident that a payment offer produced using the CFS is the result of a transparent process and, in return, money advisers can expect a consistent response from CFS sponsors and supporters.

Activity

> Obtain a budget planner used in the branch for lending applications. What other items appear on this list that are not trigger figures, mortgage or rent payments? Of these remaining items, which would you consider to be essential items?

3.3.3 Citizens Advice

Citizens Advice is a charitable organisation with an extensive network across the UK and into Europe dispensing independent and free advice to consumers to help them resolve their legal, money, and other problems. Their aim is to provide independent, confidential and impartial advice to everyone on their rights and responsibilities. It values diversity, promotes equality and challenges discrimination. Two main areas of activity are:

◆ to provide the **advice** people need for the problems they face;

◆ to **improve the policies and practices** that affect people's lives.

While having no legal authority within the UK banking services environment, Citizens Advice has a significant voice with regard to consumer lending and credit. Staffed by many volunteers (20,000 people within a total workforce of 26,000), it is able to assist its clients with advice and the best course of action in a variety of situations.

In particular, with regard to banking, it tries to mediate and help clients identify the appropriate route to follow, which might sometimes be, for example, a complaint to the Financial Ombudsman Service.

One of the many services offered by Citizens Advice is helping consumers who are struggling with **debt**: it can assist with problems of varying degrees of severity, from basic problems right through to debt management, individual voluntary arrangements and bankruptcy.

Detailed below is a description of part of the service that Citizens Advice provides in relation to debt. The adviser:

◆ helps to **empower** the client to deal with the problem themselves;

◆ gains the client's **trust** to talk about their financial situation;

◆ establishes the **extent** of the debt problem;

◆ checks whether the client is **legally liable** to pay all their debts;

◆ identifies ways in which the client could **increase their income**, including by claiming benefits and tax credits, getting benefits claims backdated, claiming on payment protection insurances and applying for charitable grants;

◆ helps the client to draw up a **budget** and advises them on reducing expenditure;

◆ identifies the debtor's most **important debts** – ie those for which, if acceptable payment arrangements are not made, the debtor could lose their home, their liberty, their fuel supply, or essential household goods on hire purchase;

◆ helps the client to decide a **suitable strategy** for dealing with their debt problem, including making arrangements with creditors, bankruptcy or individual voluntary arrangements;

◆ works out and **negotiates** fair and sustainable repayments to all the client's creditors, and if possible, arranges for the client to pay these via a payment distribution system;

◆ advises the client on **court procedures** for debt recovery, and if possible, represents the client at any debt-related hearings.

A banking adviser could suggest a customer contact Citizens Advice if they are experiencing problems and need external assistance. In the case of banks, this can be during a dispute or, more often than not, when there are problems over repayment of debt and the customer is unwilling to discuss it with the lender.

Activity

Visit the Citizens Advice website (www.adviceguide.org.uk) and review some of the information in the credit and debit factsheets.

3.3.4 Consumer Credit Counselling Service

The Foundation for Credit Counselling, based in Leeds, is the umbrella charity for the Consumer Credit Counselling Service (CCCS) in the UK. Through its free national telephone service, ten regional centres and online debt assessment tool, CCCS is able to help people with debt problems wherever they live. CCCS is well established as an important source of money advice and the focus for the repayment ethic.

The advisory service provides counselling on personal budgeting, advice on the wise use of credit and, where appropriate, managing achievable plans to repay debts. Each counsellor is trained in counselling, debt advice and the operation of systems specifically designed for debt counselling.

Over the telephone, the helpline adviser will:

◆ perform an immediate assessment of the situation, ending in emergency help, self-help material or the offer of a counselling appointment;

◆ conduct a full review of the credit and debt situation followed by a recommendation – the first priority, wherever possible, is to allow for essential expenditure, priority debts and living expenses;

◆ assess whether the client has enough left over to make an offer of repayment to other creditors.

If the client is in a position to make repayments, creditors are asked to freeze interest, stop penalties and charges, and accept a longer repayment period and, sometimes, a reduced sum. Many creditors will accept the repayment proposals without further checking and the repayment records of clients the CCCS has counselled are very good. The CCCS is able to achieve this as it follows the two key principles of **best advice** and **sustainable plans**.

As some people prefer to be counselled anonymously, CCCS introduced the online process 'CCCS Debt Remedy' in 2006. As with the telephone advice service, CCCS Debt Remedy performs an immediate assessment, which leads to emergency help, self-help material or the option of continuing to an online counselling session. Counsellors are available to answer any questions. As with a telephone appointment, CCCS conducts a full review of the credit and debt situation followed by a recommended course of action.

The benefit to clients is that CCCS brings peace of mind through education and understanding, reaching solutions to their problems and agreeing repayments that are achievable. Most importantly, the free service also means that the debt situation is not worsened with the burden of management fees. The benefit for creditors is that CCCS can improve recovery of moneys owed as a result of its independent assessment of a customer's situation.

Source: www.cccs.co.uk.

Activity

> Why might a customer choose to use the services of an organisation such as CCCS rather than discuss problems with their financial services provider?

Resources

www.adviceguide.org.uk

www.cccs.co.uk

www.citizensadvice.org.uk

www.financial-ombudsman.org.uk

www.fsa.gov.uk

www.fscs.gov.uk

www.ico.gov.uk

www.lendingstandardsboard.org.uk

Review questions

The following review questions are designed so that you can check your understanding of this topic.

The answers to the questions are provided at the end of these learning materials.

1. Why is the FSA unable to offer 100 per cent protection to consumers?

2. Why do consumers require protection?

3. What are the limits of the compensation available to consumers under the FSCS?

4. What criteria must be fulfilled before a customer can present their complaint to the FOS?

5. What products does the Lending Code cover?

6. What are the main functions of the Information Commissioner's Office (ICO)?

7. What is the purpose of the Common Financial Statement that MAT helped to develop?

8. How does Citizens Advice help consumers with debt problems?

9. What methods does CCCS use to provide its service to consumers who need help?

10. How might these methods be helpful to consumers?

Topic 4
The financial services environment and regulation

> **Learning objective**
>
> After studying this topic, students should be able to demonstrate an understanding of the financial services environment and the main bodies that provide its regulation.

Introduction

This topic gives an overview and sets the scene for the next topic, which deals in more detail with the role and activities of the Financial Services Authority (FSA). In this topic we shall look at the role of money and banks in our society, along with some of the other providers of credit, such as building societies, finance companies and credit unions. We shall look briefly at how the financial services markets have changed and the impact of the global financial crisis; however, this is a dynamic situation worth regular review.

We shall then move on to consider the role and activities of the two main regulators of the financial services industry: the FSA and the Office of Fair Trading (OFT). Both have the legal power and the profile to be able to enforce fines, penalties and, in some cases, prosecution for misdemeanours. These actions are to protect both consumers and the economy as a whole. We should, however, bear in mind that the FSA is due to be replaced by the end of 2012 and the future of the OFT is currently under review.; students should keep themselves abreast of these changes.

4.1 The role and function of banks and lending institutions in society

Before considering banks and lending institutions, let us first consider the commodity in which they deal – **money**. The existence of money is taken for granted in all advanced societies today. Most people are unaware of the enormous contribution that the concept of money, and the industry that has developed to manage it, have made to our present way of life.

In earlier civilisations, the process of bartering was adequate for exchanging goods and services. In modern society people still produce goods or provide services that they could, in theory, trade with others for the things they need.

The complexity of life, however, and the sheer size of some transactions make it virtually impossible for people today to match what they have to offer against what others can supply to them. What is used is a separate commodity that people will accept in exchange for any product (a **medium of exchange**). It also forms a common denominator against which the value of all products can be measured (a **unit of account**). These two important functions are carried out by the commodity we call **money**. In order to be acceptable as a medium of exchange, money must have certain properties. In particular it must be:

◆ sufficient in quantity;

◆ generally acceptable to all parties in all transactions;

◆ divisible into small units, so that transactions of all sizes can be precisely carried out;

◆ portable.

Money also acts as a **store of value**. In other words, it can be saved because it can be used to separate transactions in time. Money received today as payment for work done or for goods sold can be stored in the knowledge that it can be exchanged for goods or services later when required. To fulfil this function, money must retain its **exchange value** or purchasing power and the effect of **inflation** can adversely affect this function. Inflation is a rise in the general level of prices of goods and services over a period of time. When the general price level rises, each unit of money buys fewer goods and services; consequently, inflation is a decline in the real value of money – a loss of purchasing power.

Notes and coins are **legal tender** – they have the backing of the government and the central bank – but measuring the amount of money in the financial system involves much more than counting the cash. It includes amounts held in current accounts and deposit accounts, and other forms of investments.

Activity

> Many countries in the eurozone have adopted the euro as their legal tender. What benefits does the euro bring to these countries as a group?

The financial services industry exists largely to facilitate the use of money. It 'oils the wheels' of commerce and government by channelling money from those who have a surplus, and wish to lend it for a profit, to those who wish to borrow it, and are willing to pay for its use. Of course, the financial services organisations want to make a profit from providing this service and, in the process of so doing, they provide the public with products and services that offer among other things:

◆ **convenience**, such as current accounts for receiving and making payments;

◆ a means of achieving otherwise difficult **objectives**, such as buying a house by using a mortgage loan to raise the funds;

◆ **protection** from risk, using insurance products.

Activity

> What other benefits do financial services providers give to their customers through the provision of products and services?

4.1.1 Intermediation

In any economy there are **surplus** and **deficit** sectors. The surplus sector comprises those individuals and organisations that are cash-rich; they own more liquid funds than they currently wish to spend. Their aim is to lend out their surplus funds to gain a return on their loan and so earn more money (**credit interest**). The deficit sector comprises those who own fewer liquid funds than they want to spend. These people are prepared to pay a cost for money (**debit interest**) to anyone who will lend to them.

Activity

> What organisations act as financial intermediaries?

In this context, a **financial intermediary** is an institution that borrows money from the surplus sector of the economy and lends it to the deficit sector. A lower rate of interest is paid to the person with the surplus and a higher rate of interest is charged to the person with the deficit. An intermediary's **profit margin** is the difference between the two interest rates. Banks and building societies are the best-known examples of a financial intermediary that undertakes this function.

This 'middleman' role is not always used and the surplus and deficit sectors make a deal directly. This is known as **disintermediation**. An example of disintermediation is when companies issue shares to raise funds from the public. Recent examples of this are where financial services organisations wished to raise capital and approached existing shareholders for funds in exchange for discounted shares or borrowed directly from the government.

There are, however, several reasons why both individuals and companies need the services of the intermediaries. The four main reasons relate to the following factors.

1. **Geographic location**: there is the physical problem that individual lenders and borrowers would have to find each other and would probably be restricted to their own area or circle of contacts. An individual potential borrower in London is unlikely to be aware of a person in Edinburgh with money to lend, but each may have easy access to a branch of a high-street bank.

2. **Aggregation**: even if a potential borrower could find a potential lender, the latter might not have enough money available to satisfy the borrower's requirements. The majority of retail deposits are relatively small, averaging under £1,000, while loans are typically larger, with many mortgages being for £50,000 and above. But intermediaries can overcome this size mismatch by combining (or aggregating) small deposits.

3. **Maturity transformation**: even supposing that a borrower could find a lender who had the amount they wanted, there is a further problem. The borrower may need the funds for a longer period of time than that for which the lender is prepared to lend them. The majority of deposits are very short term in instant access accounts, whereas most loans are required for longer periods. Personal loans are often for two or three years, while companies often borrow for five or more years and many mortgages are for twenty or twenty-five years. Intermediaries are able to overcome this maturity mismatch by offering a wide range of deposit accounts to a wide range of depositors, thus helping to ensure that not all of the depositors' funds are withdrawn at the same time.

Intermediaries are also able to access funds from institutional **money markets** to bridge gaps in depositors' and borrowers' requirements.

4. **Risk transformation**: individual depositors are generally reluctant to lend all their savings to another individual or company, principally because of the risk of default or fraud. But intermediaries enable lenders to spread this risk over a wide variety of borrowers so that, if a few fail to repay, the intermediary can absorb the loss. In recent times we have seen in the UK that if a financial intermediary does get into difficulty the government will step in to help so that consumers' deposits are not put at risk.

Activity

> Make a list of the deposit and savings accounts that your bank offers. How do the maturity dates or notice periods match the lending offered?
>
> How does your organisation manage any mismatches?

4.1.2 Banks

A great majority of banks are large public limited companies (plcs) often comprising groups of companies, and not just based in the UK – some have a global presence, such as HSBC. They are owned by their shareholders, who have the right to share in the distribution of the company's profits in the form of dividends and can contribute to decisions about how the company is run by voting at shareholders' meetings.

Prior to the 1980s, which saw the **deregulation** of the financial services industry and **demutualisation** of societies, there were more clearly defined boundaries between different kinds of financial organisation: some were retail banks, some wholesale banks; others were life assurance companies or general insurance companies, although a few (known as composite insurers) offered both types of insurance. Yet others were investment companies. Today, many of the distinctions have become blurred, if they have not disappeared altogether. Increasing numbers of mergers and takeovers have taken place across the boundaries and now even the term **bancassurance**, which was coined to describe banks that owned insurance companies (or vice versa), is inadequate to describe the complex nature of modern financial management groups. For example, one major UK 'bank' offers the following range of services:

◆ retail banking services;

◆ mortgage services through a subsidiary that is a former building society;

◆ payment card services, split into: UK customers; international customers; corporate chargecards; and merchant services;

◆ wealth management services, for high-net-worth individuals;

◆ financial asset management (fund management) for institutional customers;

◆ investment banking, including financing, risk management and corporate finance advice;

◆ insurance services, by acting as an independent intermediary in relation to general insurance and as an appointed representative in relation to life assurance, pensions and income protection.

Activity

> For your own bank or that of a competitor, list the different types of product and service available across the whole group of companies.

4.1.2.1 The Bank of England

The Bank of England (often referred to simply as 'the Bank') was founded by a group of wealthy London merchants in 1694 and later granted a Royal Charter by William III. It developed a unique relationship with the Crown and Parliament, which was formalised in 1946 when it was nationalised and became the UK's **central bank**. A central bank is an organisation that acts as banker to the government, supervises the economy and regulates the supply of money. In the United States, for example, these tasks are the responsibility of the US central bank, which is known as the Federal Reserve. Within the eurozone, the European Central Bank (ECB) acts as central bank for those states that have accepted monetary union.

The Bank of England has a number of important roles within the UK economy. Its main functions are as follows.

◆ **Issuer of banknotes**: the Bank of England is the central note-issuing authority and is charged with ensuring that an adequate supply of notes is in circulation.

◆ **Banker to the government**: the government's own account is held at the Bank of England. The Bank provides finance to cover any deficit by making an automatic loan to the government. If there is a surplus, the Bank may lend it out as part of its general debt management policy.

◆ **Banker to the banks**: all the major banks have accounts with the Bank of England for depositing or obtaining cash, settling clearing, and other transactions. In this capacity, the Bank can wield considerable influence over the rates of interest in various money markets, by changing the rate of interest it charges to banks that borrow or the rate it gives to banks that deposit.

◆ **Adviser to the government**: the Bank of England, having built up a specialised knowledge of the UK economy over many years, is able to advise the government and help it to formulate its monetary policy. The Bank's role in this regard has been significantly enhanced since May 1997, with full responsibility for setting interest rates in the UK having been given to the Bank's **Monetary Policy Committee (MPC)**. This committee meets once a month and its mandate in setting the base rate is to ensure that the government's inflation target is met.

◆ **Foreign exchange market**: the Bank of England manages the UK's official reserves of gold and foreign currencies on behalf of the Treasury.

◆ **Lender of last resort**: the Bank of England traditionally makes funds available when the banking system is short of liquidity, in order to maintain confidence in the system. This function became very important in 2007/2008 following a run on Northern Rock and subsequent liquidity problems for a number of banks.

◆ **Promoting the stability of the UK financial system:** the Financial Policy Committee (FPC), the Prudential Regulation Authority (PRA) and the Financial Conduct Authority (FCA) will take over the former responsibilities of the FSA during 2012.

Activity

> Visit the Bank of England website and review what happens at MPC meetings and how accountability to the public is ensured.

4.1.3 Building societies

A building society is owned by its customers, who are classed as 'members' , and it is termed a **mutual organisation**. This type of organisation is not constituted as a company and does not, therefore, have shareholders. The most common types of mutual organisation are building societies, co-operatives, friendly societies, credit unions and a small proportion of life assurance companies. This is in contrast to a bank, which is owned by shareholders and aims to make a profit that it can pay out to them as a dividend.

If a mutual organisation makes money on the products and services that it provides to its customers, this surplus is shared out among them by reducing the interest that they pay on their loans, giving them more interest on savings or retaining it in reserves to strengthen the business. The members can determine how the organisation is managed through general meetings similar to those attended by shareholders of a company. In the case of a building society, the members comprise its depositors and certain classes of borrowers.

Since the Building Societies Act 1986, a building society has been able to **demutualise**: in other words, to convert to a bank with its legal status changed to that of a public limited company. Such a change requires the approval of its members, but this approval has in practice generally been readily given, not least because of the **windfall** of free shares to which the members have been entitled following conversion to a company. The Abbey National Building Society, for instance, demutualised to become, first, the 'Abbey' and then the 'Abbey Bank'.

The possibility of a windfall on conversion led in the 1990s to a spate of **carpetbagging**. This refers to the practice of opening an account at a building society that it is believed will soon convert, purely to obtain the subsequent allocation of shares on conversion. Societies considering conversion have, in response, sought to protect the interests of their long-term members by placing restrictions on the opening of new accounts.

At one time, banks and building societies had quite different ranges of products. Building societies mostly undertook residential mortgage lending, while banks offered current accounts, overdrafts and personal loans. As a result of the deregulation brought about by the Building Societies Act 1986, building societies are able to offer many products that are similar to retail banks.

An advantage of converting into a bank is that shares are offered for sale to new investors – that is, to people who are not customers. In this way new shareholders lend the organisation money in exchange for a share in the profits. The new bank can use this extra funding to develop its business – buildings, employees, computer systems, and so on.

There are, however, disadvantages of converting from a building society to a bank. The new bank must pay shareholders from its profits and there will be pressure to do so. There may be a conflict between how the shareholders and customers want the organisation to operate. In a mutual organisation the members are the customers and have the opportunity to make their feelings known about the management of the organisation at the annual general meeting.

Organisations that are owned by shareholders are at risk of being taken over by another organisation. The Abbey, mentioned above, was taken over by the Santander Group from Spain and rebranded as Santander UK.

Activity

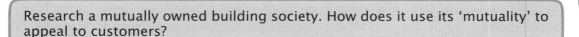

Research a mutually owned building society. How does it use its 'mutuality' to appeal to customers?

4.1.4 Finance companies

Finance companies offer lending facilities to consumers and as such would appear to be in direct competition with retail banks because they deal in consumer loans. They also lend to businesses. Sometimes, the finance company is part of a leading bank (Black Horse Finance is part of Lloyds Banking Group, for example), but they may also be independent and specialise in car loans, furniture loans, holiday loans, etc – in fact any purchase where a consumer might feel that they would like to spread payments over a period of time.

Another example is where a customer is buying a new car. The garage might offer finance terms through hire purchase or leasing, so that the car could be paid for over a number of years. If the customer were to accept the terms, however, it would be a finance company, rather than the garage, that provided the finance.

Before taking out loans with such companies, customers should check the terms carefully, because it may be cheaper to take out a bank loan. A number of these companies do, however, manage to run **0 per cent finance** deals. A '0 per cent finance deal' is a loan on which no interest is charged provided that payment is made in full by the due date.

Some of these loans, particularly car loans, are different from loans made by banks, as they are **hire purchase** agreements. This means that the ownership of the asset, in this case the car, does not pass to the borrower until the loan has been paid in full. Customers need to be aware of the nature of the loan into which they are entering. This type of finance provides considerable competition for retail bank personal loans, particularly as it is offered at **point of sale** when the customer wishes to take ownership of their new purchase.

Many finance companies belong to the **Finance and Leasing Association (FLA)** which is the leading trade association for the asset, consumer and motor finance sectors in the UK. They all subscribe to the FLA's code of conduct. At the end of 2010 FLA members financed £69.8bn of new business. Of this, £19.6bn was provided to the business sector and UK public services, representing almost 25 per cent of all fixed capital investment in the UK in that year (excluding real property and own-account software). The remaining £50.2bn was provided to the consumer sector, representing almost 30 per cent of all unsecured lending in the UK. FLA members provided £18.4bn of motor finance in 2010 and financed more than 50 per cent of all new car registrations in the UK. We will look at the FLA again in section 7.6.2.

4.1.5 Credit unions

Another example of a mutual organisation is the credit union. Credit unions are **financial co-operatives** run for the benefit of their members, who are all linked in a particular way, for instance by living in the same area or belonging to the same club, church, employer or other association. A co-operative is an autonomous (self-governing) group of people who have come together to meet common economic, cultural and social needs by forming a jointly owned, democratic organisation.

In order to join a credit union, the member (customer) must meet the membership requirements, pay any required entrance fee and buy at least one £1 share in the union. All members are equal, regardless of the size of their shareholding.

Credit unions are owned by the members and controlled through a voluntary board of directors, all of whom are members of the union. The members elect the board members at the annual general meeting. Although the directors control the organisation, the day-to-day management is usually carried out by the union's employees. Credit unions are authorised and regulated by the FSA, and savers are protected through the Financial Services Compensation Scheme.

Credit unions offer simple savings and loan facilities to members. Savers invest cash in units of £1, with each unit buying a share in the credit union. Each share pays an annual dividend, typically 2–3 per cent, although the maximum permitted by law is 8 per cent. These savings create a pool of money that can be lent to other members; the loans typically have an interest rate of around 1 per cent of the reducing balance each month (with a legal maximum of 2 per cent of the reducing capital).

A unique feature of credit unions is that members' savings and loan balances are covered by **life assurance**. This means that any loan balance will be paid off on death, and a lump sum equal to the savings held will also be paid, subject to overall limits. In order to compete in today's financial services marketplace, many credit unions offer additional services, often in conjunction with partners, including basic bank accounts, insurance services and mortgages.

Traditionally, credit unions operated in the poorer sections of the community, providing savings and reasonably priced short- and medium-term loans to their members as an alternative to 'loan sharks'. In more recent years it has been recognised that credit unions have a strong role to play in combating financial exclusion and delivering a range of financial services and financial education to those outside the mainstream. It has also been recognised that the image of credit unions needs to be improved in order to encourage participation from a wider range of consumers. As a result, the government has funded a number of initiatives to widen the scope of the movement. An example of how the government has helped is given in the case study below.

Case study – cheque replacement and financial inclusion

This Department will continue to work with the Post Office to explore further opportunities for them to support new ways of delivering welfare, including playing an important role in supporting the delivery of universal credit – building on the work on pilots already underway.

We also see real opportunities for the Post Office network in building closer links with credit unions. Credit unions have made great progress in recent years in bringing affordable financial services to people who would not otherwise be able to access them. I want to see credit unions – in partnership with the Post Office – providing more services, more efficiently, to more people.

I am therefore pleased to announce this Department's continuing support for credit unions, building on the existing growth fund, and providing the new funding required for further expansion. This modernisation fund, worth up to £73m over the next four years, will support those credit unions who are ready and prepared to step up to the plate – to expand their service to benefit more customers.

My Department will work with the credit unions to look at ways in which the future progress of this sector can best be supported. This includes the possible development of a shared banking platform, for which funding has already been set aside. Subject to successful feasibility studies, this will open up opportunities for many more people to access credit union services, including through the Post Office network.

Making credit union services available to more people who could benefit from them is an important part of our welfare reforms: making work pay; reforming crisis loans; making people better off for every pound they earn through universal credit; and simplifying the benefits system.

From a statement by the Minister of State, Department for Work and Pensions (Chris Grayling), March 2011. Source: www.abcul.org

4.2 The changing profile of financial services and the impact of the global financial crisis

Earlier in this topic we looked at how financial intermediaries bring together people with surplus funds and those who have a deficit and are prepared to pay a cost for borrowing these funds.

Retail banks and the larger mutual societies are the main intermediaries for the general public and businesses, being primarily concerned with common services such as deposits, loans and payment systems. They deliver their products through traditional branch networks, call centres or the Internet and, more increasingly, mobile devices.

With the widespread replacement of cheques by payment cards, the traditional suppliers of retail banking are experiencing increasing competition from major stores, such as Tesco and Sainsbury, and well-known brands such as Virgin, which are offering their own banking facilities, credit cards and other financial services.

Wholesale banking refers to the process of raising money through the wholesale money markets in which financial institutions and other large companies buy and sell financial assets. The distinction between 'retail' and 'wholesale' in financial services is much less obvious than it used to be, however, with many institutions operating in both areas. This is a feature of how the financial services industry is changing, as organisations look for opportunities for growth and revenue.

In June 2010, the government announced the creation of the Independent Banking Commission (IBC). Its role is to consider whether to separate retail and wholesale banking in the UK in order to promote financial stability and competition. It is due to make recommendations to the government by September 2011.

The main retail banks are heavily involved in wholesale banking in order to top up deposits from their branch networks as necessary. For example, if a bank has the opportunity to make a substantial profitable loan but does not have adequate deposits, it can raise the money very quickly on the **interbank market**. This is a very large market encompassing over 400 banking institutions, which serves to recycle surplus cash held by banks, either directly between banks or more usually through the services of specialist money brokers. The rate of interest charged in the interbank market is the **London Interbank Offered Rate (Libor)**. It acts as a reference rate for the majority of corporate lending, for which the rate is quoted as Libor plus a specified margin. Libor rates are fixed daily and vary in maturity from overnight through to one year.

It was the failure of the interbank market that led to the financial crisis. The financial system came close to collapse in the autumn of 2008, following the failure of **Lehman Brothers**. Other banks refused to trade with the company and, without the ability to trade or investors prepared to bet on its long-term viability, Lehman effectively had no business. The resulting shock to the global financial system led to unprecedented action by governments and central banks, which injected $14 trillion into financial systems around the world to prevent disaster. This was the equivalent of half the gross domestic product (GDP — the total value of all goods and services produced) of Europe and the USA.

As a result, almost half the world's largest 20 banks received **direct government investment**, and central bank lending to the economy more than doubled. Losses at major UK banks soared from £150bn to £400bn between October and December 2008, and outpaced bank attempts to raise additional capital of around £100bn.

The impact of these huge losses was to make banks **reluctant to lend**. UK banks found it difficult to bridge the gap between what they lent out and what they were receiving from savers. They faced difficulty in raising money cheaply on the capital markets from wholesale sources, a situation made worse because the UK and other governments still have large budget deficits. This has made the cost of borrowing more expensive for everyone.

Another outcome of the global financial crisis has been **increased regulation** of banks and a requirement for them to hold more capital and liquidity reserves. We have seen further consolidation through mergers and acquisitions, although there has been much debate about the appropriate size and structure of banks. Some people argue that banks should not be allowed to become so large that they are '**too big to fail**': if a bank becomes so big that its failure would have a catastrophic impact on the national or international economy, the government would have no choice but to rescue it. This might encourage the bank to carry out its business irresponsibly, knowing that the government would always bail it out if it runs into difficulties. The IBC is considering how best to address these issues.

There has been a **loss of confidence** in the financial services industry around the world, evidenced by the drop in company values on stock markets and consumer scepticism about the benefits of investing in stock-based products. The difficulty consumers have faced in accessing credit has led to a loss of confidence in the housing market, and **property prices** have fallen as a result. The downturn in the economy has seen consumers lose their jobs, leading to financial hardship with increasing numbers of people in debt. We shall look at this further in Topic 12. However, historically, recession and boom tend to be **cyclical**, so at some point the economy will recover.

In the next section we shall take a more in-depth look at regulation and some of the reasons why it is likely to increase.

4.3   Regulation of financial services in the UK

Let us look at how the regulation of financial services is organised in the UK. Broadly speaking, it is a five-tier process.

1. **First level**: European legislation that impacts on the UK financial industry. The two main types of European legislation are **regulations** and **directives**.

2. **Second level**: the Acts of Parliament that set out what can and cannot be done. Whenever reference is made to Acts of Parliament, it should be borne in mind that the effects of the laws are often achieved through subsidiary legislation – known as **statutory instruments** – which are made pursuant to (in accordance with) the Act. Examples of legislation that directly affect the industry are the Financial Services and Markets Act 2000, the Banking Act 1987, the Building Societies Act 1997 and the Consumer Credit Acts 1974 and 2006.

3. **Third level**: the regulatory bodies that monitor the regulations and issue rules about how the requirements of the legislation are to be met in practice. At the time of writing, the responsibilities of the FSA are being handed over to the Financial Policy Committee (FPC), the Prudential Regulatory Authority (PRA) and the Financial Conduct Authority (FCA). These bodies are expected to be operational by the end of 2012.

4. **Fourth level**: the policies and practices of the financial institutions themselves and the internal departments that ensure they operate legally and competently – for example, the compliance department of a life assurance company.

5. **Fifth level**: the arbitration schemes to which consumers' complaints can be referred. In most cases, this will be the Financial Ombudsman Service.

In the latter part of the twentieth century, there was a strong assertion in Western societies of the rights of the **consumer**. Many people believe that, as commercial organisations have grown through mergers and acquisitions, they have become more remote from their customers and more concerned with their own financial results than with customer satisfaction. Concerns about this trend are reflected in the emergence of both government-sponsored organisations, such as the Competition Commission, and consumer advice bodies such as *Which?*.

Some people believe that the pendulum has now swung too far in the other direction, and that consumers are now too powerful – notably in the USA, where there are high levels of litigation. However, the general view is that protection for the consumer is both necessary and appropriate.

One of the primary objectives pursued by most modern governments is an economic and legal environment in which a balance is established between the need for businesses to make a profit and the rights of customers to receive a fair deal. This has led to the regulation, to some degree, of most industries in the UK but, at the same time, the government recognises the right of companies to make a profit. Indeed, it recognises that it is essential that companies be permitted to make a reasonable profit; it would otherwise be impossible to attract the investment that sustains the industries on which the UK economy depends.

These twin objectives of a free market for business enterprise and the protection of the consumer are among the principles on which the European Union is based. It is not surprising to discover that these objectives have been promoted largely through European legislation, most of which impacts, either directly or indirectly, on the UK. The force of European law can be seen in most recent major developments in the regulation of UK financial institutions.

Perhaps because it deals with money, a vital common denominator both in the lives of individuals and in the national economy, the financial services industry has become one of the most regulated business sectors of all. There is no sign of a slowing down in the trend to greater supervision of the industry.

Although governments try to foresee problems and to introduce legislation as a means of 'prevention rather than cure', it remains true that most regulatory legislation in the past has been reactive rather than proactive; it has been passed in response to problems, rather than designed to pre-empt them. Examples of this include the following.

◆ Particular **scandals or crises**: for example, the events surrounding the collapse of Barings Bank in the 1990s and the problems at Equitable Life that were exposed in 2000. These have shown up the need for prudential control and for protection against mismanagement and fraud.

◆ An increase in **consumers' financial awareness** and a demand for a more customer-focused business approach; demand for a 'one-stop shop' approach to financial services sales.

◆ The need to respond to **changes in lifestyle**: more relaxed attitudes to marriage and divorce in recent years have led to a strengthening of the rights of divorcees to share in former spouses' pension benefits; the introduction of civil partnerships for same-sex couples has extended the scope of some tax benefits and other financial and social benefits.

◆ Developments in **business methods**: technological advance, in particular, has fuelled many changes in the last years of the twentieth century and the early part of the twenty-first; this is particularly true for banks and building societies, whose customers now can, and do, carry out many of their transactions electronically.

◆ Innovation in **product design**: rapid expansion has been seen in the ranges of certain products, particularly in **mortgage business** in the boom years before the financial crisis. This has made it more important than ever to provide consumers with sufficient clear information about the features and benefits of the products they are buying.

◆ The increase in the number and **complexity** of financial products: this has made it necessary to provide customers with more information and advice.

Activity

> Which of the issues above do you think are most important to customers you meet?

Now, however, there is a strong move towards a culture of recognising and preventing problems before they arise, where possible, rather than simply picking up the pieces afterwards and allocating blame and punishment (although punishment has not been discarded).

Government policy on the regulation of the financial services industry in the UK has, since the late 1970s, displayed what appears to be something of a paradox. There have been specific moves in what seem to be two opposite directions: in some areas, **deregulation** has been a key development; at the same time, many aspects of the industry have become more **closely regulated**. The aims of developments in all areas have been to benefit the consumer through greater choice, better service and stronger protection.

Deregulation was experienced mainly in the worlds of banking and building societies. Traditionally, banks had not been active in the mortgage market because government credit controls had severely restricted their lending activities, while building societies – operating under legislation that dated, in some cases, from as far back as the nineteenth century – were restricted to lending on mortgages and to offering simple personal savings products. But the world had moved on: the increase in home ownership was creating a huge demand for mortgages, and customers were demanding a much wider range of products and services from their chosen financial providers.

The deregulation introduced in the UK in the 1980s was designed to remove these barriers, enabling institutions to broaden their services and to move into new markets. Increased competition was beneficial for customers who, in addition to having a much wider choice of both products and providers, saw a reduction in the cost of many products. The increased size and complexity of the financial marketplace, however, quickly revealed the inadequate protection afforded to customers by existing legislation. Many existing laws were quite inadequate to deal with what was now a much more sophisticated and competitive industry.

4.3.1 The FSA's objectives, role and activities

Until the FSA is disbanded in 2012 (see section 4.3), its role is to oversee the regulation of the financial services industry in the UK. The FSA is not a government department – it is a limited company – but it does have statutory powers, given to it under the Banking Act 1987, the FSMA 2000 and other legislation. The FSA's board, which makes its policy decisions, is, however, appointed by the Treasury, which has overall responsibility for the UK financial services industry.

The FSA carries out its role by setting standards, developing rules and regulations, supervising their implementation, authorising firms and individuals, and providing guidance and training. These and other areas of FSA activity are covered in a range of **sourcebooks**, which make up the **Handbook**.

The FSA has also been given the following statutory objectives:

◆ **maintaining confidence in the UK financial system**, including financial markets, exchanges and regulated activities – the aim is to ensure that markets are 'fair, efficient and transparent';

◆ **promoting financial stability** – contributing to the protection and enhancement of the stability of the UK financial system;

◆ **securing an appropriate level of protection for consumers**, but it should be noted that the FSA emphasises that it cannot provide 100 per cent protection and an 'appropriate' level of protection may depend on:

   – the different level of risk that relates to different investments;

   – the different experience/expertise of different consumers;

   – the consumers' need for accurate advice and information;

   – the principle that consumers should take responsibility for their decisions;

◆ **reducing the scope for financial crime**, the three main areas that the FSA seeks to control being:

   – money laundering;

   – fraud and dishonesty, including e-crime;

   – criminal market conduct, such as insider dealing.

The performance of the FSA in regulating the industry will be judged against a set of 'principles of good regulation'. It must be seen to be:

◆ allocating its resources in the most efficient and economic way;

◆ ensuring that the costs of regulation are in proportion to the benefits;

◆ taking proper account of the responsibilities of those who manage authorised firms;

◆ facilitating innovation and maintaining industry competitiveness;

◆ taking into account the international character of financial services and the UK's competitive position;

◆ facilitating, and not having an unnecessarily adverse effect on, competition.

4.3.2 Enforcement

Under the FSMA 2000 the FSA has an extensive range of disciplinary, criminal and civil powers to take action against regulated and non-regulated firms and individuals who are failing or have failed to meet the standards they require.

These powers include being able to:

◆ withdraw a firm's authorisation;

◆ prohibit an individual from operating in financial services;

◆ prevent an individual from undertaking specific regulated activities;

- censure firms and individuals through public statements;

- impose financial penalties;

- seek injunctions;

- apply to court to freeze assets;

- seek restitution orders; and

- prosecute firms and individuals who undertake regulated activities without authorisation.

The following press release from the FSA gives an example of the types of action the FSA can take against individuals who break the rules.

Case study – Financial Services Authority (FSA) fines ActivTrades Plc for failing to protect clients' assets adequately

Under the FSA's client money rules, firms are required to keep client money separate from the firm's money in segregated accounts with trust status. This helps to safeguard and ring-fence the client money in the event of the firm's insolvency. Between 14 April 2009 and 2 September 2010, the amount of client money held by ActivTrades ranged between £3.4m and £23.6m and averaged £12.2m. ActivTrades failed to ensure that this money was fully segregated; putting some client money at risk should the firm become insolvent.

ActivTrades' failures were discovered as part of an FSA thematic review into the management of client assets and money held by firms. Based on the initial findings of this review, the FSA required ActivTrades to engage a skilled person to review its client money arrangements.

The skilled person's report highlighted that, on several occasions, client money was mixed with ActivTrades' funds. In particular between 29 January 2010 and 14 June 2010, client money totalling €800,000 was held in an account used for ActivTrades' own funds, which meant that it was not adequately protected. The skilled person's report also identified a number of other serious failings including failure to perform client money calculations or reconciliations accurately and failure to pay interest on client money. ActivTrades was also unable to monitor and assess the adequacy of its client money arrangements due to weaknesses in the information provided to senior management.

Linda Woodall, FSA director of small firms, said: 'It is essential for firms to adhere to our client money rules and our recent action in this area shows our continuing focus on the importance of managing and protecting client assets adequately. Ensuring the necessary client money safeguards are in place is a key element of consumer protection, and firms of all sizes must ensure that any client money they hold is properly segregated.'

ActivTrades co-operated fully with the FSA in the course of its investigation and has taken significant steps to rectify its client money issues.

Source: www.fsa.gov.uk, 15 March 2011.

4.4 The Office of Fair Trading

The Office of Fair Trading (OFT) is the UK's consumer and competition authority. Its role is to make markets work well for consumers. Markets work well when businesses are in open, fair and vigorous competition with each other to gain the consumer's custom. The OFT seeks to ensure that consumers have as much choice as possible across all the different sectors of the marketplace because when consumers have choice, they have genuine and enduring power (source:www.oft.gov.uk).

The OFT deals with a wide range of issues, not just those from the financial services sector. The OFT gathers intelligence about markets and trader behaviour from a range of sources and responds to super-complaints about markets from designated consumer bodies. Where there are potential problems, it undertakes market studies and recommends or takes further action where it is needed.

In relation to providers of credit, the OFT regulates lending to customers, as we shall see in later sections.

Under a reorganisation of government departments in October 2010 it was decided to merge the competition activities of the OFT with the Competition Commission. This is another independent public body whose aim is to ensure healthy competition between companies in the UK, based on the premise that the existence of healthy competition leads individual companies to charge reasonable prices and to supply good-quality products.

It is likely that the Financial Conduct Authority (formerly referred to as the Consumer Protection and Markets Authority) will take over the consumer credit licensing and enforcement activities of the OFT and students should look out for any developments in this area.

4.4.1 The OFT's objectives, roles and activities

The OFT is a non-ministerial government department established by statute in 1973.

As an independent professional organisation, the OFT plays a leading role in promoting and protecting consumer interests throughout the UK, while ensuring that businesses are fair and competitive. Their tools to carry out this work are the powers granted to the OFT under consumer and competition legislation.

The OFT pursues its goals by:

◆ encouraging businesses to comply with competition and consumer law and to improve their trading practices through self-regulation;

◆ acting decisively to stop hardcore or flagrant offenders;

◆ studying markets and recommending action where required;

◆ empowering consumers with the knowledge and skills to make informed choices and get the best value from markets, and helping them to resolve problems with suppliers through Consumer Direct.

The OFT achieves its aims through collaboration with others. Their partners include sector regulators, government, the courts, the Competition Commission, the European Commission, local authority trading standards services, and businesses, consumers and their representatives.

4.4.2 Enforcement

The **Consumer Protection from Unfair Trading Regulations (CPRs)** and the **Consumer Credit Act 2006** have made significant changes to the body of UK consumer protection law. Together with the **Unfair Terms in Consumer Contracts Regulations 1999** and the **Enterprise Act 2002**, they mark a fundamental move away from prescriptive regulation towards a principles-based consumer protection regime which encourages targeted, risk-based enforcement geared to the efficient operation of the market. At the same time, they:

◆ increase the range of enforcement tools available to enforcers;

◆ strengthen investigative powers; and

◆ enable the OFT to take criminal proceedings and seek financial penalties, alongside existing civil enforcement and compliance tools.

Though the OFT is not primarily a regulator, certain of its functions are regulatory in character, and as such are subject to the statutory provisions referred to earlier. These functions are in the areas of consumer enforcement, consumer credit licensing and anti-money-laundering supervision. A statement of principles sets out how, particularly when undertaking enforcement in these areas, the OFT seeks to comply with the requirements both of the law and of good practice.

Figure 4.1 illustrates the range of options available to the OFT. It will normally seek to use less onerous options in the first instance unless the circumstances indicate that formal enforcement action is the appropriate first step: such action may include a criminal investigation and prosecution.

Figure 4.1   Range of enforcement options open to the OFT

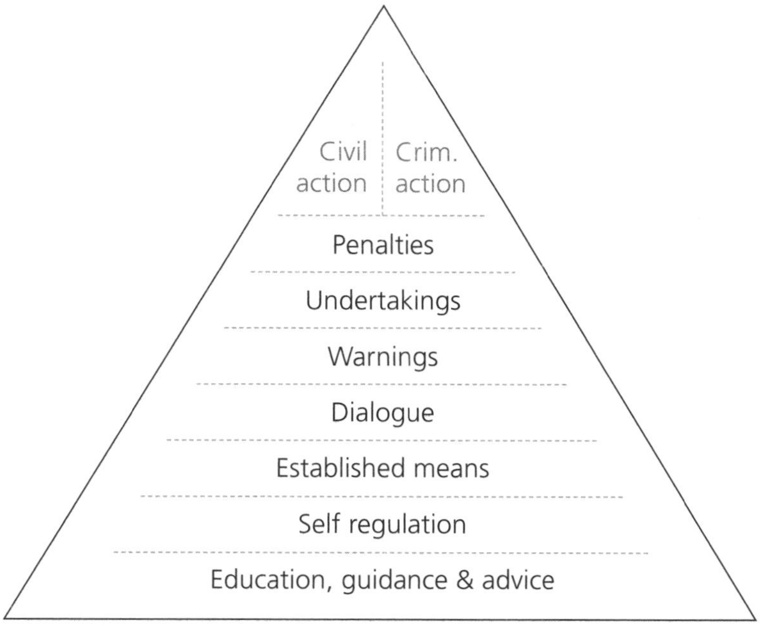

Source: Statement of Consumer Protection Enforcement Principles Crown Copyright 2008

4.4.3 The OFT and consumer credit

The OFT is responsible for enforcing the Consumer Credit Acts (CCAs) 1974 and 2006. This law regulates most lenders and people offering credit, or advising on it. Credit or finance companies, and anyone offering hire purchase credit, must obtain a **licence** from the OFT before they can operate and must **comply** with various rules once they have that licence.

The rules laid down under the Act include a set of **advertising regulations**, which aim to make sure that borrowers understand the full costs and implications of any loan before they buy it. They also lay down the formula for showing the **annual percentage rate (APR)**.

Activity

> Research the definition and formula for APR.

The rules also allow for **cooling-off periods** for certain loans. These give people time to change their minds without any penalty before they enter into the loan. Having this option might be important if they were to have made a decision in the heat of the moment, or been persuaded by a high-pressure salesperson.

The objective of the CCAs, and of the OFT's activities in general, is the **protection** of borrowers. They seek to ensure that customers are fully informed about the costs of loans and credit that they take out.

4.4.4 OFT consumer licences

The CCAs 1974 and 2006 require most businesses that offer credit or lend money to consumers to be licensed by the OFT. This includes where credit is arranged to finance the purchase of goods or services. Licensing arrangements are also required by debt collectors, debt advisers and businesses that offer goods for hire or leasing. Trading without a licensing arrangement is a **criminal offence** and can result in a fine and/or imprisonment.

The Act also requires certain credit and hire purchase arrangements to be set out in a particular way and to contain certain**information**.

If a consumer credit business deals with first-charge mortgages, payment protection insurance or other types of insurance, then it will need **permission** from the FSA to sell or administer regulated mortgage contracts and general insurance contracts. There is risk of a fine or imprisonment if a business carries on a mortgage or general insurance business without either permission or arranging to become exempt.

Resources

www.bankofengland.co.uk

www.oft.gov.uk

www.fsa.gov.uk

www.abcul.org

Review questions

The following review questions are designed so that you can check your understanding of this topic.

The answers to the questions are provided at the end of these learning materials.

1. What are the characteristics of money?

2. What is intermediation?

3. What are the functions of the Bank of England?

4. How do building societies differ from banks?

5. How do credit unions differ from banks?

6. Why has there been increased legislation in the financial services industry?

7. What problems arose for consumers following deregulation of banks and building societies in the 1980s?

8. What are the statutory objectives of the FSA?

9. What powers of enforcement does the FSA have?

10. How does the OFT regulate the financial services industry?

Topic 5
Fundamental regulatory themes

> **Learning objective**
>
> After studying this topic, students should be able to demonstrate an understanding of the fundamental regulatory themes relating to the Financial Services Authority (FSA).

Introduction

In the last topic we looked at an overview of the main regulatory bodies for the financial services industry in the UK. This topic concentrates on some of the detail of how the regulation undertaken by the Financial Services Authority (FSA) is undertaken. We shall consider some of the main themes that have been important to the FSA in achieving its objectives, such as Treating Customers Fairly, 'Know Your Customer', measures to prevent money laundering, and complaints handling.

We shall also overview legislation relating to the Retail Banking Conduct of Business and the Payment Services Directive.

5.1   To whom, why and where does regulation apply?

Any financial services organisation carrying on business in the UK must be authorised by the FSA if it carries out **regulated activities** in relation to **regulated investments**. Similarly, individuals who undertake certain specified **controlled** functions also have to be authorised.

5.2   What activities are regulated?

The activities for which firms must be authorised include:

◆ accepting deposits;

◆ effecting and carrying out insurance contracts (including funeral plans);

◆ dealing in and arranging deals in investments;

◆ managing investments;

◆ establishing and operating collective investment schemes;

◆ establishing stakeholder pension schemes;

◆ advising on investments;

◆ mortgage lending and administration;

◆ advising on and arranging mortgages;

◆ advising on and arranging general insurance.

Permission is given in the form of a list of regulated activities that the firm is allowed to undertake; it also shows the regulated investments with which the firm is allowed to deal.

5.2.1 Capital adequacy and liquidity

A vital element of the work of any industry regulator is to ensure that the firms operating in the industry are prudently managed. The aim is to protect the firms themselves, their customers and the economy, by establishing rules and principles that should ensure the continuation of a safe and efficient market, able to withstand any foreseeable problems.

One of the key areas of **prudential control** for financial institutions relates to their capital adequacy. Simply put, capital adequacy is the requirement for firms conducting investment business to have sufficient funds. There are different rules for deposit-takers (banks and building societies), investment firms and life assurance companies.

5.2.1.1 Capital adequacy regulations for deposit-takers

Regulations about capital adequacy broadly state that institutions must have sufficient **capital** to make it very unlikely that deposits will be placed at risk. The meaning of 'capital' in this context is perhaps best illustrated by the fact that it is also sometimes referred to as **own funds**, ie the bank's own capital base, obtained from shareholders and related sources, as distinct from funds deposited by customers.

Although a bank's lending is generally financed by deposits, any losses made (for instance if a loan is written off because repayment cannot be obtained) should be borne by shareholders rather than by depositors. Minimum requirements for capital adequacy are set to protect a bank's depositors so that they do not lose money, whereas shareholders are expected to take risks.

The Basel Committee on Banking Supervision, a multinational body acting under the auspices of the Bank for International Settlements, first established an international framework for deposit-takers (principally banks) in 1988. This agreement, which among other things set out minimum capital requirements for banks, was commonly referred to as the **Basel Accord**. This was superseded by a new expanded Accord, commonly known as **Basel II**, which became fully operational in 2007.

In the aftermath of the 2008 financial crisis, the Basel Committee published proposals to further improve the quantity and quality of bank capital and to discourage excessive leverage and risk taking. These rules, already commonly known as Basel III, are expected to be phased in by the end of 2012.

Basel II was implemented in the European Union via the Capital Requirements Directive (CRD). It affects banks and building societies and certain types of investment firm. The framework consists of three 'pillars':

1. Pillar 1 of the standards sets out the **minimum capital requirements** that organisations are required to meet for credit, market and operational risk.

2. Pillar 2 requires that organisations and supervisors take a view on whether the organisation should hold **additional capital** against risks not covered in Pillar 1 and take action accordingly.

3. Pillar 3 aims to improve **market discipline** by requiring organisations to publish certain details of their risks, capital and risk management.

These minimum capital requirements are specified in terms of a bank's **solvency ratio**, which means that the capital required is denominated as a proportion of the bank's assets (mainly its loans), with appropriate allowances made for the perceived risk level of different assets.

The solvency ratio is defined as *'own funds of the institution as a percentage of the risk-adjusted value of its assets'*. Current regulations require credit institutions to keep a **solvency ratio** of at least 8 per cent. This means that their own funds must amount to at least 8 per cent of their **risk-weighted assets**. In practice, institutions normally keep more than the required 8 per cent.

The 'risk weighting' of assets is a process that is largely self-explanatory. Since the solvency ratio is designed, broadly speaking, to calculate how much an institution must hold to cover the risk of loss on its lending (its credit risk), each asset is categorised according to risk.

Activity

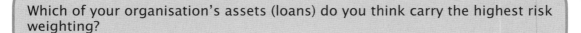

Which of your organisation's assets (loans) do you think carry the highest risk weighting?

5.2.1.2 Liquidity

Liquidity can be defined as the ease and speed with which an asset can be converted into cash. It must not be confused with insolvency, or with capital adequacy, which are different issues. In relation to banks, the definition of liquidity is a measure of a bank's ability to acquire funds immediately at a reasonable price in order to meet demands for cash outflows.

The FSA defines **liquidity risk** as the risk that a firm, though solvent, does not have sufficient financial resources available to enable it to meet its obligations as they fall due. The situation of Northern Rock in 2007 illustrates the problems that can arise.

> **Case study: Northern Rock – 2007**
>
> The bank had a business plan that involved borrowing money short term on the wholesale money markets on a regular basis to fund a proportion of its much longer-term mortgage lending. The success of the plan depended on the continuing availability of short-term interbank lending. When this dried up, the bank's liquidity quickly disappeared.

At that point, a different aspect of liquidity risk appeared, when a large number of depositors chose to withdraw their savings (a so-called '**run**' on the bank). Banks do not, of course, retain all the funds deposited with them in a readily accessible form – most of their deposits are lent to customers who wish to borrow. Only a small proportion is kept in cash or assets convertible into cash. If a run on the bank occurs, their liquidity can be quickly used up, so making the problem more acute.

Some argue that if Northern Rock had remained a building society then it would not have been so reliant on the wholesale markets for funding, as 50 per cent of its funding would have been from depositors.

As we can see from the case study above, in assessing liquidity risks, banks need to consider the timing of both their assets and their liabilities and endeavour to match them as far as possible.

◆ **Asset liquidity**: a firm's assets (loans made to customers) can provide liquidity in three main ways: by being sold for cash, by reaching their maturity date, and by providing security for borrowing. *Asset concentrations*, where a large number of receipts from assets are likely to occur around the same time, should be avoided.

◆ **Liability liquidity**: similarly, banks try to avoid *liability concentrations*, where a single factor or a single decision could result in a sudden significant claim. A wide spread of maturity dates of deposits taken from customers is one obvious way to achieve this.

5.3   What products are regulated?

Regulated investments include:

◆ deposits;

◆ electronic money (e-money);

◆ insurance contracts, including funeral plans;

◆ shares, company loan stocks and debentures, and warrants;

◆ gilt-edged stocks and local authority stocks;

◆ units in collective investment schemes;

◆ rights under stakeholder pension schemes;

◆ options and futures;

◆ mortgage contracts.

The FSA defines two key categories of regulated investments: **securities**, such as shares, debentures and gilts; and **contractually based investments** including life policies, personal pensions, options and futures.

Activity

> In the retail branch setting, what qualifications does an adviser who sells contractually based investments need to have?
>
> Why do you think this qualification is important?

5.4   Treating Customers Fairly

The FSA has established a very large body of rules, many of which are found in the Sourcebooks. A selection of the important rules affecting financial advisers and mortgage advisers is also included.

The establishment of rules and regulations can, however, carry with it one very serious drawback, which is that people and organisations make it their aim to comply with the letter of the law rather than to operate according to its spirit. There is also the danger that it is sometimes possible for firms to 'hide behind' the rules, using loopholes or technicalities to their own advantage.

The FSA quickly became aware of this potential drawback to its complex system of rules and introduced an initiative known as **Treating Customers Fairly** (TCF). The aim of the scheme is to develop a more ethical frame of mind within the industry, leading to more ethical behaviour at every stage of firms' and individuals' relationships with their customers.

Activity

> What exactly is meant by Treating Customers Fairly?

The FSA has declined to supply a definition of 'fair', claiming that fairness is a concept that is 'flexible and dynamic' and that it can 'vary with particular circumstances'. Instead, firms will have to decide for themselves exactly what TCF means within their own context. What is clear is that the FSA intends that TCF will apply at every stage throughout the life cycle of financial products, beginning with product design. All the stages that follow, including sales and marketing, advice and selling, and administration, must also be carried out with TCF in mind. This carries through into all post-sales activities such as claims handling and, where necessary, dealing with complaints. The FSA has stressed that firms and employees must 'embed the principle of Treating Customers Fairly into the firm's culture and day-to-day operations'.

Despite failing to specify what 'fairness' entails, the FSA has given some guidance on the types of behaviour it would wish to see and has suggested a number of areas that a firm should consider. These include:

◆ considering specific target markets when developing products;

◆ ensuring that communications are clear and do not mislead;

- honouring promises and commitments that it has made;

- identifying and eradicating the root causes of complaints.

Responsibility for the introduction of TCF lies with a firm's senior management, which is required to ensure that TCF is 'built consistently into the operating model and culture of all aspects of the business'.

One of the key issues to be addressed is the extent to which customers are helped to understand the financial products they are buying. Firms are expected to be clear about the services they offer and about the true cost to the customer. It is vitally important, for instance, that information is provided to customers in a way that is clear, fair and not misleading. Firms should always consider the ways in which the customer will assess their product against others in the market, and ensure that a fair comparison can be made. This means not only that product literature should be clear and appropriate to the expected financial sophistication of the customer, but also that the advice given should be of a sufficiently high quality to reduce the risk of mis-selling.

In summary, TCF is designed to deliver six 'improved outcomes' for retail financial consumers, which the FSA has described as follows:

- Consumers will be confident that the firms they are dealing with are committed to fair treatment of customers.

- Products are designed to meet the needs of properly identified customer groups.

- Consumers are provided with clear information at all stages, before, during and after a sale.

- Any advice given is suitable for the customer, taking account of their circumstances.

- Products perform as customers have been led to expect, and associated services are of an acceptable standard.

- There are no unreasonable barriers to switching product or provider, making a claim, or complaining.

Firms must be able to demonstrate that they are consistently treating their customers fairly. This can be done by means of a review and report showing how they are delivering the six consumer outcomes described above.

5.5 Financial promotions

A **financial promotion** is defined as an 'invitation or inducement to engage in investment activity'. This includes:

- advertisements in all forms of media;

- telephone calls;

- marketing during personal visits to clients;

- presentations to groups.

Financial promotions can be 'communicated' only if they have been prepared, or approved, by an authorised person.

There is a distinction between:

◆ **non-written financial promotions**, such as personal visits and telephone conversations; and

◆ **written financial promotions**, such as newspaper advertisements and those on Internet sites.

Activity

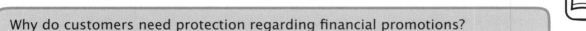

> Why do customers need protection regarding financial promotions?

The overall principle is that financial promotions to retail clients and professional clients must be fair, clear and not misleading. In the case of retail clients, this means specifically that information supplied must:

◆ be accurate – this includes the requirement not to emphasise potential benefits without giving a fair and prominent indication of the risks;

◆ be understandable by an 'average' member of the group it is aimed at;

◆ **not** disguise or obscure important terms or warnings.

Activity

> Why do you think this last point is so important?

5.5.1 Comparisons

Comparisons with other products must be meaningful, and presented in a fair and balanced way. Firms that fall within the remit of the Markets in Financial Instruments Directive (MiFID) are subject to additional requirements to detail the source of information and the assumptions made in the comparison.

5.5.2 Past performance

Past performance information must **not** be the most prominent part of a promotion. It must be made clear that it refers to the past, and it must contain a warning that past performance is not necessarily a reliable indicator of future results. Past performance data must be based on at least five years' results (or the period since the investment commenced, if less, but not less than one year).

Activity

In what ways might customers be at risk if past performance claims are exaggerated?

5.5.3 Unsolicited promotions

There are particular rules about **unsolicited non-written** promotions ('cold calls'), as follows:

◆ They are permitted only in relation to **certain investments**, including packaged products, such as life assurance policies and unit trusts. They are not permitted in relation to higher volatility funds (which use gearing) or life policies with links to such funds, due to the increased investment risk involved. Cold calls are not permitted in relation to mortgage contracts.

◆ Unsolicited telephone calls or visits must not be made during **unsocial hours**, generally taken to mean between 9.00pm and 9.00am Monday to Saturday, and not on a Sunday.

◆ The caller must **check** that the recipient is happy to proceed with the call.

Activity

Why do you think cold calls on mortgage contracts are not allowed?

5.6 Know Your Customer

One of the most important elements in the financial services industry's action against money laundering is the process of confirming the **identity** of customers. The FSA has called the need for this confirmation 'Know Your Customer' or KYC.

Evidence of identification is required:

◆ when entering into a **new business relationship** (particularly when opening a new account, investment or policy);

◆ in the case of new customers (and any existing customers whose identity has not been verified previously), when the **value of a transaction exceeds €15,000**, whether as a single transaction or as a series of linked transactions. For **life assurance policies** the limits are €1,000 for annual premiums and €2,500 for single premiums.

Evidence of identification must be obtained in every case where there is suspicion of money laundering. If there is suspicion that the applicant may not be acting on their own behalf, reasonable measures must be taken to identify the person on whose behalf the applicant is acting.

If a client is introduced to the firm by a financial intermediary or other authorised firm, it is permissible to accept the written assurance of the intermediary that they have obtained sufficient evidence of identity. This is important to, for instance, financial advisers and mortgage advisers.

The definition of what constitutes satisfactory evidence of identity is rather vague – it requires that it should be reasonably capable of establishing that the applicant is the person that they claim to be, to the satisfaction of the person who obtains the evidence. Acceptable forms of identification include:

◆ current passport;

◆ national identity card with photograph;

◆ driving licence with photograph;

◆ entry on electoral roll;

◆ recent utility bill or council tax bill.

Activity

> What rules does your organisation follow for identifying and verifying new customers?

There is also a requirement to 'know your customer' when giving financial advice. Advisers must take reasonable steps to find out and record all the details of the customer in relation to the services they are offering. The information must be collected before any recommendation is made. The areas to be considered may include the following:

◆ **Advice**: Do the adviser and the customer share a common understanding of the areas on which advice will be given? Has the adviser warned the customer of the potential limitations and risks if they do not provide advice on all the identified needs?

◆ **Customer details**: this could include information on customer needs and objectives, attitude to risk, affordability, tax status and entitlement to state benefits.

◆ **Risk**: has the adviser explored their customer's attitude to risk across all their objectives and ensured there is a common understanding of what this means in practice? Has the adviser explored all aspects of risk, including product risks and underlying fund risks, where applicable, as well as the circumstances in which these risks might occur?

◆ **Customer needs**: Is the customer asking for a product or service that does not suit their needs? The adviser is responsible for telling the customer if that product is not suitable for them. Does the customer need to buy a new product? Has the adviser identified significant needs?

◆ **Change in circumstances**: the adviser should consider whether the advice they provide remains suitable if the customer's circumstances change, for example changes in income, employment, residence and health.

Activity

> Where does a financial adviser record all this information?
>
> Why is it important for the adviser to make accurate records?

5.7 Prevention of money laundering

There is no formal definition of 'financial crime'. It includes:

◆ many kinds of financial fraud;

◆ criminal market conduct such as insider trading;

◆ the funding of terrorism; and

◆ money laundering.

The prevention of the use of financial systems for money laundering purposes has, for many years, been a key objective of most national, European and international communities. In 1989, the **Financial Action Task Force on Money Laundering** (FATF) was created as an international body dedicated to the fight against criminal money. The FATF has over 30 members including the European Commission and many of the EU member states.

One indication of the scale of the problem is that from October 2009 to the end of September 2010, the Serious Organised Crime Squad received 240,500 suspicious activity reports (SARs).

The UK's laws and regulations about money laundering were developed in a number of Acts and amendments over a period of more than 15 years before they were consolidated in the **Proceeds of Crime Act 2002**. The 2002 Act no longer separates the proceeds of drug-related crimes from others, and deals with the laundering of the proceeds of all forms of crime. In particular, the 2002 Act extends the obligation to report suspicions about the laundering of proceeds of all forms of crime, where previously it had been restricted to those about the proceeds of drug or terrorism offences.

Under the Proceeds of Crime Act 2002, there are three principal money laundering offences:

◆ **Concealing criminal property**: criminal property is property that a person knows, or suspects, to be the proceeds of any criminal activity; it is a criminal offence to conceal, disguise, convert or transfer criminal property – clearly, money laundering is included in those definitions.

◆ **Arranging**: this happens when a person becomes involved in a process that they know or suspect will enable someone else to acquire, retain, use or control criminal property (where that other person also knew or suspected that the property derived from criminal activity).

◆ **Acquiring, using or possessing**: it is a criminal offence for a person to acquire, use or possess any property when that person knows or suspects that the property is the proceeds of criminal activity.

These definitions lead to a number of practical procedures designed to ensure that persons working in the financial services industry do not become 'involved' in money laundering. The rules require that all authorised firms must:

◆ establish accountabilities and procedures to prevent money laundering;

◆ educate their staff about potential problems;

◆ obtain satisfactory evidence of identity for individual transactions (or a series of linked transactions) over €15,000 – the sterling equivalent is set each year and is around £10,000;

◆ report suspicious circumstances;

◆ refrain from alerting persons being investigated;

◆ appoint a **money laundering reporting officer**: this post is a 'controlled' function, and must be filled by a person of 'appropriate seniority';

◆ give regular training to staff about what is expected of them under the money laundering rules, including the consequences for the firm and for themselves if they fail to comply;

◆ take reasonable steps to ensure that procedures are up to date and reflect any findings contained in periodic reports on money laundering matters issued by the government or by the FATF;

◆ requisition a report at least once in each calendar year from the money laundering reporting officer. This report must assess the firm's compliance with the sourcebook, indicate how FATF findings have been used during the year and provide information about reports of suspected money laundering incidents submitted by staff during the year;

◆ take appropriate action to strengthen its procedures and controls to remedy any deficiencies identified by the report.

Contravention of any of the money laundering rules is a **criminal offence**.

When assessing a firm's compliance with its money laundering requirements, the FSA will take into account the extent to which the firm has adhered to the following guidelines:

◆ The **Joint Money Laundering Steering Group**'s (JMLSG) guidance notes for the financial sector. These describe the steps that firms should take to verify the identity of their customers and to confirm the source of their customer's funds. The JMLSG is made up of the leading UK trade associations in the financial services industry. Its aim is to promote good practice in countering money laundering and to give practical assistance in interpreting the UK money laundering regulations. This is primarily achieved by the publication of guidance notes.

◆ The publications of the FATF, which highlight any known developments in money laundering and any deficiencies in the money-laundering rules of other jurisdictions.

◆ The FSA's own guidance on financial exclusion.

Two areas of particular concern to financial advisers are **failure to disclose** and **tipping off**.

Activity

> Visit the 'Case studies' section of the JMLSG website to research how money launderers use bank accounts to commit financial crime.

5.7.1 Failure to disclose

All suspicions of money laundering must be reported to the authorities. The Proceeds of Crime Act 2002 introduced the requirement for a person to disclose information about money laundering if they have **reasonable grounds** for knowing or suspecting that someone is engaged in money laundering. The FSA will determine this on the basis of whether a reasonable professional should have known – so the importance of good-quality, appropriate training of staff is obvious.

5.7.2 Tipping off

It is also an offence to disclose to, or **tip off**, a person who is suspected of money laundering that an investigation is being, or may be, carried out.

5.8 Record keeping

The maintenance of clear and readily accessible records is vital at all stages of the relationship between financial services professionals, their clients and the FSA, from details of advertisements to information collected in factfinds, to the reasons for advice given and beyond. Record-keeping requirements for the different stages can be found at appropriate points within the Conduct of Business sourcebook, with details of what must be kept and the minimum period for which it must be retained.

There are many good business reasons for maintaining accurate records. From a regulatory point of view, the most important reason is to be able to demonstrate compliance with the regulations. Records can be kept in any appropriate format, which includes storage on computer, although the rules say that records stored on computer must be 'capable of being reproduced on paper in English'.

Firms are expected to take reasonable steps to protect their records from destruction, unauthorised access and alteration. We saw in Topic 3 how sometimes organisations fail to do this adequately.

5.9 Complaints handling

The Financial Services and Markets Act 2000, which consolidated and enhanced the arrangements under the previous regulatory regime, introduced new rules on complaint-handling arrangements. The rules require firms to deal properly and promptly with consumer complaints. The **key requirements** for firms' complaints procedures are that firms must:

◆ have appropriate and effective complaint-handling procedures;

◆ make consumers aware of these procedures – this is normally done through the client agreement or initial disclosure document;

◆ aim to resolve complaints within eight weeks;

◆ notify complainants of their right to approach the Financial Ombudsman Service (FOS) if they are not satisfied;

◆ report to the FSA on their complaint handling, on a regular six-monthly basis.

Complaints may be received orally (in person or by telephone) or in writing. In either case, the complaint should be acknowledged promptly and in writing. Complaints covered by the FSA rules are those that are received from **eligible complainants**, which means:

◆ private individuals; or

◆ small businesses (with an annual turnover of under €2m or employing fewer than 10 people); or

◆ charities with an annual income of under £1m; or

◆ trustees of a trust with assets of under £1m.

It is also necessary to distinguish between **soft** and **hard** complaints. Hard complaints are those involving 'an allegation that the complainant has suffered financial loss, material distress or material inconvenience'. Soft complaints are any other complaints and are, for the most part, subject to the same rules as hard complaints – the only differences are that they are not subject to the usual deadlines and they do not have to be reported to the FSA.

All complaints must be promptly and thoroughly investigated by a person of sufficient competence who, wherever possible, was not directly involved in the matter under complaint. The overall aim should be to ensure that any specific problem identified by the complainant is remedied.

The firm's response to the complainant is in the form of a **final response letter**, which must 'adequately address the subject matter of the complaint'. It must also inform the complainant that if they are not satisfied, they can refer their complaint to the FOS within **six months** of the date of the letter.

The firm should keep the complainant informed of the progress of the complaint. If, after **eight weeks**, a final response still cannot be given, the client must be told that they can refer the matter to the FOS if they are dissatisfied about the delay.

Records of hard complaints have to be retained for at least three years.

Six-monthly reports about the progress of hard complaints are required, showing how many were satisfactorily concluded within four weeks, between four and eight weeks, and after more than eight weeks.

Activity

> What is the complaint process for your organisation?

5.10   Banking conduct of business

The Banking Conduct of Business Sourcebook (BCOBS) and the Payment Services Regulations (PSRs) (see section 5.11) were launched by the FSA on 1 November 2009.

◆ BCOBS introduced principles-based regulation to deposit-taking products and services for consumers.

◆ The PSRs implemented in the UK the EU Payment Services Directive, which prescribes the way that payments are to be undertaken within the European Economic Area (EEA). These regulations relate directly to the retail banking sector and improve protection for consumers.

Those areas not covered by BCOBS are covered by the Lending Code (see section 3.2.3), which is overseen by the Lending Code Standards Board.

The changes were required for a number of reasons:

◆ With the FSA, as the 'competent authority' for the UK at the time, taking responsibility for the PSR, it seemed commonsense that it should also take responsibility for customers' core financial services relationships through BCOBS.

◆ There were concerns that the provisions of the Banking Code meant responsibility was spread between a number of organisations, with the result that no single organisation had clear accountability.

◆ The Treating Customers Fairly (TCF) principle did not have any regulatory backing, which could have proved detrimental to customers.

◆ UK branches of credit institutions authorised in other EEA states would now be caught under BCOBS rules, so affording better protection for customers.

◆ There was increased pressure from government and the public for more controls over the financial services sector due to recent regulatory failures. It has been necessary to bolster public confidence in the UK financial services industry and further regulation has been necessary to go some way in doing this.

There are six chapters to this sourcebook:

◆ **BCOBS 1: Application.** The sourcebook applies to a firm with respect to the activity of accepting deposits from banking customers carried on from an establishment maintained by it in the UK and activities connected with that activity.

◆ **BCOBS 2: Communications with banking customers and financial promotions.** This chapter reinforces these requirements by requiring a firm to pay regard to the information needs of banking customers when communicating with, or making a financial promotion to, them and to communicate information in a way that is clear, fair and not misleading.

© *ifs School of Finance 2011*

◆ **BCOBS 3: Distance communications and e-commerce.** This section applies to a firm that carries on any distance marketing activity from an establishment in the UK, with or for a consumer in the UK or another EEA state. It contains many of the provisions of the Distance Marketing Directive.

◆ **BCOBS 4: Information to be communicated to banking customers and statements of account.** This section contains details about how a firm must provide or make available to banking customers appropriate information about a retail banking service and any deposit made in relation to that retail banking service.

◆ **BCOBS 5: Post-sale requirements.** A firm must provide a service in relation to a retail banking service which is prompt, efficient and fair to a banking customer and which has regard to any communications or financial promotion made by the firm to the banking customer from time to time. This includes dealing with customers in financial difficulty, those who wish to move bank accounts, and lost and dormant accounts.

◆ **BCOBS 6: Cancellation.** This section sets out the customer's rights to cancel in various circumstances and also when there are no rights to cancellation.

5.11 Payment Services Regulations 2009

We covered the Payment Services Regulations in outline in section 3.2.4. The FSA issued a guidance document for firms in May 2010 that explained its general approach to payment services regulation, and to help firms understand how they should interact with them. They also set out the requirements for credit institutions and e-money issuers, which must comply with parts of the PSRs. The FSA has compiled a handbook that:

◆ sets out complaints handling procedures that payment institutions (PIs) must have in place;

◆ establishes the right of certain customers to complain to the Financial Ombudsman Service (FOS)

◆ sets out the FSA's policy and procedures for taking decisions relating to enforcement action and when setting penalties; and

◆ contains rules on application, the FSA's ongoing fees, and FOS levies.

We will look in more detail at the types of payment that fall under these regulations, the currencies that are affected and the issue of value dates as these areas are of most interest to customers.

Table 5.1 shows the types of payment service and gives examples.

Table 5.1   Types of payment service

Payment service	Examples
Services enabling cash to be placed on a payment account and all of the operations required for operating a payment account.	Cash deposits on a payment account over the counter and through an ATM.
Services enabling cash withdrawals from a payment account and all of the operations required for operating a payment account.	ATM cash withdrawals and over-the-counter withdrawals.
Execution of the following types of payment transaction: ◆ direct debits, including one-off direct debits; ◆ payment transactions executed through a payment card or a similar device; ◆ credit transfers, including standing orders.	◆ Transfers of funds with the user's payment service provider or with another payment service provider. ◆ Direct debits (including one-off direct debits). ◆ Transferring e-money. ◆ Credit transfers, such as standing orders, BACS or CHAPS payments.
Execution of the following types of payment transaction where the funds are covered by a credit line for a payment service user: ◆ direct debits, including one-off direct debits; ◆ payment transactions through a payment card or a similar device; ◆ credit transfers, including standing orders.	◆ Direct debits using overdraft facilities. ◆ Card payments. ◆ Credit transfers using overdraft facilities.
Issuing payment instruments or acquiring payment transactions.	◆ Card issuing services (other than mere technical service providers who do not come into possession of funds being transferred). ◆ Card merchant acquiring services (rather than merchants themselves).
Money remittance.	Money transfer/remittances that do not involve payment accounts.
Execution of payment transactions where the consent of the payer to execute a payment transaction is given by means of any telecommunication, digital or IT device and the payment is made to the telecommunication, IT system or network operator, acting only as an intermediary between the payment service user and the supplier of the goods and services.	◆ Mobile or fixed phone payments. ◆ Payments made from handheld devices (for example, BlackBerry).

Source: www.fsa.gov.uk/pubs/other/PSD_approach.pdf (p 12).

Firms are required to be authorised for payments made from the UK in any currency, and the FOS will also accept complaints about payments made from the UK in any currency. For payment transactions provided from a UK establishment where both the payer and payee's payment services provider are in the EEA, then the regulations cover payment transactions in:

◆ euro; or

◆ (within the UK) in sterling; or

◆ where there is only one currency conversion between euros and sterling, provided that:

  – the coin version is carried out in the UK; and

  – where there is a cross-border payment the cross-border transfer takes place in euros.

If the payment transaction that does not satisfy any of the above conditions (say, for example, it is denominated in an EEA currency other than euros or sterling), the customer may agree with its provider the above rules do not apply. (*Source:* www.fsa.gov.uk/pubs/other/PSD_approach.pdf (p13))

The date on which a payment is credited to a customer's account and the funds are available for their use is called the **value date**.

◆ **For EEA transactions involving euros/sterling or a conversion between euro and sterling**, payments must be credited to the payee PI's account by close of business on the business day following the time that the payer's PI receives the payment instruction (ie D+1). However, until 1 January 2012, the payer customer and their PI may expressly agree to extend this period to the end of the third business day following the time of receipt of the payment instruction. An extra business day may be added to each of the above periods when the payment order is initiated on paper, rather than in electronic form.

◆ **For EEA transactions involving EEA currency other than sterling or euros**, where a payment transaction is to be executed wholly within the EEA but does not meet the currency criteria outlined above (ie where a payment transaction is carried out in another currency), the payment must be credited to the payee PI's account by the end of the fourth business day following the payer PI's receipt of the payment instruction.

While the parties to this type of transaction may contract out of most of the requirements of the regulations relating to currency (see above), they cannot contract out of this requirement.

The value date for the payee's payment account must be the same business day on which the amount of the payment transaction is credited to the account of the payee's PI. The payee's PI must ensure that the amount of the payment transaction is available to the payee as soon as the amount has been credited to them. PIs must have systems in place to identify the funds immediately as they are received in their own account with their settlement provider. If funds are received outside business hours, the funds must be identified and credited to the payee customer's account immediately at the start of the next business day.

Where a payee customer does not hold a payment account with a provider (which would be the case where the payee is receiving cash via money remittance services), the payee's PI must again make the funds available to the payee customer immediately after the funds have been credited to that provider's account.

Figure 5.1 sets out the payment process.

Figure 5.1   The payment process

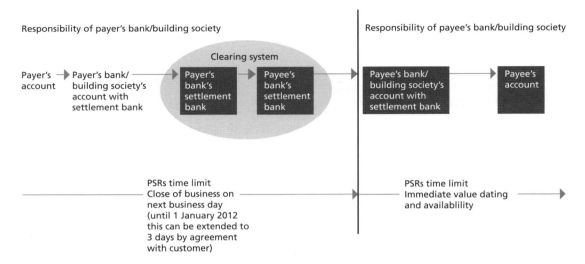

Resources

www.fsa.gov.uk

www.jmlsg.org.uk

www.soca.gov.uk

Review questions

The following review questions are designed so that you can check your understanding of this topic.

The answers to the questions are provided at the end of these learning materials.

1.   Why is it important that financial services providers are prudently managed?

2.   What is liquidity risk?

3.   What is the purpose of ''Treating Customers Fairly'?

4.   What is a financial promotion?

5.   What are the rules relating to unsolicited promotions?

6.   To what two areas does 'Know Your Customer' relate?

7.   Under the Proceeds of Crime Act 2002, what are the three principal money-laundering offences?

8.   What is the difference between a 'hard' and a 'soft' complaint?

9.   What were the reasons for introducing BCOBS?

10. Why is it important for PIs to have systems in place to identify payees' funds as soon as they are received?

Topic 6
Legal concepts relating to banking – general

Learning objective

After studying this topic, students should be able to demonstrate an understanding of key legal concepts that relate to all businesses and how they impact on financial services providers. Banking-specific legal concepts will be covered in Topic 7.

Introduction

The provider/customer relationship has a number of different facets depending on which products and services have been taken out by the customer. The customer may choose to split their banking and financial services between providers, making it difficult for any one provider to have a full overview of the customer's circumstances. There has been a raft of legislation affecting provider/customer relationships, and in this topic we will concentrate on legislation that affects *all* businesses, not just those in the financial services industry. We will look at the implications of such legislation for financial services providers and their customers.

There are a number of areas that are important – equality and discrimination legislation, unfair trading regulations, unfair contract terms, data protection, electronic and distance selling and, finally, codes of practice on advertising that affect all businesses.

6.1   The customer relationship

From a legal perspective we need to define what is meant by a customer in the context of a bank. The FSA's Banking Conduct of Business Sourcebook defines a banking customer as:

◆ a consumer;

◆ a micro enterprise that employs fewer than ten people, with a turnover of less than €2m;

◆ a charity that has an annual income of less than £1m;

◆ a trustee of a trust that has a net asset value of less than £1m.

There is no statutory definition of a banking customer as such; however, there are a number of points that help to make the meaning of the term clearer. There are a variety of different legal aspects to the banker—customer relationship. These are as follows:

◆ **Offer and acceptance**: where a person requests the opening of an account, for example by completing and submitting an application form, they are in effect making an **offer** to enter into a banker—customer contract. When the bank agrees to open the account it is **accepting** that offer. From that point o, the contract is legal and binding, so it is important that all the account formalities have been completed correctly. Some banker—customer contracts (such as those for insurance) have '**cooling-off**' periods to allow the customer to look at alternative quotations and consider their decision.

◆ **Need for the account to be in existence**: for someone to be a customer they must have an account, although there is no need for the account to have been in existence for very long. The fact that the account has become operational is sufficient evidence that the relationship has been established.

◆ **Need for the intention to establish a banker—customer relationship**: there must be the intention to create a relationship. For example, if an account were to be opened in someone's name without their knowledge, they would have no right to any money deposited there.

◆ **Debtor/creditor**: where the customer deposits money, the banker is the debtor; where the customer borrows money, the banker is the creditor. We shall look at this aspect of the relationship further when we consider lending products.

◆ **Mortgagor/mortgagee**: where a customer borrows from their bank, securing the loan against property by way of legal mortgage, the relationship with the bank changes, in that it also becomes that of mortgagor (customer) and mortgagee (lender). A **legal mortgage** is created by the parties signing a deed and gives each of the parties certain rights relating to the borrowing arrangements.

◆ **Bailor/bailee**: the term 'bailment' covers the legal relationship between two parties where goods are delivered by one (the bailor) to another (the bailee). In financial services the most common example is in hire-purchase arrangements. For instance, it may involve the bailment of an asset — say, a car — by a bailor such as a motor-finance company to the hire purchaser (the bailee) by way a of hire-purchase agreement. The rent on this hire is paid through a number of instalments and, when the agreed number of payments have been made, the hire purchaser becomes the absolute owner of the car. This means the customer does not actually become the owner of the vehicle until the last instalment is paid. A bank holding property in safe custody for a customer is acting as bailee only and derives no rights over the property it is holding for the customer in its vaults.

Activity

What procedures are in place in your organisation to ensure that account formalities are undertaken correctly?

6.2 Equality and discrimination legislation

The Equality and Human Rights Commission opened in October 2007. A key aim of the commission is to end discrimination and harassment of people because of their disability, age, religion or belief, race, gender, or sexual orientation. The new commission brings together the work of three former equality commissions. They were the:

◆ Disability Rights Commission;

◆ Commission for Racial Equality;

◆ Equal Opportunities Commission.

As an employee, you experience the impact of the legislation with which the Commission is involved in your workplace. However, it also affects the way that customers are treated. In both situations, **equal treatment** and not discriminating against individuals is key. The following sections describe relevant legislation and what financial services providers do to comply with the requirements of the legislation.

6.2.1 Disability Discrimination Acts

While the Disability Discrimination Act (DDA) 2005 has been largely replaced by the Equality Act 2010 (see section 6.2.2), some aspects are worth considering separately as they affect customers directly.

Disabled people have specific rights in the areas of:

◆ employment;

◆ education;

◆ access to providers of everyday goods and services, such as shops, cafes, banks, cinemas and places of worship;

◆ buying or renting land or property, including making it easier for disabled people to rent property and for tenants to make disability-related adaptations;

◆ accessing or becoming a member of a larger private club (25 or more members);

◆ accessing the functions of public bodies, such as the issuing of licences for example.

The DDA made it illegal for service providers to treat disabled people less favourably than other people for a reason related to their disability. Service providers have to make '**reasonable adjustments**' to the way they deliver their services so that disabled people can use them.

Access to services is not just about installing ramps and widening doorways for wheelchair users – it is about making services easier to use for all disabled people, including people who are blind, deaf or have a learning disability.

Other examples of reasonable adjustments include:

◆ installing an induction loop for people who are hearing impaired;

◆ giving the option to make enquiries by email as well as by phone;

◆ providing disability awareness training for staff who have contact with the public;

◆ providing larger, well-defined signage for people with impaired vision.

What is considered a 'reasonable adjustment' for a large organisation like a bank may be different from a reasonable adjustment for a small local shop. It is about what is practical in the service provider's individual situation and what resources the business may have. They will not be required to make changes that are impractical or beyond their means.

Activity

> Make a list of non-branch-based delivery channels used by financial service providers.
>
> ◆ What particular disabilities does each of these delivery channels help to overcome?
>
> ◆ What disabilities do they *not* help to overcome?

Failure or refusal to provide to a disabled person a service that is offered to other people is discrimination unless it can be justified.

6.2.2 The Equality Act 2010

The Equality Act 2010 strengthens further the rights of disabled people and in addition:

◆ provides a new legislative framework to protect the rights of individuals and advance equality of opportunity for all;

◆ updates, simplifies and strengthens the previous legislation; and

◆ delivers a simple, modern and accessible framework of discrimination law which protects individuals from unfair treatment and promotes a fair and more equal society (*source:* www.equalities.gov.uk/equality_bill.aspx).

Most of the provisions came into force in October 2010 and the remaining ones will be phased in over time. The Act introduces a number of key concepts:

◆ **Protected characteristics**: The Act offers protection to people with 'protected characteristics'. The list below covers all those characteristics covered by existing anti-discrimination laws. The protected characteristics are:

  — age;

  — disability;

  — gender reassignment;

  — marriage and civil partnership;

  — pregnancy and maternity;

  — race;

— religion or belief;

— sex;

— sexual orientation.

◆ **Associative discrimination** : this is an aspect of direct discrimination and involved discrimination against a person because they have an association with someone with a particular protected characteristic. This already applied to race, religion or belief, and sexual orientation, and has been extended to cover age, disability, gender reassignment and sex. An example of associative discrimination might be a non-disabled employee who is discriminated against because of activities she needs to undertake to care for a disabled dependant.

◆ **Perceptive discrimination**: this is an aspect of direct discrimination. It involves discrimination against a person because the discriminator believes the person possesses that characteristic, even if they do not. Perceptive discrimination already applied to age, race, religion or belief and sexual orientation, and has been extended to cover disability, gender reassignment and sex.

◆ **Indirect discrimination**: this form of discrimination occurs where an employment policy applies to everybody, but the policy has more impact on people with a protected characteristic. Indirect discrimination has been extended to cover disability discrimination and gender reassignment.

◆ **Harassment**: this is defined as 'unwanted conduct related to a relevant protected characteristic, which has the purpose or effect of violating an individual's dignity or creating an intimidating, hostile, degrading, humiliating or offensive environment for that individual'. Under the Act:

— employees can complain of harassment even if they do not possess the protected characteristic or the harassment is not directed at them;

— employers can be liable for harassment of their staff by non-employees (for example, customers).

In the case of third-party harassment (from a customer, for example), an employer will only be liable if the harassment has occurred on at least two previous occasions, they know that it has taken place and have not taken reasonable steps to prevent it happening again. Harassment applies to all protected characteristics except for pregnancy and maternity and marriage and civil partnership. Because of the overlap with sex and sexual orientation discrimination, for practical purposes, employers should assume the same protection will be given to people with these characteristics as for other protected characteristics.

Direct discrimination and **victimisation** are other key concepts that are carried over from the anti-discrimination laws and are largely unchanged by the Act. (*Source*: adapted from CIPD factsheet Equality Act 2010)

Activity

Visit the Government Equalities Office website to review the 'Quick Guides' for employers and consumers.

6.3 Consumer Protection from Unfair Trading Regulations and Business Protection from Misleading Marketing Regulations

We will see that there are many laws to protect customers from being treated unfairly. The **Trading Standards Institute** (TSI) enforces many of these regulations.

Many existing consumer laws — including most of the Trade Descriptions Act — have been replaced by the **Consumer Protection from Unfair Trading Regulations 2008** since May 2008. The new regulations ban traders in all sectors from engaging in unfair commercial (mainly marketing and selling) practices against consumers. The regulations also set out how commercial practices can be unfair by being misleading (by action or omission) or aggressive, and list 31 specific practices that are banned. The **Business Protection from Misleading Marketing Regulations 2008** replaced the Trade Descriptions Act insofar as that Act protects businesses.

6.3.1 Fair trading

To protect both consumers and other businesses, businesses must comply with a number of fair trading laws. This is to **prevent false claims** being made about products and services and to ensure a **fair environment** for commerce.

The main areas covered by fair trading laws are:

◆ safety;

◆ pricing;

◆ weights and measures;

◆ descriptions of products and services;

◆ the contract between a buyer and seller;

◆ competition between businesses;

◆ intellectual property and counterfeiting.

As well as general laws, there are sector-specific laws. We will see in the next topic what the sector-specific laws are. Complying with these laws is good business practice; not complying with them represents a reputational risk to the business. Penalties include **fines** and even **imprisonment**.

6.3.2 Describing products and services

Any description of goods and services that are sold or hired out must be accurate. That description could be:

◆ in writing — for example, in an advertisement for a financial product its interest rate must be described in terms of its annual percentage rate (APR);

◆ in an illustration, for example on packaging;

◆ given orally, for example in a sales pitch.

A range of factors that fall within the scope of fair trading legislation might be included within an advertisement. These might include, for example, references to the:

◆ quantity and size;

◆ composition;

◆ method, place and date of manufacture;

◆ fitness for stated purpose;

◆ endorsements by people or organisations.

The regulations make it an offence to mislead consumers about goods and services, including immoveable property, rights and obligations. The Business Protection from Misleading Marketing Regulations 2008 make it an offence to mislead other businesses. People found guilty of an offence could face an **unlimited fine** and two years' **imprisonment**. The Regulations apply to directors, managers and employees of a business, who can all be liable.

This press release from June 2009 gives an example of how the TSI monitors the financial services arena.

Case study – Consumers paying the price for antiquated insurance law

An archaic law leaving consumers vulnerable at their hour of need must urgently be reformed, says the Trading Standards Institute (TSI).

Current legislation enables insurers to reject a critical illness policy claim if an undisclosed condition is discovered – even if it is unrelated to the illness suffered by the claimant. The case of a leukaemia sufferer whose claim was not paid because she had omitted to mention in her application form unrelated ear infections suffered in the past is a typical example.

Paul Ramsden, deputy chief executive of TSI, said: 'People claiming on a critical illness policy will be going through a very difficult time in their lives and should not have this additional worry. The law needs amendment to treat the claim in an appropriate manner in the first place.

'The current legal situation is letting down consumers through a significant imbalance against consumers. We would like to see swift government action to act upon this by reforming the current law and creating better regulation for consumers and business.'

Law Commission commissioner David Hertzell is keen to support TSI's campaign to push for a law reform as soon as possible.

He said: 'Current insurance law dates back to a time when there were no consumers. The economic and social context was very different from what we have today.

'The insurance industry has recognised the problem and has issued guidelines to limit this. However these are voluntary and unlike law reforms do not provide a comprehensive solution.'

Consumers can take their case to the Financial Ombudsman Service, which will take a fair and reasonable view, and is likely to uphold the initial claim. The service received 50,000 insurance disputes last year.

> But lead financial ombudsman Peter Hinchliffe said: 'Settlement through the financial ombudsman gives consumers good protection, but not all cases qualify for this route. Some consumers might also be deterred by insurers or by their own advisers' explanation of the legal position, leaving the consumer with little chance of an appropriate redress.'

Source: www.tradingstandards.gov.uk, June 2009.

Activity

> Why do you think it is important to describe products and services accurately?

6.4   Unfair contract terms

We have already seen in earlier topics that consumers need protection from powerful organisations that can dictate their own terms. The following two sections show which general business laws deal with unfair contract terms and how these may impact on the provision of banking services.

6.4.1   Supply of Goods and Services Act

The Supply of Goods and Services Act 1982 applies to all contracts (except those entered into before 1995) involving the supply of services, including those for the supply of financial services. Its terms mean that, in the absence of anything specific, the following provisions are automatically deemed to be included in all such contracts.

◆ The service will be performed with reasonable care.

◆ The work will be done within a reasonable time.

◆ A reasonable charge will be made.

6.4.2   Unfair Terms in Consumer Contracts Regulations

Consumers can sometimes find themselves in a position where their rights are being adversely affected in a contract with a supplier, particularly when a supplier is a large and powerful organisation. In fact they may not even realise that their rights are being affected until it is too late — when they have taken up a service and something has gone wrong. There are, however, regulations that protect consumers from imbalances of this nature.

Contract terms are often what people refer to as the 'small print' and generally set out the rights of each party under their agreement. The regulations governing unfair terms in consumer contracts are intended to protect consumers from the types of imbalance that generally act in favour of the supplier of goods or services; in fact, the word **'imbalance'** is actually used in the regulations. In the case of financial services there is considerable scope for such imbalances. After all, wherever the provider uses standard terms, they could draft them with an eye to their own interests.

The current law on unfair contract terms is covered by two pieces of legislation:

◆ **Unfair Contract Terms Act 1977**;

◆ **Unfair Terms in Consumer Contracts Regulations (UTCCRs) 1999**.

They aim to protect consumers from terms that impose unfair burdens on them, or reduce their statutory or common law rights. The **Office of Fair Trading** (OFT) currently deals with complaints under these regulations and the FSA also oversees the UTCCRs.

Where a term is 'unfair' as defined under the regulations, it is not binding on the consumer. However, if the remainder of the contract is capable of continuing despite the removal of that unfair term, then it will do so.

The UTCCRs apply where the terms of a contract have not been individually negotiated. Terms that have not been individually negotiated include any standard contract terms, such as those in account opening forms, or personal loan, investment or insurance agreements. These are examples of the terms having been drafted in advance. Even if some terms of a contract have been individually negotiated, the regulations will apply to the rest, if overall the contract's terms are standardised. The onus is on the provider to prove that a term was individually negotiated. If this is in dispute, then it is a good reason for ensuring that providers keep detailed notes when negotiating terms with prospective customers.

Activity

> What would be the effect of negotiating every single term with a customer when opening a new account?
>
> Why have financial services providers standardised many of the terms in their contracts with customers?

One unfair term mentioned in the regulations is of particular interest to financial service providers. It is one that requires the consumer, if they fail to fulfil their obligations, to pay a **disproportionately high sum in compensation**. In the context of penalties applied on non-performing loans and overdrafts, for instance, high penalties would be deemed unfair. Lenders authorised by the FSA have a direct responsibility to their authorising body to use fair terms.

The regulations also state that written contracts must be in **plain, intelligible language**, something that financial institutions should be mindful of achieving. This is an important requirement, because the regulations state that where there is doubt about the meaning of any term, the interpretation most favourable to the consumer will prevail. This shows that clarity is not only in the interests of the customer, but also the supplier.

The following is an example of how a customer was able to use the regulations to his advantage in challenging the power of a large organisation.

Case study — the UTCCRs and bank charges

In 2005 Stephen Hone, who was then a law student at Plymouth University, was charged two fees of £32 for going 5 pence over his current account overdraft limit with his bank. As a law student he realised that the charges were likely to be illegal under the Unfair Terms in Consumer Contracts Regulations 1999.

When he asked for a refund of the charges the bank offered to refund one of the £32 charges as a 'gesture of goodwill'. They refused to refund the other. Hone worked out that the £32 fee on 5p was still equivalent to being charged interest at a rate of 64,000 per cent. He threatened to take action against his bank through the county court unless both the charges were refunded, but the bank refused to oblige.

As we have seen, the Unfair Terms in Consumer Contracts Regulations do not allow any organisation to charge customers with 'unreasonable' penalties even if those charges are spelt out in a signed contract. The charges must be proportionate to the costs incurred by the provider and any more is considered to be profiteering.

The bank did not send representatives to the hearing, claiming that it did not know that the case was going to be heard. It then appeared to decide to settle as quickly as possible, offering Hone £5,000 in compensation. Hone refused to sign a confidentiality agreement and has publicised what he has done via his website (www.penaltycharges.co.uk) to other banking customers who may feel aggrieved by their own financial services provider's charges.

6.4.3 Legal challenges to bank charges

The OFT has acknowledged that the public has the right to be concerned about the level and incidence of unarranged overdraft and charging terms. In August 2008 it wrote to eight banks setting out its approach to the assessment of fairness and, for seven of them, its concerns about their particular terms. This included a provisional view on the unfairness of particular terms and conditions that impose charges.

The OFT looked at whether, under a specific European regulation, it was *legally possible* for bank charges to be 'unfair', and came to the provisional conclusion that it was. In the High Court and then in the Court of Appeal, the banks lost their case, showing there was real strength in the OFT's argument. However, with a turnaround decision in November 2009, the new Supreme Court overturned the earlier judgments on a technicality and decided that 'fairness rules' did not apply. At this point, the OFT decided not to continue its case — which was unfortunate for around 15,000 consumers whose claims had been put on hold while the court case was underway and who were hoping to reclaim the money they had paid in bank charges. The Financial Ombudsman Service said it would still hear cases from those in hardship. The issue of fairer fees remains topical and, in certain circumstances, consumers are still able to recoup these from their providers.

Activity

> Visit the websites www.penaltycharges.co.uk and www.moneysavingexpert.com.
>
> How much have users of these sites reclaimed from banks to date, according to the details they have registered? What help is available for consumers who wish to make a claim?
>
> This has probably caused much additional work for the banks. How could they have avoided this work if they had handled the initial complaints differently?

6.5 Data Protection Act and confidentiality

We looked at the role of the Information Commissioner's Office in Topic 3 and its role in enforcing the Data Protection Act. In this section we will consider the Act and the need for confidentiality.

The **Data Protection Act 1998** replaced an earlier Act (the Data Protection Act 1984) when it became necessary for UK law in this area to comply with an EU data protection directive issued in 1995. The 1998 Act is much wider in its scope than the earlier Act: in particular, it extends the regulations to cover not only **computerised** data (as in the 1984 Act) but also 'any structured set of personal data'. It can therefore include data held in **manual filing** systems.

The purpose of the legislation is, broadly speaking, to give private individuals **control** over the use of personal data about themselves held by commercial (and other) organisations. It does so by establishing a series of data protection principles, together with enforcement processes.

6.5.1 Definitions

The Data Protection Act 1998 uses a number of words and phrases that have precise meanings within its terms. These include the following:

◆ **Data subject**: an individual whose personal data (see below) is processed.

◆ **Personal data**: the Act relates only to personal data, which is defined as 'information relating to a living individual who can be identified from that information or from a combination of that information and other information in the possession of the data controller' (see below).

◆ **Sensitive personal data**: this data can only be processed if the individual has given *explicit* consent (in other words, it is not sufficient to claim that the individual has never specifically withheld their consent). Sensitive data includes information about an individual's:

  – racial origin;

  – religious beliefs;

  – political persuasion;

  – physical health;

- mental health;

- criminal (but not civil) proceedings.

◆ **Processing**: this has a very broad meaning, covering all aspects of owning data, including:

- obtaining the data in the first place;

- recording of the data;

- organisation or alteration of the data;

- disclosure of the data by whatever means;

- erasure or destruction of the data.

◆ **Data controller**: this is the 'legal person' who determines the purposes for which data is processed and the way in which this is done. It is normally an organisation/employer, such as a company, partnership or sole trader. The data controller has prime responsibility for ensuring that the requirements of the Act are carried out.

◆ **Data processor**: this is a person who processes personal data on behalf of the data controller.

6.5.2 Data protection principles

The basis of the Data Protection Act is a set of eight **data protection principles**. These are described below; they all relate to the processing of personal data.

1. Data must be **processed fairly and lawfully**. This includes the specific requirement for the data controller to tell the individual what information will be processed and why, and whether it will be disclosed to anyone else. Data must not be processed unless the data subject has given their consent or the processing is necessary for one of the following reasons:

   ◆ to perform the data controller's contract with the data subject or to protect the interests of the data subject;

   ◆ to fulfil a legal obligation or to carry out a public function;

   ◆ to pursue the legitimate interests of the data controller — unless this could prejudice the interests of the data subject.

2. Data must be obtained only for a **specified lawful purpose** or purposes and must not be processed in any way that is not compatible with the purpose(s) — this includes the use of the data by any person to whom it is later disclosed.

3. Data must be **adequate** (but not excessive) and **relevant** to the purpose for which it is processed. This should be borne in mind by advisers when determining how much information it is appropriate to collect and retain in a factfind document.

4. Data must be kept **accurate and up to date**.

5. Data must **not be kept for longer than is necessary**. This will be dictated to some extent by FSA rules on how long information must be kept.

6. Data must be processed in accordance with the **rights of data subjects**. These include:

   ◆ the right to receive (on payment of a fee of £10) a copy of the information being held (the information must be provided within 40 days of a written request);

   ◆ the right to have the information corrected if it can be shown to be incorrect.

7. Data controllers must take appropriate technical and organisational measures to keep data **secure** from accidental or deliberate misuse, damage or destruction. This includes taking reasonable steps to ensure the reliability of any employees of the data controller who have access to the data.

8. Data must **not be transferred** to a country outside the European Economic Area (EEA) unless that country's data protection regime 'ensures an adequate level of protection for the rights and freedoms of data subjects'. Broadly speaking that means that it should be comparable to that within the EEA.

Activity

> Within the retail banking environment, what steps are taken to comply with these principles?

6.5.3 Enforcement

The **Information Commissioner** oversees the application of the Data Protection Act. The Commissioner's responsibilities are:

◆ to educate organisations about their responsibilities under the Act, and individuals about their rights;

◆ to take action where necessary to enforce the provisions of the Act.

The Commissioner can issue one of two types of notice to a data controller if the Commissioner believes that there has been an infringement of the terms of the Act:

◆ An **information notice** is the milder of the two and requires the data controller to specify the steps that the organisation must take to comply with the Act.

◆ An **enforcement notice** requires the organisation either to take some specified action or to refrain from certain activities.

The enforcement powers of the Information Commissioner include the power to prosecute a data controller that fails to comply with an information notice or enforcement notice. This is a criminal offence and there are two further criminal offences under the Act.

◆ It is an offence to **fail to make a proper notification** to the Information Commissioner. **Notification** is the way in which a data controller effectively registers with the Office of the Information Commissioner, by acknowledging that personal data is being held and by specifying the purpose(s) for which the data is being held.

◆ It is also an offence to process data without authorisation from the Commissioner.

The maximum penalty for these offences is £500,000 (from April 2010), unless the case goes to the Crown Court, in which case there is no limit on the possible fine.

6.6 Electronic and Distance Selling Directive

Many people buy goods and services over the Internet, by phone or by mail order. These are all examples of **distance** selling. An increasing range of goods and services are available to consumers shopping in these ways. Businesses that normally sell by distance means and have systems in place for trading in this way (for example by having standard letters or emails that they send to consumers they deal with at a distance) need to comply with the **Consumer Protection (Distance Selling) Regulations 2000** (DSRs).

Businesses that sell **electronically** (such as over the Internet or via mobile phone texts) also need to know about the:

◆ **Electronic Commerce Regulations** (ECRs); and

◆ **Privacy and Electronic Communications Regulations** (PECRs), where, for example the business is engaged in direct marketing activity by phone, fax, automated calling systems, and electronic mail (this means text/video/picture messaging and email).

Activity

> What are the difficulties with buying products and services over the Internet?

The DSRs implement a European Council Directive and for most goods and services provide additional rights to consumers buying at a distance to encourage confidence in this method of buying. The protection the DSRs offer is important because consumers cannot inspect goods or services before they buy when they shop at a distance. The DSR made changes to the requirements to provide information when supplying services and to cancellation periods for the supply of services.

The DSRs say that consumers must be provided with clear information so that they can make an informed choice about whether or not they wish to buy from an organisation. In most cases businesses must also give consumers the right to a cancellation period.

One aim of the Directive is to ensure that consumers enjoy the same minimum level of protection no matter where a supplier is based in the EU. If businesses make distance sales to consumers in other member states they should be aware that the Directive may have been implemented differently elsewhere in the EU.

However these DSRs do not apply to the sale of land, construction of a building or contracts relating to financial services to consumers. The latter are likely to be subject to the information giving and cancellation provisions contained in the Financial Services (Distance Marketing) Regulations 2004 and, where relevant, the Consumer Credit Acts 1974 & 2006.

6.6.1 The Distance Marketing of Consumer Financial Services

The UK implemented the European Union's Directive on the Distance Marketing of Financial Services in October 2004 with the implementation of the Financial Services (Distance Marketing) Regulations.

The regulations govern the sale of pensions, mortgages and other financial products by means of distance communication. This includes online sales and sales by telephone, fax or post – essentially, any sale where the contract is concluded yet the parties never meet face to face.

The regulations aim to protect the consumer by ensuring that the supplier discloses sufficient information both before and after the contract is concluded. The consumer must also have an opportunity to withdraw from the concluded contract without incurring liability during a specified cancellation period (often referred to as a 'cooling-off' period).

Activity

Which products and services does your organisation offer as a 'distance' sale?

6.6.1.1 Required information

Before the consumer is bound into the contract, the supplier (or their intermediary) must inform the consumer of the following:

- the supplier's identity;
- details of the product; and
- details of the contract.

6.6.1.2 Telephone marketing

Of course it is impractical to suggest that all this information could be provided sufficiently by telephone. So for marketing or selling using the telephone, less extensive information tends to be supplied. However the more information that is supplied, the easier it is defend the provider's position later should a dispute occur. Similarly, the more information that is provided, the clearer the contract will be to the consumer, who will be less likely to dispute anything later. This is one of the reasons that has led to the use of scripts by providers for both incoming and outgoing calls.

Activity

> What are the advantages and disadvantages of using scripts for telephone calls?

6.6.1.3 Following up

As well as providing the information listed above, the supplier should also ensure that they communicate all the contractual terms and conditions to the consumer on **paper** or another **durable medium** (email is permitted). This should be done in good time, prior to the conclusion of the contract. Where the consumer has requested that the contract be concluded using a means of distance communication, then the terms and conditions should be provided immediately after conclusion of the contract. The consumer must also be provided with a copy of the terms and conditions when requested, unless these have already been communicated to the consumer and they have not changed.

The cancellation period (discussed below) only begins when the paper or other durable medium copy of the contract terms and conditions is received by the consumer. If the supplier provides the required information in a timely manner the cancellation period will be kept to a minimum and the consumer will have as little time as possible to cancel the contract.

6.6.1.4 Cancellation or cooling-off period

The regulations allow consumers to withdraw from financial services contracts entered into at a distance. This terminates the contract from the notice of termination being given.

The cancellation period begins on the date of **conclusion** of the contract and ends 14 days from that date. The contract is concluded at the point at which the copy of the information previously provided is sent on paper or other durable medium, hence the commercial interest in sending the information as soon as possible.

In life insurance contracts the cancellation period runs from the date the consumer is informed that the contract has been concluded. The cancellation period in life insurance or personal pension contracts runs for 30 days instead of 14 days.

Activity

> Why do you think life insurance and personal pension contracts have a longer cancellation period?

The regulations also cover a number of areas including:

◆ methods of cancellation;

◆ exceptions to the right to cancel;

◆ payment for services provided before cancellation;

◆ payment by card;

◆ unsolicited services.

6.7 Codes of practice

The last section in this topic relates to a body that oversees many of the activities relating to marketing of products and services across all industries.

6.7.1 Advertising Standards Authority

The Advertising Standards Authority (ASA) is the independent body set up by the advertising industry to police the rules laid down in the advertising codes. The strength of the self-regulatory system lies in both the independence of the ASA and the support and commitment of the advertising industry, through the Committee of Advertising Practice (CAP), to the standards of the codes, protecting consumers and creating a level playing field for advertisers.

The ASA can stop misleading, harmful or offensive advertising. They ensure sales promotions are run fairly. Also they can help reduce unwanted commercial mail, either sent through the post, by email or by text message, and they can resolve problems with mail order purchases.

The ASA investigates complaints made about ads, sales promotions or direct marketing. Anyone can complain to the ASA and they publish their adjudications (http://www.asa.org.uk/asa/adjudications/) on complaints on their website every Wednesday.

They undertake research in many areas to help with the work of the agency, including research into people's attitudes towards advertising and compliance with the advertising standards codes within specific sectors and media.

This gives another avenue of protection to consumers, who can highlight areas where they feel promotional material is misleading or inaccurate, particularly from a consumer perspective. The ASA has the power to ban advertisements, whether this is on TV, online, in regional or national press or via direct mail. (Source: www.asa.org.uk),

Activity

> Search in the adjudications section of the ASA's website under 'financial' to see what types of advertisement are complained about and on what grounds.

Resources

www.tradingstandards.gov.uk

www.equalities.gov.uk

www.asa.org

Review questions

The following review questions are designed so that you can check your understanding of this topic.

The answers to the questions are provided at the end of these learning materials.

1. How does the Banking Conduct of Business Sourcebook define a banking customer?

2. How do banks make reasonable adjustments to their services to meet the needs of disabled people?

3. What is the purpose of the fair trading laws?

4. How do the Unfair Terms in Consumer Contracts Regulations (UTCCRs) provide protection for consumers?

5. What is 'sensitive' personal data?

6. How can customers obtain information an organisation may hold about them?

7. What are the enforcement powers of the Information Commissioner?

8. Which regulations are in place for organisations that deal with their customers at a distance?

9. How should financial services sold at a distance be followed up?

10. Over what types of advertising media does the Advertising Standards Authority have jurisdiction?

Topic 7

Legal concepts relating to banking
– specific

Learning objective

After studying this topic, students should be able to demonstrate an understanding of key legal concepts and codes of practice relating specifically to banking.

Introduction

In the last topic we looked at various pieces of legislation that affect all businesses. In this topic we shall look at legislation that is specifically aimed at the financial services sector. Some of this legislation led to regulation by the FSA following the Financial Services and Markets Act 2000. The other main pieces of legislation relate to the provision of credit to customers.

If a customer experiences financial difficulty and is unable to keep up with the repayment of their debts they may find themselves 'insolvent'. We shall explore the various routes, underpinned by further legislation, that are open to customers when this happens. The topic concludes by looking at two codes of practice relating to the financial services industry.

7.1 The creation of the Financial Services Authority

By the mid-1990s it was becoming clear that the self-regulatory aspects of the financial services system had not been wholly successful and that the overall structure of regulation was too fragmented for the increasingly integrated world of financial services. For example, many large banking groups, now providing a wide range of financial products and services, were regulated by the Bank of England and also by several other organisations relating to fund management, investments and marketing. This sometimes led to confusion over where regulatory responsibility lay. The collapse of Barings Bank in 1992 highlighted many of these anomalies, with both the Bank of England and the body then regulating stock market organisations (the Securities and Futures Authority) being criticised.

The first major step in the development of a new regulatory regime came in June 1998, when responsibility for the regulation of the UK banking sector was transferred from the Bank of England to a **new single regulator**, the Financial Services Authority (FSA). The next stage was achieved in December 2001, when the FSA assumed regulatory responsibility for almost all of the financial services industry. A wide-ranging new Act, the Financial Services and Markets Act (FSMA) 2000, gave effect to the new regulatory regime.

This Act provides the legislative framework through which the FSA is able to regulate the professional and business behaviour of all parts of the industry, from the largest institutions (including around 800 insurance companies and 600 banks) to individual employees and sole traders. It covers a wide range of matters, including solvency, capital adequacy, sales and marketing practices, prevention of crime, competence of managers and sales staff, complaints and compensation.

Two sectors of the industry that did not come under the wing of the FSA in 2001, however, were mortgages and general insurance. Regulation of mortgage sales continued on a voluntary basis, overseen by the Mortgage Code Compliance Board (MCCB), until their regulation under the FSA in October 2004. Similarly, general insurance continued to be the responsibility of the General Insurance Standards Council (GISC), until its regulation under the FSA in January 2005.

7.2   The FSA Handbook

The FSA's Handbook sets out all the FSA's rules made under powers given to the FSA by FSMA 2000, and are entirely binding. This section is to give a high-level overview of the contents of the FSA's Handbook.

The Handbook consists mainly of 'rules' and 'guidance', and it is important to understand the difference between them.

◆ Most of the **rules** in the Handbook create binding obligations on authorised firms. If a firm contravenes a rule, it may be subject to **enforcement** action and, in certain circumstances, to an action for damages.

◆ The purpose of the **guidance** is to explain the rules and to indicate ways of complying with them. The guidance is **not binding**, however, and a firm cannot be subject to disciplinary action simply because it has ignored the guidance. It is helpful, however, for firms to know that, if they have acted in accordance with the guidance 'in circumstances contemplated by that guidance' (in the FSA's words), it will be presumed that the firm has complied with the relevant rule.

7.2.1   High level standards

The 'High level standards' section of the FSA's Handbook covers:

◆ the threshold conditions;

◆ the statements of principle for approved persons;

◆ the 'fit and proper' test for approved persons;

◆ the principles for business;

◆ senior management arrangements, systems, and controls.

7.2.2 Business standards

Business standards are described in the following sourcebooks:

◆ **Prudential sourcebooks** are concerned with the financial soundness of the various types of firm (such as valuation of a firm's assets and liabilities, its reserves, and financial reporting);

◆ **Conduct of Business sourcebooks** address the standards applied to the marketing and sale of financial services products. In November 2007, a new conduct of business sourcebook (COBS) was introduced, centred on a principles-based approach.

◆ The **Market Conduct sourcebook** concerns investment markets and is therefore primarily of interest to investment firms. It covers such issues as insider dealing;

◆ **Training and Competence sourcebook**.

7.2.3 Regulatory processes

The third section of the Handbook covers regulatory processes, including rules and guidance for firms wishing to seek authorisation. It also includes the **Supervision manual**, which sets out the way that the FSA will regulate and monitor the compliance of authorised firms.

7.2.4 Redress/specialist sourcebooks

The two remaining sections of the Handbook cover:

◆ **redress** (including investor complaints and compensation); and

◆ **specialist sourcebooks** (including arrangements for credit unions, professional firms such as solicitors and accountants, and the supervision of Lloyd's of London).

7.2.5 Mortgage Conduct of Business rules

The Mortgage Conduct of Business rules for first-charge lending came into effect in October 2004. They regulated the four activities of lending, administering, advising on and arranging regulated mortgage contracts. A regulated mortgage contract is defined as being a contract under which:

◆ the lender provides credit to an individual or to trustees (the borrower); and

◆ the obligation of the borrower to repay is secured by a first legal mortgage on land (other than timeshare accommodation) in the United Kingdom, at least 40 per cent of which is used, or is intended to be used, as or in connection with a dwelling by the borrower or (in the case of credit provided to trustees) by an individual who is a beneficiary of the trust, or by a related person.

The rules adopt a 'cradle to grave' approach throughout the relationship between consumers, intermediaries and lenders.

◆ They begin with a financial promotions regime on advertising.

◆ They then lay great emphasis on providing consumers with intelligible information, provided in a consistent format that will enable consumers to shop around, compare different products, and make informed choices.

◆ Every consumer *must* be given pre-contractual information, in a highly prescribed format — the **key facts illustration** — before they can apply for a particular loan.

◆ Lenders are under a duty to lend **responsibly**: that is, they must be able to show that they have given proper consideration to a prospective borrower's ability to repay the loan for which they are applying.

◆ Information must continue to be given to consumers in a prescribed format at mortgage offer stage and throughout the life of the loan.

◆ Consumers who fall into arrears must be given prescribed information, including an official FSA leaflet.

◆ The rules set out how firms must deal with arrears and possessions cases.

No person may carry on a regulated activity without permission. Any person who does so will be guilty of an offence and may be liable to imprisonment for a term of up to two years, or a fine, or both.

Activity

> Obtain a copy of a key facts illustration to review what information is contained within it.
>
> Why is this information important to customers?

7.2.6 Banking Conduct of Business Sourcebook

We looked at the Banking Conduct of Business Sourcebook (BCOBS) in section 5.10. This section expands on these regulations further as they are very important in the relationship between retail financial services providers and their customers.

BCOBS applies to accepting deposits to the extent that it does not overlap with the requirements of the PSRs (see section 5.11 relating to payment transactions and payment accounts. This means that where a retail banking service:

◆ is not a payment service within the scope of the PSRs, BCOBS applies in full;

◆ is a payment service within the scope of the PSRs, parts of BCOBS would not apply.

If you visit the FSA's website and look at BCOBS you will see that it is split into 'rules' (R) and guidance' (G). The text that follows is a synopsis of both; however, some of the actual 'rules' that have to be followed have been highlighted in text boxes.

7.2.6.1   BCOBS 1: General application

The main rules under this section are self-explanatory:

This sourcebook applies to a *firm* with respect to the activity of *accepting deposits* from *banking customers* carried on from an establishment maintained by it in the *United Kingdom* and activities connected with that activity.

Deposit-taking is covered in Topic 8.

Exclusion of liability

A *firm* must not seek to exclude or restrict, or rely on any exclusions or restriction, of any duty or liability it may have to a *banking customer* unless it is reasonable for it to do so and the duty or liability arises other than under the regulatory system.

The other legislation covering unfair terms regulations that forms guidance for this rule is covered in section 6.3 and section 6.4. BCOBS does not explain what is 'reasonable' and it will be up to each individual organisation to interpret what this means.

7.2.6.2   BCOBS 2: Purpose and application: who and what?

In addition to the general application *rule*, this chapter applies to the *communication*, or *approval* for *communication*, to a *person* in the *United Kingdom* of a *financial promotion* of a *retail banking service* unless it can lawfully be *communicated* by an *unauthorised person* without *approval*.

Financial services providers are required to pay due regard to the interests of their customers and treat them fairly (section 5.4). They are also required to pay due regard to the information needs of clients (this may need to take account of cultural and language issues – section 2.5.1) and communicate information to them in a way that is clear, fair and not misleading.

Chapter 2 of BCOBS reinforces these requirements by requiring financial services providers to:

◆ pay regard to the information needs of banking customers when communicating with or making a financial promotion to them (section 5.5); and

◆ communicate information in a way that is clear, fair and not misleading.

This rule applies in a way that is appropriate and proportionate and will be dependent on the means of communication and the information conveyed. This could mean, for example, that information going to personal customers may need to be expressed slightly differently from that going to small business customers.

There are some general requirements for communicating with customers. For example, financial promotions must:

◆ include the name of the provider;

◆ be accurate and not emphasise any potential benefits of a retail banking service without also giving a fair indication of any risks in a prominent place within the communication;

◆ be presented in a way that is likely to be understood by an average member of the group of people to whom it is directed or by whom it is likely to be received; and

◆ not hide important information, statements or warnings.

Any comparisons made between banking services must be made in a fair and balanced way. Similarly the tax treatment of, and interest rates applicable under, a service must be stated. The promotion must also state that the amount of tax due will depend upon the individual circumstances of each customer, and that it could change in the future. The payment of tax is dealt with in section 8.2.

7.2.6.3 BCOBS 3: Distance marketing

The existing distance marketing regulations are covered in section 6.6 and you will see that the BCOBS rules follow these regulations closely.

> This section applies to a *firm* that carries on any distance marketing and e-commerce activity from an establishment in *the United Kingdom*, with or for a *consumer* in *the United Kingdom* or other *EEA state*.

In this context distance marketing relates to telephone and postal marketing. The various different delivery channels are covered in section 9.5.

For distance marketing there are rules that cover the following:

◆ **Disclosure of information**: information must be provided to the consumer in good time, before the consumer is bound by that information, and the information must be given in a clear and comprehensible manner.

> When a *firm* makes a telephony communication to a *consumer*, it must make its identity and the purposes of its call explicitly clear at the beginning of the conversation.

◆ **Terms and conditions, and form**: these must be communicated to the consumer in good time and in a durable medium (either by post or by email).

◆ **Commencing performance of the distance contract**: the contract may only begin after the consumer has given their approval.

◆ **Exception: successive operations**: where a distance contract is made up of an initial service agreement followed by successive operations of the same nature, the rules in BCOBS 3 only apply to the initial agreement. For example, the initial service agreement includes the opening of a bank account and operations include the deposit or withdrawal of funds from a bank account. However, if a new element of the service is added, such as using an electronic payment service, this is not an operation. It is considered to be an additional contract to which the rules apply.

◆ **Consumer's right to request paper copies and change the means of communication**: the consumer can request and receive the contractual terms and conditions on paper at any time and can request a change to the means of distance communication, unless it is incompatible with the contract concluded or the nature of the service provided. For example, it may not be possible for a customer to request a postal service from an Internet bank.

◆ **Unsolicited services**: where a customer does not reply to an unsolicited service a firm cannot enforce a contract against a consumer. However, this rule does not apply to the implicit renewal of a distance contract.

7.2.6.3.1 e-commerce

There are some additional rules that relate to e-commerce:

◆ **Information about the firm and its products or services**: a firm must make certain information easily, directly and permanently accessible. This includes its name, the geographic address at which it is located and how it may be easily and quickly contacted. It must also state its FSA authorisation and any registration with professional bodies.

  If the price of services is mentioned then this must be clear and unambiguous. Any promotional offers must be clearly identified as such, and the conditions that have to be met for customers to qualify for them must also be clearly stated.

◆ **Requirements relating to the placing and receipt of orders**: these ensure that customers are made aware of the technical steps they need to follow to place orders, and that firms have means of amending errors, acknowledging orders and sending the necessary contractual terms and conditions to customers so that they can store them.

◆ **Exception**: contract concluded by email.

> The requirements relating to the placing and receipt of orders do not apply to contracts concluded exclusively by exchange of email or by equivalent individual communications.

7.2.6.4 BCOBS 4: Enabling bank customers to make informed decisions

We considered the problem of financial literacy in section 2.1 and the need for customers to have access to information in an understandable format so that they can manage their finances. This rule ensures that all customers' needs are met:

> A *firm* must provide or make available to a *banking customer* appropriate information about a *retail banking service* and any *deposit* made in relation to that *retail banking service*:
>
> 1. in good time;
>
> 2. in an appropriate medium; and
>
> 3. in an easily understandable language and in a clear and comprehensible form so that the banking customer can make decisions on an informed basis.

When considering the above, a financial services provider needs to consider the importance of the information to the decision-making process of the customer and the time at which the information may be most useful. So, for example, if a customer opens a bank account, the provider should ensure that the customer has a written copy of the terms and conditions of that account in good time, before that customer is bound by them. In a situation where a provider wishes to make changes to the terms and conditions of an existing account that will be to the disadvantage of the customer, then the provider should give reasonable notice to the customer in writing.

With changes of interest rates that will be to the disadvantage of the customer, the notification should:

◆ give details of a comparable service for which the customer is eligible;

◆ indicate that the customer may move their account to another provider; and

◆ indicate that the provider will help the customer to move their account if they wish.

Where introductory offers have been made, such as preferential rates of interest on deposit accounts, the provider should give written notice of the expiry of that offer within a reasonable period before that rate ceases to apply.

Appropriate information provided to customers should include:

◆ information relating to the provider;

◆ the different services offered by the provider that share the main features of the service the customer has enquired about or those features that the customer has expressed an interest in (unless the customer has expressly indicated that they do not wish to receive this information);

◆ the terms and conditions of the contract and any changes to them;

◆ the rate of interest payable on any deposit, how and when the interest is calculated and applied and any changes to the rates;

◆ any charges payable and changes to these charges;

◆ the time at which any funds placed or transferred to the provider for the credit of the customer's account will be made available to the customer;

◆ how a customer may complain (section 15.7);

◆ the terms of any compensation scheme if the provider cannot meet its obligations (section 3.2.1);

◆ details of any basic bank accounts (section 8.1.3) (but only if the provider offers this type of account and the customer meets the eligibility criteria); and

◆ the timescales for each stage of the cheque-clearing process (section 11.4).

The information required by the 'appropriate information' rule may vary according to the customer's actual or likely commitment, the information needs of a reasonable recipient, the distance communication requirements, and if the information has already been provided to that customer recently.

7.2.6.4.1 *Statements of account*

The rules regarding bank accounts are very clear:

◆ The provider must make regular statements of account available on paper to customers appropriate to the type of service provided. However, it need not do so where:

— the provider has given the customer a pass book in which to record transactions;

— the service is provided at a distance using electronic means, such as the Internet, where the customer can access their account balance, view transactions and give instructions online;

— a customer has elected not to receive statements of account; or

— the provider has reasonable grounds to believe that the customer is not resident at their last known address and it is not possible to ascertain the customer's new address.

◆ A provider must not charge for providing statements.

◆ A provider must provide statements within a reasonable time of the customer requesting them.

◆ A provider and customer may agree on a charge for providing copy statements or providing statements more frequently. However, any such charge must correspond to the provider's actual costs.

7.2.6.5   BCOBS 5: Post-sale requirements

There are a number of post-sale requirements:

◆ **Service**:

A *firm* must provide a service in relation to a *retail banking service* which is prompt, efficient and fair to a *banking customer* and which has regard to any communications or *financial promotion* made by the *firm* to the *banking customer* from time to time.

When considering the order in which to process payment instructions, providers must ensure that they treat customers fairly.

◆ **Dealing with customers in financial difficulty**: a provider should deal fairly with a customer whom it has reason to believe is in financial difficulty (section 12.3 and section 14.7).

◆ **Moving a retail banking service**:

A *firm* must provide a prompt and efficient service to enable a *banking customer* to move to a *retail banking service* (including a *payment service*) provided by another *firm*.

Where there are no arrangements between the existing provider and the new provider to which the customer wishes to move their account, then the service given by the existing provider need only be prompt and efficient. For an account, for example, this would be the closing of the account and returning the deposit (plus any interest) to the customer. Where there are arrangements between the two providers, then the service would include transferring any account balance and making arrangements in respect of direct debits and standing orders.

◆ **Lost and dormant accounts**:

A firm must make appropriate arrangements to enable a banking customer, so far as is possible, to trace and, if appropriate, to have access to a deposit held (or formerly held) in a retail banking service provided by the firm. This applies even if:

1. the banking customer may not be able to provide the firm with information which is sufficient to identify the retail banking service concerned; or

2. the banking customer may not have carried out any transactions in relation to that retail banking service for an extended period of time.

◆ **Firm's liability for unauthorised payments**: this strengthens existing legislation (section 11.2 and section 11.3) in that, where a customer denies having authorised a payment, it is for the provider to prove it was authorised. Where an unauthorised payment has been made, the provider must, within a reasonable period, refund the amount and restore the customer's account to the state it would have been in had the payment not been made.

◆ **Banking customer's liability for unauthorised payments**:

— A customer will be liable for a maximum amount of £50 for a lost or stolen payment instrument such as a cheque or payment card or where the customer has failed to keep the PIN safe.

— A customer will be liable for all losses where they have acted fraudulently. They will also be liable for all losses where they have intentionally or with gross negligence failed to comply with their obligations under the banking agreement in relation to the issue or use of the payment instruments. Similarly, they will be liable for all losses if they have failed to take all reasonable steps to keep their PINs safe.

— Where the customer has not acted fraudulently the provider must not make the customer liable for any losses arising after the customer has notified the provider of a payment instruction or PIN loss. The provider must ensure that the customer has the means to report the loss at all times. The provider must also not make the customer liable for any unauthorised payments for distance contracts.

◆ **Value date**:

The reference date used by a firm for the purpose of calculating interest in funds credited to an account of a banking customer held with it must be no later than:

— the business day on which the funds are credited to the account of the firm; or

— in the case of cash placed with a firm for credit to a banking customer's account in the same currency as that account, immediately after the firm receives the funds.

The above rule does not apply to funds credited to a customer's account by means of a cheque, in which case the normal clearing cycle will apply.

◆ **Non-execution or defective execution of payments**: where a customer claims that a payment has not been correctly executed it is for the provider to prove that the payment was authenticated, accurately recorded, entered in the provider's accounts and not affected by a technical breakdown or other problem. Where a payment has been made incorrectly the provider must refund the customer the amount of the defective payment and restore the customer's account to the state in which it would have been had the defective payment not taken place.

If the payment reaches the same bank as the recipient's bank but not their account, the recipient bank must make the amount immediately available to the recipient and credit their account.

Where a refund has been made, the provider must also refund any charges or interest due to be paid by the customer as a result of the error made by the provider.

7.2.6.6 BCOBS 6: The right to cancel

A customer has the right to cancel a contract for a retail banking service without penalty and without giving any reason within 14 calendar days. There are some exceptions to this rule. The customer has no right to cancel:

◆ a contract (other than a cash ISA) where the interest rate payable on the deposit is fixed for a period of time;

◆ a contract whose price depends on the fluctuations in the financial market outside the provider's control (such as fluctuations in the stock market) that may occur during the cancellation period; or

◆ a cash deposit child trust fund (other than a distance contract).

The cancellation period begins on the day that the contract for the service is concluded or the day on which the customer receives the contractual terms and conditions if it is later than this date.

Providers are obliged to inform customers of their right to cancel.

There are various other requirements regarding the customer's right to cancel:

◆ **Exercising the right to cancel:** the customer must exercise their right to cancel within the notice period. In the case of a dispute, where the evidence is unclear, the provider must treat the date that the notification was given as the date when the customer dispatched their letter of cancellation.

◆ **Effects of cancellation:** cancellation allows the customer to withdraw from the contract and the contract is terminated. The customer may only be required to pay for any service actually given by the provider. The provider is not allowed to charge a penalty fee.

◆ **Obligations on cancellation:** the provider must return funds to the customer, less any fees for services due, within 30 calendar days of receipt of the notice of cancellation. In the same way, the customer is obliged to return to the provider any sums or property they have received within 30 calendar days.

Activity

> Visit the FSA's website and review the BCOBS Q&As.

Resources

http://fsahandbook.info/FSA/html/handbook/BCOBS

www.lendingstandardsboard.org.uk

7.3 The Financial Ombudsman Service

We looked at the Financial Ombudsman Service (FOS) in section 3.2.2; however, it would be useful to repeat some of the key points here.

◆ The FOS settles individual complaints between consumers and businesses providing financial services.

◆ Set up as independent experts, the service is free to consumers.

◆ The FOS looks at complaints about a wide range of financial matters — from insurance and mortgages to investments and credit..

◆ Being independent and impartial, the FOS looks at all complaints carefully from both sides and considers all the facts.

◆ If the FOS decides a business has treated the consumer fairly, it will explain why. However if it decides the business has acted wrongly, and the consumer has lost out as a result, it can order matters to be put right.

◆ It can resolve many disputes informally, but some cases are more complex and take more time. They aim to settle most disputes within six to nine months.

◆ Consumers do not have to accept any decision made. They are free to go to court instead. However, if they do accept an ombudsman's decision, it is binding both on them and on the business.

◆ The FOS does not write the rules for businesses — or fine them if rules are broken. That is the job of the regulator — which, at the time of writing, is the FSA.

The FOS looks at complaints regarding the following:

◆ banking;

◆ insurance;

◆ mortgages;

◆ pensions;

◆ savings and investments;

◆ credit cards and store cards;

◆ loans and credit;

◆ hire purchase and pawnbroking;

◆ financial advice;

◆ stocks, shares, unit trusts and bonds.

7.4   Consumer Credit Acts

The regulation of consumer credit in the UK (with the exception of most mortgage lenders) is the result of the Consumer Credit Acts of 1974 and 2006. The 1974 Act established the basic principles of consumer credit regulation, many of which are still in force today. The 2006 Act consolidated, expanded and brought up to date the earlier Act.

7.4.1   Consumer Credit Act 1974

The purpose of the Consumer Credit Act 1974 (CCA 1974) was to **regulate**, **supervise** and **control** certain types of lending to individuals, and to provide borrowers with **protection** from unscrupulous lenders. The provisions of the Act, and those of the 2006 Act, are regulated by the Office of Fair Trading (not the FSA).

There are many types of lender in the market for financial services, ranging from large multinational banks to individual moneylenders. The Act sets out standards by which all lenders must conduct their business. It includes a number of safeguards under which potential borrowers must be made aware of the nature and conditions of the borrowing, and of their rights and their obligations.

The Act affects most aspects of a bank's lending activities, including personal loans and revolving credit such as credit cards. Not all loans are covered by the Act. Loans for the purchase of a private dwelling are *exempt* and further loans for the improvement or repair of a private dwelling are also exempt, provided that they are from the same lender as the original mortgage loan. Loans raised on the security of a dwelling but used for other purposes are *not exempt*.

The main elements of the Act's provisions are as follows.

◆ Suppliers of loans and credit as defined in the Act must be **licensed** by the Office of Fair Trading.

◆ Clients must receive a copy of the **loan agreement** for their own records.

◆ Prospective borrowers have a **cooling-off period** during which they can review the terms of the loan and, if they wish, decide not to proceed with the transaction. This applies to all loans regulated by the Act, unless the loan agreement is signed on the **lender's premises**.

◆ Undesirable **marketing practices** are forbidden: for instance, advertisements must not make misleading claims.

◆ **Credit reference agencies** must, on request, disclose information held about individuals and must correct it if it is shown to be inaccurate.

One of the Act's most significant innovations was a system for comparing the price of lending. This is the **annual percentage rate** (APR), which must be quoted for all regulated loans. The APR represents a measure of the total cost of borrowing and its aim is to allow a fair comparison, between different lenders, of the overall cost of borrowing.

The calculation of the APR is specified under the terms of the CCA 1974 and it takes account of two main factors:

◆ the **interest rate** – whether it is charged on a daily, monthly or annual basis;

◆ the **additional** costs and fees charged when arranging the loan, eg an application fee.

The result is that the APR is higher than the interest rate being charged on the loan because of the inclusion of the additional fees.

7.4.2 Consumer Credit Act 2006

Following a three-year review of consumer credit law, the Government decided to reform the CCA 1974 in order to better protect consumers and to create a fairer and more competitive credit market. The aim was to make improvements in three broad areas, as follows:

◆ To enhance **consumer rights and redress** – consumers will be able to challenge unfair lending and will have access to more effective options for resolving disputes.

◆ To improve the **regulation** of consumer credit businesses by ensuring fair practices and through 'targeted action to drive out rogues'.

◆ To make regulation more appropriate for all kinds of consumer credit transaction. The plan is to **extend protection** to all consumer credit and to create a **fairer regime** for businesses.

This reform was implemented through primary and secondary legislation. The primary legislation is the Consumer Credit Act 2006.

The 2006 Act was introduced in three stages, the main elements of which were as follows.

◆ **April 2007**: The scope of the Financial Ombudsman Service was expanded to incorporate consumer credit disputes. At the same time, the **Unfair Relationships Test** was introduced for new agreements: this enables borrowers to challenge credit agreements in court on the grounds that the relationship between themselves and the lender is 'unfair'. This replaced the previous concept of 'extortionate' credit and broadens the rest of the agreement to include relevant factors other than cost, which might include, for example, the financial skill/experience of the borrower.

◆ **April 2008**: The upper limit on the size of loans regulated by the Act was removed (it had previously been £25,000), so that all new credit agreements – unless exempt – are now regulated. The Unfair Relationships Test, introduced a year earlier, was extended to cover both new and existing credit agreements.

◆ **October 2008**: New rules require lenders to supply borrowers with more information about their accounts on an ongoing basis, for instance annual statements, and arrears notices if they fall into arrears.

Activity

> Obtain a quotation prepared under the CCA regulations.
>
> What information is supplied to the customer?
>
> How does this information enable them to make comparisons with another competitive quote?

7.4.3 Consumer credit regulations 2004

The Consumer Credit (Advertisements) Regulations 2004 relate to the form and content of advertisements for credit. They replaced the old distinction between simple, intermediate and full-credit advertisements, and established a single list of items of information that must be included in all credit advertisements. They also introduced new provisions relating to the calculation and presentation of APR in advertisements, including a requirement to display the APR more prominently than other financial information. Other requirements of the regulations are that:

◆ all advertising must be in plain English and must be easily read or clearly heard;

◆ the name of the advertiser must be included;

◆ the **typical** APR must be displayed, meaning that at least two-thirds of those responding to the advert would qualify for it;

◆ if a loan is to be a secured loan, the advertisement must state clearly the nature of the required security.

The Consumer Credit (Agreements) (Amendments) Regulations 2004 seek to make the agreements signed by customers clearer and easier to understand, by making some changes to content and layout.

The Consumer Credit (Disclosure of Information) Regulations 2004 specify what information must be disclosed to prospective borrowers, and the way in which it must be disclosed.

The Consumer Credit (Early Settlement) Regulations 2004 confirm the entitlement of borrowers, under regulated credit agreements, to a rebate when all or part of the debt is repaid earlier than when it is due. They also change the calculation method for such rebates.

7.4.4 The Consumer Credit Directive 2008

The Consumer Credit Directive (CCD) adapts the European consumer credit regime to enable it to deal with modern forms of credit. It is also designed to bring a greater level of harmonisation to the regulation of consumer credit across Europe, and to increase consumer protection. It became law in the UK in February 2011. The following outlines the key changes.

7.4.4.1 Advertising and APRs

◆ Under the new Advertisements Regulations, if an advertisement includes an interest rate or any amount relating to the cost of credit, it must also include a representative example. This must contain certain standard information including a representative APR. The example must be clear and concise and must be more prominent than the other APR information.

◆ The representative APR must reflect at least 51 per cent of business expected to result from the advertisement. The standard information must be representative of agreements to which the representative APR applies.

◆ The rules for the calculation of the total charge for credit (TCC), and hence the APR, differ slightly from the previous requirements, and there are some new assumptions.

7.4.4.2 Creditworthiness and adequate explanations

◆ Lenders are required to assess the borrower's creditworthiness before granting credit or significantly increasing the amount of credit. The assessment must be based on sufficient information, obtained from the borrower where appropriate, and from a credit reference agency (CRA) where necessary.

◆ Lenders must ensure that the borrower is provided with an adequate explanation of the proposed credit agreement — for example, the particular features of the agreement, the cost and the consequences of failure to make payments — to enable the borrower to assess whether the agreement is suited to their needs and financial situation. The explanation must cover certain specified matters, and must be provided orally in certain circumstances. The borrower must be able to ask questions about the agreement, or to ask for further information or explanation.

7.4.4.3 Pre-contractual information and agreements

◆ The Disclosure Regulations require pre-contractual information to be given in good time before the borrower enters into the agreement. The information must be clear and easily legible, and the borrower must be able to take it away to consider and to shop around if they wish. In most cases the information must be provided in a standard format, the Pre-contract Credit Information form, to help the customer make comparisons and to aid their understanding. In the case of overdrafts, a different standard form may be used. If this form is not used, all the information must be equally prominent.

◆ The Agreements Regulations prescribe the information that must be included in the document that the borrower signs. It must be clear, concise and easily legible. There are new rules regarding the provision of copies of executed agreements.

◆ There is a new right for consumers to request a statement of account for a fixed-term loan. The statement can be requested at any time during the life of the agreement but not more frequently than once a month

7.4.4.4 Right of withdrawal

◆ The borrower can withdraw from an agreement within 14 days following conclusion of the agreement or (if later) once the borrower has received a copy of the agreement or notification of the credit limit on a credit card. The borrower must repay the credit and must also pay interest for each day the credit was drawn down.

7.4.4.5 Other key changes

◆ The borrower must be notified of changes in the rate of interest payable under the agreement. This must generally be done in writing before the change takes effect.

◆ The borrower is entitled to seek redress from the lender in certain circumstances if they are unable to obtain satisfaction from the supplier of goods or services. This applies in cases where section 75 of the CCA (joint and several liability) does not apply, provided that the cash value of the goods or service is more than £30,000 and the credit does not exceed £60,260.

◆ The existing right to settle a credit agreement early is extended to a right to make partial early settlements at any time. Under the CCA the lender may claim compensation in certain circumstances provided that this is fair and objectively justified and does not exceed 1 per cent or 0.5 per cent of the amount repaid early.

- The borrower can terminate an open-end agreement at any time, subject to notice of no more than one month. The lender must give at least two months' notice of termination, and give justified reasons for termination. This requirement is waived in certain situations, for example where giving notice would prejudice the prevention of crime.

- The borrower must be informed if the debt is sold or transferred to a third party, unless the arrangements for servicing the debt are unchanged.

- A number of changes have been made in the requirements on overdrafts. These largely relate to the information that the creditor must give to the borrower about both authorised overdrafts and overdrafts that are not prearranged

- Credit intermediaries must disclose the extent to which they are acting independently or work exclusively with one or more creditors. If a fee is payable by the borrower to the credit intermediary for their services, this must be agreed in writing with the borrower before the credit agreement is entered into. The fee must be notified to the creditor if the creditor is calculating the APR.

- If an application for credit is declined on the basis of information from a CRA, the creditor must notify the borrower of this and provide contact details for the CRA.

Source: www.bis.gov.uk, 2011.

7.5   Personal insolvency

When a person is experiencing financial hardship they may become **insolvent**, which means they are in a position where they cannot pay their debts as they fall due or have an excess of liabilities over assets (negative equity). These debts may be rent or mortgage payments, loan and credit card repayments, utility bills, household expenditure such as food, and other living expenses.

This will be an extremely stressful time and many people find themselves unable to repay all their creditors in full and don't know where to turn. A useful step would be to take advice from one of the agencies discussed inTopic 3. If, after receiving advice, they are unable to make an arrangement with their creditors there are a number of routes open to them, as we shall see below.

Over recent years, there has been an upward trend in individual insolvencies (although some of the figures given below for the fourth quarter of 2010 indicate a year-on-year decline). In part, the increase in insolvencies has been the result of a change in legislation, which made it easier for people to start afresh after making arrangements with their creditors. As more people have taken this route, the **social stigma** of doing so has reduced. Another reason is the **worsening economic climate**, which has led to people losing their jobs – and therefore their income – through redundancy.

Activity

> What other reasons may there be for people having financial difficulty?

According to the information available at the time of writing, there were 30,729 individual insolvencies in England and Wales in the fourth quarter of 2010 on a seasonally adjusted basis. This was a decrease of 13.6 per cent on the same period in 2009.

The total number of individual insolvencies was made up of :

◆ 12,049 bankruptcies (down 29.2 per cent on the corresponding quarter of the previous year);

◆ 12,508 individual voluntary arrangements (IVAs) (down 5.4 per cent on the corresponding quarter of the previous year); and

◆ 6,172 debt relief orders (DROs) (up 15.4 per cent on the corresponding quarter of the previous year).

Source: Insolvency Service

Figure 7.1 shows how the numbers have increased since 2000.

Figure 7.1   Personal insolvencies in England and Wales, 2000–2010

Thousands, not seasonally adjusted

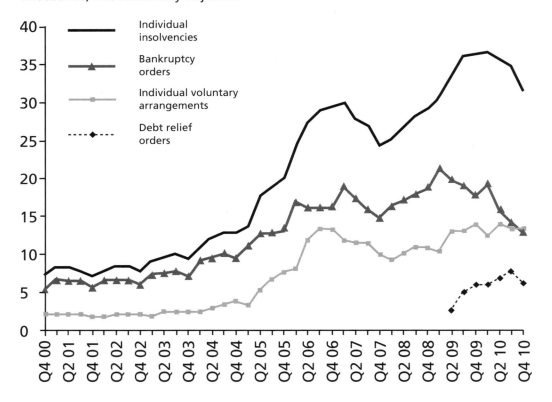

There are three main ways in which a person can deal with their debts and make a fresh start (outlined in section 7.5.1 to section 7.5.3).

7.5.1 Debt relief orders

Debt relief orders (DROs) provide debt relief, subject to some restrictions. They are suitable for people who

◆ do not own their own home;

◆ have little surplus income and assets; and

◆ less than £15,000 of debt.

An order lasts for **12 months**. In that time creditors named on the order cannot take any action to recover their money without permission from the court. At the end of the period, if the person's circumstances have not changed they will be freed from the debts that were included in the order. DROs do not involve the courts. They are run by the **Insolvency Service** in partnership with skilled debt advisers, called **approved intermediaries**, who will help people apply to the Insolvency Service for a DRO.

To apply for a DRO, an individual must meet certain conditions:

◆ They must be unable to pay their debts.

◆ They must owe less than £15,000.

◆ They can own a car to the value of £1,000 but the total value of other assets must not exceed £300.

◆ After taking away tax, National Insurance contributions and normal household expenses, their disposable income must be no more than £50 a month.

◆ They must be domiciled (living) in England or Wales, or at some time in the last three years have been living or carrying on business in England or Wales.

◆ They must not have been subject to another DRO within the last six years.

◆ They must not be involved in another formal insolvency procedure at the time they apply.

Activity

> Who might find this type of process useful ?

7.5.2 Individual voluntary arrangements

An individual voluntary arrangement (IVA) is a formal version of a DRO. The process begins with a formal proposal to the creditors to pay part or all of an individual's debts. The debtor will need to apply to the court and must be helped by an **insolvency practitioner**. Any agreement reached with the creditors will be binding on them.

7.5.2.1 How does it work?

◆ The debtor first has to find an authorised insolvency practitioner prepared to act for them.

◆ Then they apply to the court for an 'interim order'. This prevents the creditors from presenting or proceeding with a bankruptcy petition against the debtor while the interim order is in force. It also prevents them from taking other action against the creditor during the same period without the permission of the court.

◆ The insolvency practitioner tells the court the details of the debtor's proposals and whether in their opinion a meeting of creditors should be called to consider it.

◆ If a meeting is to be held, the date of the meeting and details of the proposals are sent to the creditors.

◆ At the meeting, the creditors vote on whether to accept the proposals. If enough creditors (over 75 per cent in value of the creditors present in person or by proxy (substitute), and voting on the resolution) vote in favour, the proposals are accepted. They are then binding on all creditors who had notice of, and were entitled to vote at, the meeting.

◆ The insolvency practitioner supervises the arrangement and pays the creditors in accordance with the accepted proposal.

◆ Insolvency practitioners are usually accountants, some are solicitors and their fees are similar to those charged by members of these professions for other kinds of work.

An IVA may be useful where:

◆ the debtor has friends or relatives prepared to help pay or contribute towards paying their debts;

◆ their income enables them to pay regular sums to creditors.

There are some **advantages** of an individual voluntary arrangement compared with bankruptcy:

◆ It gives the debtor more say in how their assets are dealt with and how payments are made to creditors. The debtor may be able to persuade their creditors to allow them to retain certain assets (such as their home).

◆ They avoid the restrictions that apply to a bankrupt (see next section).

◆ The debtor does not have to pay some of the fees and expenses that are charged in a bankruptcy, and so the overall costs are likely to be less.

Activity

> Research the costs of an IVA for an individual who has decided to take this route out of insolvency.

7.5.3 Bankruptcy

The bankruptcy proceedings will:

◆ free someone who is insolvent from overwhelming debts so that they can make a fresh start, subject to some restrictions; and

◆ make sure their assets are shared out fairly amongst their creditors.

Anyone can be made bankrupt, including individual members of a partnership. There are different insolvency procedures for dealing with companies and for partnerships themselves.

A court makes a bankruptcy order only after a bankruptcy petition has been presented. It is usually presented either by:

◆ the debtor; or

◆ one or more creditors who are owed at least £750 and that amount is unsecured.

An **official receiver** or an **insolvency practitioner** (known as the trustee) can be appointed to take responsibility for administering the bankruptcy process and protecting the bankrupt's assets from the date of the bankruptcy order. They are also responsible for looking into the bankrupt's financial affairs for the period before and during their bankruptcy. They may report to the court and have to report to the creditors. They must also report any matters that indicate the bankrupt may have committed criminal offences in connection with their bankruptcy or that their behaviour has been dishonest or they have been in some way to blame for their bankruptcy.

The trustee will tell the creditors how much money (if any) will be shared out in the bankruptcy; however, the costs of the bankruptcy proceedings are paid first from the money that is available. The bankrupt no longer controls their assets, although they will be allowed to keep certain assets, such as those required for their business and basic items needed by the family at home. Other assets will be disposed of to raise funds to meet the creditors' claims.

If a bankrupt owns their own home, their interest (share) in it will form part of the assets available to the trustee. In the case of a married couple or partners living together it may be possible for the sale of the property to be put off until after the first year of bankruptcy, which gives time for other housing arrangements to be made. However, the spouse or civil partner who is not made bankrupt should take legal advice as soon as possible.

There are a number of restrictions on a bankrupt as mentioned above. Briefly, these are that it is a **criminal offence** for an undischarged bankrupt to:

◆ obtain credit of more than £500 without disclosing their bankruptcy;

◆ carry on a business in a different name from that in which they were made bankrupt;

◆ be involved with a limited company or act as a director without the court's permission.

There are other **restrictions**; those that relate to conducting a banking relationship are as follows.

◆ When opening a new bank or building society account, the provider should be advised that the individual is bankrupt.

◆ A bankrupt should not obtain overdraft facilities without informing the bank that they are bankrupt nor write cheques that are unlikely to be paid by the bank.

◆ They must tell the trustee about any money they have in their bank account that is more than they need to pay for reasonable living expenses. The trustee can claim any surplus to pay the creditors.

Activity

> What is your bank's policy on opening accounts for bankrupts?

Since April 2004, anyone made bankrupt will automatically be discharged (freed from the bankruptcy) after a maximum of 12 months. This period may actually be shorter if the trustee concludes their enquiries and files a notice in court. On the other hand, if the bankrupt does not co-operate, the period can be longer.

7.6 Codes of practice

As we have seen, there is a large amount of legislation designed to protect consumers. There are some areas, however, that are still governed by codes of practice, and we shall look at two of these below.

7.6.1 UK Payments Administration

The UK Payments Administration (UKPA) was formerly known as APACS (Association for Payment Clearing Services). It is the UK trade association for payments and for those institutions that deliver payment services to customers. It provides the forum for its members to come together on non-competitive issues relating to the payments industry.

One of UKPA's key responsibilities is co-ordinating a whole range of activities to tackle **payment-related fraud**. One of the most visible recent initiatives has been the introduction of chip and PIN, which has been achieved hand in hand with the retail industry.

7.6.1.1 UKPA guidelines

Guidelines are **advisory** rather than mandatory. They set a standard that the industry should aim to achieve, and give examples of implementation strategies that may help members to meet requirements. Adoption of guidelines by individual members will be affected in the short term by matters such as investment cycles and product design.

The areas that the guidelines cover are:

◆ plastic cards – matters such as billing best practice, credit card limit increases, debt advice health warning and direct sales of credit cards;

◆ CHAPS (Clearing House and Payments) guidelines;

◆ cheque guidelines.

7.6.2 Finance and Leasing Association

The Finance & Leasing Association (FLA) is the major UK representative body for the UK finance and leasing industry. It campaigns for best practice in lending and leasing. We looked at the FLA in relation to finance companies in section 4.1.4.

7.6.2.1 FLA Lending Code 2006

The Lending Code of the Finance and Leasing Association sets out standards of good practice for the finance and leasing industry.

It has various sections, depending on the type of provider from whom the customer took out the loan:

◆ direct from the finance company;

◆ through a supplier of goods and services, for example in a shop or a motor dealership;

◆ through a credit broker (a third party who arranges finance).

The code is intended to assure those who obtain finance from full members that they are doing business with reputable organisations. The FLA monitors members' performance in line with this code.

The **Key Commitments** of the code are as follows.

'We will:

◆ act fairly, reasonably and responsibly in all our dealings with you;

◆ make sure that all services and products meet the requirements of this Code;

◆ make sure that all services and products meet all the relevant laws and regulations, including the Consumer Credit Acts and all regulations made under it;

◆ not discriminate against you because of your race, sex, disability, ethnic background or sexuality;

◆ help you when you need information and guidance, including explaining how the products will affect your finances;

◆ act honestly and try to make sure that credit brokers, and all other suppliers of goods and services we do business with, do the same;

◆ not pressurise you to enter into any agreement with us and try to make sure that credit brokers, and all other suppliers of goods and services we do business with, do not pressurise you;

◆ correct mistakes, handle complaints quickly and sympathetically, and tell you how to take your complaint forward if you are still not satisfied;

◆ co-operate with regulators (such as the Office of Fair Trading (OFT) or the Financial Services Authority (FSA)) and organisations that handle complaints (such as FLA or the Financial Ombudsman Service);

◆ consider cases of financial difficulty sympathetically and positively;

◆ follow any guidance notes that FLA issues, where relevant to the products and services we offer;

◆ treat all your personal information as private and confidential, and run secure and reliable systems;

◆ train our staff to make sure that the procedures they follow reflect the commitments set out in this Code; and

◆ publicise the Code and make copies freely and readily available to you.'

Source: FLA Lending Code 2006

Activity

Review the list above and compare it with the key commitments of the Lending Code in Topic 3.

Resources

www.apacs.org.uk

www.bis.gov.uk

www.financial-ombudsman.org.uk

www.fla.org.uk

www.insolvency.gov.uk

Review questions

The following review questions are designed so that you can check your understanding of this topic.

The answers are provided at the end of these learning materials.

1. Which of the FSA's sourcebooks describe the business standards to which financial service providers should adhere?

2. What activities do the Mortgage Conduct of Business rules regulate?

3. What six areas does the Banking Conduct of Business Sourcebook cover?

4. Which parties are bound by the FOS's decisions?

5. What was the purpose of the CCA 1974?

6. What is the role of the OFT in relation to the Consumer Credit Acts?

7. What factors caused the increase in insolvencies from 2003 onwards?

8. List the differences between the three main ways in which a person can deal with their debts and make a fresh start.

9. What is the role and purpose of UKPA?

10. What types of provider does the FLA Lending Code of practice cover?

Topic 8

Key retail financial products and services

Learning objective

After studying this topic, students should be able to demonstrate an understanding of the key retail financial products and services.

Introduction

So far we have looked at the underpinning framework for the financial services industry. We are now going to move on and consider, in this topic, the key retail financial products and services including current accounts, deposit and savings accounts, overdrafts, payment card services and unsecured/personal loans. We will return to bank lending again in Topics 12–14 as it is a large part of many banks' and building societies' business.

Both personal and small business customers will use the services described in this topic. However, some services such as structured deposits and personal loans are aimed specifically at personal customers. The equivalent of a personal loan for a business customer would be a business development loan and perhaps even a commercial mortgage. Larger businesses that are likely to require these sorts of facilities are more complex and therefore not likely to be dealt with by the 'retail' part of the organisation.

8.1   Current accounts

As we saw in Topic 1, people open bank accounts primarily as a safe place to store their money and so they can access various payments systems. The basic features of a current account are as follows.

◆ It allows the customer to hold credit balances with a bank or building society and, sometimes, receive a small amount of interest on credit balances over a certain amount.

◆ The customer receives regular statements showing transactions in and out of the account.

◆ It provides a means of making payments to third parties: all of the banks and building societies provide a chequebook and/or a debit card, plus the ability to set up standing orders and direct debits.

♦ A debit card enables account holders to draw cash from cash machines around the country in a variety of public locations outside normal banking hours and also overseas.

♦ It may allow overdrafts, although this may only be offered to customers with a good track record with the provider, up to a pre-set agreed overdraft limit.

♦ There will be certain charges, for example, in relation to overdrafts or for duplicate statements, and interest will be charged on overdrawn balances.

♦ Most banks and building societies offer online or telephone access to their accounts.

Transactional accounts such as bank current accounts are regarded as being very safe for customers. They have little or no element of risk, usually pay little or no interest, and so offer little or no reward. What they do offer is a low-cost (sometimes no-cost) service for accepting and making payments.

Activity

For what reason do banks and building societies want customers to open current accounts?

8.1.1 Customer segmentation

In order to cross sell more financial services products, providers segment their customer base by offering **packaged** current account products with features and benefits that match the characteristics of that segment. Examples of a range of packaged accounts from one high street provider are listed below.

♦ **Current Account**: £12.95 per month, interest-free overdraft up to £300, slightly cheaper rate on overdrafts over £300 (eg 19.9 per cent EAR), up to £100 per year on additional benefits such as extended warranty cover on domestic appliances and cardholder protection.

♦ **Mass Affluent Current Account**: £15 per month, better rate on overdrafts over £300 (eg 17.9 per cent EAR), up to £100 per year on additional benefits such as extended warranty cover on domestic appliances and cardholder protection.

♦ **Premier Account**: a current account with no monthly fee that offers personalised banking and professional guidance. A dedicated manager, personal financial planning manager and mortgage adviser. Eligibility criteria require account holders to earn £100,000 or have £50,000 to save or invest. Agreed overdrafts up to £500 interest- and fee-free, preferential interest rate (eg 11.9 per cent EAR variable) on agreed overdrafts over £500, a range of benefits including home emergency cover, extended warranty cover, travel insurance, vehicle recovery cover, access to airport lounges and meeting rooms, premier debit and credit cards.

Activity

> Why are providers prepared to offer free and cheap overdrafts to 'premier' customers?

The current account is a platform that enables sales of other products. Credit scoring of the customer details at account opening gives the provider an indication of what those products could be.

Activity

> What additional products does your organisation offer at account opening if customers fulfil the appropriate criteria?

8.1.2 Children's accounts

We noted in section 1.1.3 that financial providers market accounts aimed at children because they provide a good source of future business. Children's accounts are segmented by age; a range from a high street provider is listed below.

◆ **Children's savings**: a current account for parents and guardians wanting to save for a child up to the age of 18.

◆ **Children's plus**: a current account for children aged 11–17 who can manage their account themselves. This account pays interest and provides a cash card.

◆ **Young person's account**: a current account with special offers for young people aged 16–19. It provides a cheque book and a card that allows withdrawal from ATMs and shopping online. Customers can access the account online.

We can see that the facilities available on the young person's account are very similar to an account for adults that relies on technology for most of its delivery.

Activity

> Why do providers want to encourage the use of technology to service this type of account?

8.1.3 The basic bank account

The government's objective is to make all benefit and pension payments direct to bank accounts. This is to tackle issues of financial exclusion as discussed in section 2.1. Basic bank accounts are simplified current accounts, designed for people who might not otherwise open a current account, or want anything more sophisticated. They are particularly appropriate for people receiving state benefits or pensions who have been used to collecting their payments in cash at the post office.

Basic bank accounts are able to receive money by a wide variety of methods, but the methods of withdrawing money are limited. Cash can be obtained with a card from ATMs and also from post offices. Payments can be made by direct debit, but no chequebooks are issued on these accounts, and there is no overdraft facility. The simplicity of operation is to ensure those with less financial capability feel comfortable using them and in control.

Activity

> Why do providers not want to authorise overdraft facilities on this type of account?

8.2 Deposit/savings accounts

These are among the most straightforward types of account that banks offer. This may be the first type of account that customers open as children (or have opened for them by family members). Depositors (whether individuals or corporate bodies) can invest from as little as £1 with no maximum. They receive a return on their investment in the form of interest.

Interest is normally variable and is usually linked to the bank's base lending rate. It is calculated daily and added to the account on a periodic basis (normally quarterly, half-yearly or yearly).

Some deposit accounts offer higher interest rates provided a certain minimum sum is paid in. Deposits can be subject to **notice of withdrawal** – typical notice periods being from seven to ninety days. Often the requirement for notice will be waived subject to a penalty, which is normally equal to the amount of interest that could be earned over the notice period, as this means that the bank will not have those funds available to lend out **and create a turn, as it will affect its capital adequacy ratio**.

Deposit accounts may be considered as an investment of funds kept for an **emergency** or other cases of need. Over the longer term, however, they have proved to be unattractive when compared with asset-backed investments (those that rely on stock exchange investments). This is because the returns on deposit accounts over time are comparatively low and the effects of inflation erode the exchange value of money, which we considered in section 4.1.

A tax-free type of deposit account is available, subject to certain limitations, in the form of **individual savings accounts** (ISAs). The ISA is a government attempt to encourage saving, by allowing people to save tax-free within certain limits.

Another form of deposit account is a **money market deposit account** – which is usually offered by a centralised department of the provider and for large amounts, usually over £50,000. These accounts typically attract a higher rate of interest than ordinary deposit accounts. The rate of interest reflects current money market interest rates and may vary according to the amount invested.

There are two basic types of money market account: fixed accounts and notice accounts.

1. **Fixed accounts** are **term** deposit accounts, where a sum of money is invested for a fixed period during which time it cannot normally be withdrawn. This period can vary from overnight to five years. The rate of interest is normally fixed for the whole period.

2. **Notice accounts** have no fixed term but, as the name implies, there is a requirement on the investor to give an agreed period of **notice of withdrawal**. Similarly, the bank normally must give the investor the same period of notice of a change in interest rate. A typical period of notice could be anything from seven days to six months, although twelve-month notice periods are available.

Interest rates may be quoted net of basic rate tax, with a gross rate or annual equivalent rate (AER) for comparison. This is because HM Revenue and Customs (HMRC) requires providers in the UK to deduct basic rate tax **at source** before paying the interest over.

Interest may be added to the account whenever it is due. Alternatively, some of the banks and building societies give the option to have interest paid to another account (for example, a current account).

Activity

> Research the range of savings/deposit accounts offered by your organisation.
>
> What are the differences?
>
> What are the criteria that are required for higher interest rates to be paid to savers?

8.2.1 Structured deposits

Structured deposit accounts combine **capital protection** with the potential for **capital growth**. Such growth is dependent on the performance of the underlying investment, eg the FTSE (Financial Times Stock Exchange) index, being at a certain level at the end of the fixed term.

This type of deposit is a fixed-term investment, issued by banks, that guarantees to return at least 100 per cent of the capital invested at the end of the term (before charges). It also offers the potential for higher returns than traditional deposit accounts. This is because the returns are usually linked to the performance of higher-risk investments, such as equity indices. The returns are not guaranteed, and customers may only get back their initial investment. It is possible to invest via an international bond that has the added advantage that any growth is virtually tax-free. This type of bond is attractive to customers when credit interest rates are low and the economic climate is uncertain.

8.3 Overdrafts

An overdraft is a **line of credit** on a current account, offered by all retail banks and some building societies, which enables the customer to continue to use the account in the normal way, even though their funds have been used up. The bank sets a limit to the amount by which the account can be overdrawn. An overdraft:

◆ is a convenient form of short-term temporary borrowing;

◆ with interest calculated on a daily basis; and

◆ assists the customer over a period in which expenditure exceeds income – for instance, an unexpectedly high utility bill, or to fund the purchase of Christmas gifts.

As it is essentially a short-term facility, the agreement is usually for a fixed period, after which it must be renegotiated or the funds repaid.

Overdrafts are **on demand**. This means that although the limit is granted for an agreed period before the next review, technically the lender can demand repayment of the amount outstanding at any time. This is in contrast to a loan account where the term is agreed over a number of years, the benefit to the customer being certainty that repayment can be spread over a longer period. Overdrafts that have been agreed in advance (**authorised**) with the provider are normally a relatively inexpensive form of borrowing, although there may be an arrangement fee.

Unauthorised overdrafts (those that have not been agreed in advance), on the other hand, attract a much higher rate of interest, and can also attract large fees. This can vary from £10 to £25 and can be by transaction or on a monthly basis. A bank can return items (cheques and direct debits) unpaid to stop an unauthorised overdraft. However, it may have a long-term relationship with the customer and, given this history, may prefer to allow the debits to the account. There are no guarantees that the bank will do this, however, and customers should always be encouraged to obtain an authorised overdraft.

Overdrafts are regulated by the Consumer Credit Acts 1974 and 2006 and by the Consumer Credit Regulations 2010. The APR must be published to enable customers to make comparisons with alternative borrowing methods and providers.

Activity

> Research the fees that are levied by your organisation on customers when:
>
> ◆ they take an unauthorised overdraft;
>
> ◆ your organisation returns a cheque unpaid.

8.4 Credit, debit, prepaid and charge cards

The development of plastic cards, and their impact, has gone hand in hand with the rapid advance, over the past 30 years or so, of the electronic processing technologies on which their systems now largely depend. Cards are a convenient way to buy goods and services, and their development has led to a considerable reduction in the use of cash and cheques. They are acceptable in a wide range of locations, including most major retailing chains, and come in a number of different forms.

8.4.1 Credit cards

Credit cards enable customers to shop without cash or cheques in any establishment that is a member of the credit card company's scheme. Originally, all credit card transactions were dealt with manually at the point of sale, but most retailers now have terminals linked directly to the credit card companies' computers, enabling online credit limit checking and authorisation of transactions.

Most credit cards are issued under the umbrella of MasterCard or Visa and they are generally branded to the organisation that issued the card to its customer, eg banks, building societies, stores, motor manufacturers, and others.

Activity

What other types of organisation use their own branding on credit cards?

Why do they do this?

As well as providing cash-free purchasing convenience, credit cards are a source of **revolving credit**. The customer has a credit limit and can use the card for purchases or other transactions up to that amount, provided that at least a specified minimum amount (usually 3 per cent of the outstanding balance) is repaid each month. The customer receives a **monthly statement**, detailing recent transactions and showing the outstanding balance. If the balance is repaid in full within a certain period (usually up to 25 days or so), no interest is charged. This can give the customer a period of up to 56 days **interest-free credit**. If a smaller amount is paid, the remainder is carried forward and interest charged at the company's current rate.

However, credit cards can be an **expensive** way to borrow, with rates of interest considerably higher than most other lending products. There is also normally a charge if the card is used to obtain cash either over the counter or from an automated teller machine (ATM).

Activity

Research a number of credit cards.

What is the interest charged on each of them?

How does this compare with overdraft facilities on different types of current account?

Credit card providers offer interest-free periods for customers transferring their credit card balances to them from a competitor in order to attract new business. There is often a 'handling fee' of around 3 per cent of the balance. Some customers can be very astute at regularly swapping providers to take advantage of these marketing offers. Some customers could be in danger of never making any repayments to this debt and subsequently the amount becomes so large that their credit rating from credit reference agencies does not allow them to swap to a new provider. At this point they may find repayment of the debt quite expensive and therefore difficult to manage.

Activity

> If this situation occurs, how much at fault are providers for encouraging this behaviour in customers?

Credit card companies charge a fee to the retailers for their service. This is deducted as a percentage (typically around 2 per cent) of the value of transactions when the credit card company makes a settlement to the retailer. There are, however, a number of advantages to retailers, in addition to the fact that more customers may be attracted if payment by credit card is available. The retailer can reduce its own bank charges because the credit card amounts paid into a bank account are treated as cash. Some retailers no longer accept cheques, making card and cash the only options for payment.

8.4.2 Debit cards

Debit cards, such as Maestro, enable cardholders to make payments for goods by presenting the card and entering their **PIN** (personal identification number), in just the same way as with credit cards or charge cards. In the case of debit cards, however, the effect of the transaction is that funds equal to the amount spent are transferred electronically from the cardholder's current account to the account of the retailer. This is known as **EFTPOS** (electronic fund transfer at point of sale), although at present the funds are not transferred instantaneously. The system replaces the use of cheques and reduces handling costs for business customers.

Debit cards are also used to withdraw cash from ATMs, and many debit cards have a dual role as cheque guarantee cards. It is possible for providers to control the spending of customers by blocking transactions on the card at the point of sale via the electronic system. This gives an added benefit of certainty of payment to the suppliers of goods and services, because customers who cannot afford to pay have their transaction declined.

8.4.3 Prepaid cards

A prepaid card is a payment card that can be **loaded with money** for the customer themselves or to give to someone else.

A prepaid card looks just like a normal credit or debit card, with a card number, signature strip and company branding. However, they are very different from debit cards that are linked to a bank account with an overdraft facility. This is because it is only possible to spend the money loaded onto the prepaid card.

A prepaid card can be used in the same way as a debit or credit card. When the card is used, the money is immediately taken from the amount loaded onto the card, not from a line of credit or a bank account. As long as there is enough money available on the card, or in the host system, the cardholder can continue to use it.

When the amount remaining on the card is low or at zero, the card may be reloaded (or 'topped up') in a number of ways, such as:

◆ cash top-up at post offices or convenience stores;

◆ funds transfer from a bank account;

◆ online through an Internet account.

However, not all prepaid cards have this facility.

There are many types of prepaid card with a variety of features. Some have online account management, different ways in which the card can be reloaded and the availability of additional cards on the same account. There are also different fees and charges to be considered. For example, when using a prepaid card for travelling abroad, a card that has low foreign exchange fees and low overseas charges is likely to be the most appropriate.

A prepaid card is a good solution for:

◆ giving someone a gift;

◆ travelling abroad without having to carry cash or travellers' cheques – a prepaid card is more secure because it can be blocked if it is lost or stolen;

◆ helping younger family members to learn about managing their money – they can only spend the money that has been loaded onto the card, and the spending can be viewed online;

◆ managing money by separating it into different places for different purposes – for example, a customer could have one card for everyday shopping, one for travel, and one for online purchases;

◆ someone who is having difficulty opening a bank account or getting a credit or debit card for some reason. There is no need to pass a credit check to get a prepaid card, so it can be useful to have benefits or wages payments loaded onto them.

Activity

> Make a list of the features of a credit card. Compare these with the features of a prepaid card. Consider the groups of people for whom each type of card would be appropriate.

8.4.4 Charge cards

Although a charge card is used by the customer in the same way as a credit card to make purchases, the outstanding balance on a charge card must be **paid in full** each month, usually by direct debit to a bank account. The best-known example is American Express. Charge cards may be subject to a subscription fee.

8.5 Loans and personal loans

Many financial service providers offer personal loans. They come in two forms – the **secured** and the **unsecured** loan. They are a better and, in some cases, an easier form of borrowing than an overdraft, which is considered to be a short-term, fluctuating form of borrowing. A loan has a repayment structure and as such is ideal where funds are required for a **specific purpose** – such as a major holiday or new car. They can also be used to **reschedule and consolidate debts** that have become a problem (overspending on credit cards, out of control overdrafts, etc), offering just one regular monthly payment that is easier to manage.

With a secured loan, borrowers offer something of value so that, in the event of default, the lender can take the asset, sell it (**realise the security**) and obtain repayment out of the proceeds. The asset has to be something that is readily realisable, such as a life policy or property. The most common secured loan is a mortgage loan and this will be covered in the next topic.

An unsecured loan however, relies on the borrower's **personal promise to repay**. For the banks, this is a higher-risk loan and will therefore attract a higher rate of interest to reflect this.

Of the two types of loan, the unsecured loan is one that the majority of consumers will readily recognise. A customer calling at a branch, telephoning a call centre, or applying on the Internet will generally be offered a personal unsecured loan. Such loans generally have the following features:

◆ They are for a fixed amount;

◆ They are provided for a fixed period of time, generally between one and five years, although in some cases up to ten.

◆ They have a fixed interest rate.

◆ Fixed monthly payments cover interest and capital.

◆ They are assessed centrally by a credit scoring technique.

◆ They are regulated under the Consumer Credit Acts 1974 and 2006, and the Consumer Credit Regulations 2010.

Activity

> Obtain the interest rates charged for overdrafts and personal loans by your organisation.
>
> Why are the rates different?
>
> Why might a lender prefer to lend money on a personal loan rather than an overdraft?

Review questions

The following review questions are designed so that you can check your understanding of this topic.

The answers are provided at the end of these learning materials.

1. What are the basic features of a bank account?

2. Why do banks 'segment' their customers?

3. What is the purpose of a 'basic' bank account?

4. Why might a customer chose a 'fixed-term' deposit account over a 'notice' deposit account?

5. Compare borrowing money on an overdraft with borrowing on a credit card.

6. What might attract a customer to borrowing on a credit card?

7. When would a prepaid card be useful for a customer?

8. What are the risks of an unsecured loan from the lender's perspective?

9. What benefits are there to the customer in taking out a personal loan to pay for a holiday rather than adding the amount to an overdraft facility?

10. What is a potential disadvantage of borrowing on a personal loan (rather than an overdraft), particularly if the customer has credit balances for part of the month?

Topic 9

Key retail financial products, services and the methods of service delivery

---

Learning objective

After studying this topic, students should be able to demonstrate an understanding of the key retail financial products, services and channels, and the method of delivery – branch-based, Internet, postal and telephone.

Introduction

In Topic 8 we considered the simpler financial products and services that most customers will be familiar with and are most likely to use in their relationship with their financial provider. In this topic we will look at some of the more complex products, such as mortgages, investments, pensions and insurance, which are not necessarily taken up by every customer. These more complex products require specialist advice from authorised financial advisers and would be outside the remit of most customer service staff. However, it is important to understand these products in order to give good customer service by directing the customer to the relevant adviser.

We will also look at how services are delivered, whether this is via staff at the branch, through a call centre, or over the Internet. In reality many customers will require access to all of these different delivery channels and use them to suit their own preferences. Providers need to consider what type of channel suits which segment of their customer base, or product to be delivered, and weigh this against the associated costs of providing this type of service.

Most of the products discussed in this topic are aimed at the personal customer; however, pensions and insurance products are important for business customers, too. Where applicable, the relevance of a product to business needs is mentioned.

9.1 Mortgage loans

Mortgage loans are the most common method of purchasing **residential property** in the UK. Historically, building societies were the main providers of mortgage loans. Since the deregulation of the financial markets in the 1980s, banks and specialist mortgage finance companies have also offered mortgages and a range of related products.

House purchase loans are usually known as mortgage loans because the borrower creates a **legal charge** over the title deeds to the lender as **security** for the loan. This is called a **mortgage** and is referred to as '*charge by deed expressed to be* *by way of a legal mortgage*'. A legal charge is referred to as a 'standard security' in Scotland. When referring to mortgages, the common terms used are those of mortgagor and mortgagee. A **mortgagor** is the person who owns the property and the **mortgagee** is the lender. We looked at this as part of the provider/customer relationship in section 6.1. A simple way of remembering the difference is the 'o' in 'mortgagor' representing the 'o' in 'owner'.

Although the lender does not own the buildings or land, which remains the property of the borrower, a lender with a legal charge is given **rights over the property**, and is in a very strong position. If the borrower defaults on mortgage repayments, the lender is entitled to **take possession** of the property and sell it to recover the money owed, although that step would normally be taken only as a last resort. Before resorting to possession, lenders explore all avenues by which an arrangement could be reached, taking into account the borrower's circumstances. There are, in any case, a number of drawbacks for a lender in possessing a property, for instance:

◆ the difficulty of obtaining a good price;

◆ the administrative costs; and

◆ the possibility of reputational damage.

Activity

> In what circumstances might a lender attract negative publicity when taking possession of a property?

While the mortgagee acquires a number of rights over the property, the mortgagor retains certain rights, too, in particular the following:

◆ They have the legal **right to repay** the loan at any time. This may be subject to an early repayment penalty if the borrower has chosen a fixed-rate, capped-rate, or discounted mortgage rate deal. The lender will have obtained matched funds to create these sorts of deals so will incur costs in releasing the customer from the agreement.

◆ Borrowers whose properties have been taken into possession by a lender are still entitled to **repay the loan** right up to the time when the property is sold.

◆ Borrowers are entitled to the remainder of the sale price after a loan has been repaid, so if the lender sells the property to repay the loan, any **surplus** remaining after the first and any subsequent charges have been met must be paid over to the borrower. In many cases the property is sold at auction and the price obtained is relatively low to reflect the quick sale. This means there may well be little or no surplus to return to the customer.

Mortgage loans are long-term loans, normally for between 10 and 30 years, with the most common terms being 20 or 25 years, which will usually run into retirement age. The amount of the loan could be anything up to 95 per cent of the property value, although it is usually prudent to advance a lower percentage, depending on the prevailing market conditions. In recent times most lenders have been reluctant to lend such a high percentage as confidence in the property market has fallen and prices deflated. The percentage of the property value advanced is generally known as the **loan-to-value** (LTV) ratio. If the value of a property falls, a lender could find that the amount outstanding on the mortgage loan is greater than the value of the asset on which that loan is secured. This is known as **negative equity** and can bring problems for both the lender and the borrower. If the borrower, for example, defaults on the payments and the property is taken into possession, the lender may be unable to sell the property for a sufficient amount to repay the loan.

Other factors also affect the amount a lender may be prepared to lend, particularly the lender's assessment of the borrower's ability to repay the loan over the specified period. The maximum loan is often based on a simple **loan-to-income** (LTI) ratio (eg three times gross (amount before tax) salary for a single earner), although in reality a borrower's 'likelihood of repaying' depends on a complex combination of factors. These factors include the:

◆ **affordability** of the loan, based on the prospective borrower's income and outgoings;

◆ nature and stability of the borrower's **employment**;

◆ borrower's previous **history** of credit repayments.

We will consider mortgage finance again in further depth in section 13.2.

Activity

Research your organisation's criteria for assessing mortgage loan applications.

9.1.1 Further advances

A further advance is a way of **releasing equity** in a borrower's property. In this context, equity refers to the excess value of the property over the outstanding amount of any loans secured on it. The borrower may have a house valued at £200,000 with a mortgage of £100,000. The equity in the property is therefore £100,000. By taking a further advance, of say £50,000, with their existing lender, the customer can release some of the equity in the value of their home for a variety of purposes that do not necessarily have to be property related.

This can be done in two ways:

◆ a physical advance of funds by the lender (as above, say a £50,000 further advance) with a specific repayment term;

◆ an offer from the lender to allow the borrower to draw funds from their mortgage up to a level determined by the mortgagee (as above, the customer has equity of £100,000 but may be allowed to borrow only, say, 80 per cent of the value of the property).

In the latter example the mortgagee may allow the borrower to borrow up to, say, a further £60,000 of that equity either as a whole or in specific amounts. This type of facility can be undertaken on an interest-only basis, although any part of the equity released can be placed on a repayment basis at any time. It is important to note that, although funds can be released in this way, they have to be repaid in full by the time the original mortgage is repaid.

The advantage to the borrower of an equity release by the first mortgagee is that generally they will be able to obtain a rate that is similar to the mortgage rate. This will usually be significantly lower than personal loan lending rates. The advantage to the lender is that they:

◆ are fully secured at all times;

◆ can undertake this type of facility with the minimum of administration; and

◆ are lending to borrowers who have had a satisfactory repayment history with them in the past.

9.1.2 Second mortgages

A second mortgage is one that is created when the borrower/owner (mortgagor) offers the property as security for more borrowing with a **new lender** while the first lender still has a mortgage loan secured on the property. The new lender (the second mortgagee) takes a **second charge** on the property; the original lender retains the deeds, and their charge takes precedence over subsequent charges. This means that in the event of a sale due to default, the original lender's claims will first be met in full; if sufficient surplus then remains, the second mortgagee's charge will allow them to claim against these remaining proceeds.

Clearly, a lender will only agree to a second mortgage if there is sufficient equity in the property. Since second mortgages represent a higher risk to the lender, they are likely to be offered at higher rates of interest than first mortgages. There are also likely to be more costs and charges with this type of loan as there will be more administration involved.

Activity

> Why might a customer approach a new lender for this type of finance?

9.2 Investments

Investments are usually a place to deposit funds over the **longer term** and they should be surplus to any emergency or 'rainy day' money the customer holds. This means the customer should expect a higher rate of return either in interest, capital growth or a combination of the two. Customers should be happy to tie up these funds for a minimum of **five years** and in most cases longer to ensure a reasonable chance of a good return.

Banks are able to give advice to customers on investments, through their **financial advisers**, who are authorised and regulated by the FSA. A huge range of investment products is provided by banks, with many different variations. To make the approach to investments more logical, investment should be considered in three layers.

1. The underlying investment itself will fall into what are referred to as '**asset classes**'. There are four main asset classes — cash deposits, shares, bonds and property. Customers can invest in each of these directly if they wish.

2. With **pooled investments**, the customer puts their money in one or more of the above asset classes, along with other investors. This spreads the risk

and saves on costs. Open-ended investment funds, investment trusts and life assurance bonds are the most common pooled investments.

3. **Tax wrappers** are tax breaks that a customer can, subject to certain rules, 'wrap around' their investment to shield it from some or all tax. The wrapper can be around either an underlying investment or a pooled investment. The two most common tax wrappers are individual savings accounts (ISAs) and pensions.

9.2.1 Underlying asset classes

◆ **Interest-bearing accounts**: these are provided by banks and building societies. They can be sold by customer advisers rather than regulated sellers and were discussed in section 8.2.

◆ **Shares**: the most common form are the ordinary share issues by public limited companies (plcs), which are traded on the stock exchange. There are some risks associated with shares in that their value can go up and down, sometimes quite dramatically in the same day. This risk will transfer across to any other form of investment based on shares.

◆ **National Savings Certificates**: these government savings bonds offer tax-free saving. They are available by direct purchase only via post offices and are considered to be a highly secure investment.

◆ **Gilt-edged securities**: these are loan bonds issued by the government and traded on the stock market. They are called 'gilt-edged' because, again, they are backed by the government and are considered very secure.

◆ **Property**: the customer could be looking for an income from a tenant or capital appreciation in the potential sale value of the property. It can be a costly investment and the funds are not necessarily easily realisable if the customer wishes to access them.

9.2.2 Pooled investments

Pooled investments are those in which a number of investors contribute to a large fund, thus 'pooling' their resources.

◆ **Unit trusts**: individuals contribute regular monthly savings or lump sums to own a part of a fund that will invest in stocks and shares. As the value of those shares moves up and down, so the value of the fund moves up and down, too. As a pooled fund, investing in a wide variety of stocks, and managed by a professional fund manager, a unit trust is considered to be less risky than an individual investing in one particular share. Unit trusts are said to be 'open-ended', which means that the number of units in issue increases as more customers invest and decreases as customers sell.

◆ **Investment trusts**: these are similar to the concept of unit trusts but instead of purchasing a unit in a trust, the customer purchases a share in a company that owns all of the shares. Investments can be made in a lump sum or on a regular monthly basis directly with the investment trust company. Investment trusts are 'close-ended' because a set number of shares are available, irrespective of how many investors wish to buy them.

9.2.3 Tax wrappers

◆ **ISAs**: ISAs succeeded personal equity plans (PEPs) as a government initiative to encourage the general public to save and invest. ISAs can have two classes of underlying asset:

— a **stocks and shares ISA** includes shares, bonds or pooled investments;

— a **cash ISA**, which may pay a higher rate of interest than an ordinary savings account. Some are instant access and some require notice.

It is possible to have a different ISA each tax year and as long as the investments are kept within an ISA no income tax or capital gains tax is payable. However, because of these tax breaks there is a limit on the amount that can be put into an ISA.

◆ **Pensions**: these are a tax-efficient way of investing for retirement which will be covered in section 9.3.

◆ **Life assurance investment products**: such as the whole-of-life policy and endowment policies (see section 9.4)

Activity

> How much can be put into an ISA each year?
>
> Which of above investments in 9.2.1 – 9.2.3 can the financial planning advisers in your organisation advise on and sell to customers?

9.3 Pensions

Pensions are a **tax-efficient** way in which customers can save for their retirement. They are tax efficient because the government will refund any income tax paid on the value of contributions by individuals to their pension. This contribution is known as '**tax relief**'. With many employers ceasing to offer company schemes whereby they contribute funds as part of a remuneration package, customers are increasingly having to make their own arrangements. The state pension provided by the government gives only a basic income in retirement. Those who can afford to pay into their own scheme should consider doing so as early as possible in their working life.

Activity

> Find out how much basic state pension a single person receives each week.
>
> Imagine that you are retired. How much of your regular outgoings would this cover?

Successive governments have been keen to encourage an increase in the number of personal pensions and hence reduce dependency on the state retirement pension.

The **stakeholder pension** (see below) was introduced in 2001, as a direct result of concern that the state retirement pension will not cope with the demands of an expanded population living longer.

Banks and building societies are able to offer pensions through a **financial adviser**, although once again, the area is tightly regulated in terms of the advice they can and cannot give.

Personal pension plans are individual pension arrangements for people who have relevant earnings from pensionable income. This includes:

◆ self-employed sole traders;

◆ business partners;

◆ employees whose employers do not provide a pension scheme; and

◆ employees who choose not join their employer's scheme.

Tax-free retirement benefits can be taken from a personal pension plan at any age between 55 and 75. It is not necessary actually to retire in order to take the benefits. Special rules apply to certain occupations: for instance HM Revenue and Customs' (HMRC) rules allow the benefits for professional sportspeople to be taken at much younger ages, in some cases as low as 35.

There is a maximum amount that can be placed in a pension each year. Tax relief on the premiums is available to all, and even people with no income can establish a pension (a parent, for instance, could set up a pension fund for a newborn baby).

The **stakeholder** pension was a new form of personal pension and aimed to provide individuals with a scheme that was **simple** and had **low costs**. The annual charges may not exceed 1.5 per cent of the total fund value for the first 10 years and 1 per cent thereafter. Employers with more than five staff have to provide acess to a stakeholder pension scheme, if they do not offer any other type of pension scheme.

The value of these pensions is determined by stock market performance over a long period of time. As with any stock-market-based investment the value can rise and fall. The events of 2007–2009 have seen pension values fall dramatically, to the detriment of people taking retirement at this time. Pension benefits can be taken as a tax-free lump sum of up to 25 per cent of the fund value, with the remainder being used to purchase an annuity that provides income for the duration of the retirement. Some people choose to use the tax-free lump sum to repay interest-only mortgages.

Activity

What is the risk of using pension fund benefits to repay an interest-only mortgage?

9.3.1 Self-invested personal pension (SIPP)

Self-invested personal pensions (SIPPs) were launched in 1989 as 'self-administered' schemes allowing a full range of investment options (approved by HMRC). HMRC has a list of **allowable** (tax-exempt) investments in which UK pension schemes can invest, and the principle of self investment is that a SIPP can utilise any of these. SIPP providers have access to these investments, which can be acquired on behalf of customers.

Customers may now also invest in other types of asset, notably **commercial property**. Some customers feel that they would prefer to invest in this type of asset rather than the stock market. A further benefit is that a SIPP fund can lend money to any unconnected third party, either an individual or company (but not a family member or the business of a family member). The SIPP holder may feel that, for example, investing in a business would be a good way of increasing their pension fund and the SIPP could lend 100 per cent of its net assets. However, in practice the trustees who run the SIPP on behalf of the customer would have a duty of care to the customer and would consider 50 per cent a more prudent figure. The trustees would have to be satisfied that the investment was a sound one and would most likely engage the services of an independent accountant to assess the proposition.

9.4 Insurance

Most people will have some form of insurance to enable them to continue their daily lives if something unforeseen occurs, whether this is car insurance (required by law), house insurance, or life insurance. The insurance market has been recognised as lucrative by banks and building societies and fits in well with their function as financial services providers. All providers are therefore able to offer protection products to customers, although we will concentrate on the protection of life (sold by authorised financial planning advisers), rather than general insurance products, such as those that protect your car or house.

This area of financial services is highly regulated in order to ensure appropriate advice is given by fully qualified financial planning advisers.

Generally, life insurance protection products can be placed into four different categories.

1. **Family protection**: the death or long-term sickness of a breadwinner can leave a family with large debts and no income to support their standard of living. The situation may be just as severe on the death or illness of a dependent spouse/civil partner, as this could leave the breadwinner with the choice between giving up work to look after the children or meeting the expense of hiring someone to look after them.

2. **Debt protection**: when a mortgage or other loan is being repaid largely from the income of one individual or the joint income of a couple, the death of an individual can result in failure to make the repayments, possibly leading to the loss of any property used as security for the loan.

3. **Business protection**: the death of a key employee could have a devastating effect on the profits of a company, and protection against the financial consequences of losing such an employee should be part of a company's planning. Another work-related circumstance is the desire of business partners to be able to buy out the share of a partner who has died, without having to realise partnership assets. In fact, a large part of the value of many partnerships, such as solicitors and accountants, is made up of that intangible asset 'goodwill', which takes account of the reputation of a business and its personnel: this could only be realised by selling the business as a whole – the

very action that the remaining partners will wish to avoid. Life assurance on each of the partner's lives can provide a solution.

4. **Tax mitigation**: when an individual leaves a substantial estate to someone after their death, the recipient may find that they have to pay inheritance tax out of the value of the estate (the only exception is if the estate is left to the deceased's spouse/civil partner). If they cannot, or do not wish to, dispose of the estate's assets in order to pay the tax, a suitable life policy of sufficient size could meet the tax bill, if it is written in trust.

The solution to the issues outlined in each of the categories above is through specific types of insurance, as detailed in sections 9.4.1–9.4.4.

9.4.1 Types of life assurance

Life assurance protection policies fall mainly into two categories: whole-of-life assurance and term assurance.

◆ **Whole-of-life assurance**: the sum assured (or guaranteed) is payable on the death of the life assured whenever that death occurs. The policy therefore has no fixed time limit and remains in force, provided that premiums continue to be paid, until it is brought to an end by the payment of a death claim, or surrendered (cashed in) by the policyholder for a reduced sum.

◆ **Term assurance**: in this case, the sum assured is payable only if the life assured dies before the end of a specified term. If the life assured survives the term, the cover ceases and no payment or refund of premiums is made. Similarly, if the policy is cancelled part way through the term, it has no cash surrender value. The term can be from one month to 30 years or more, although if a very long term is required, it may be better to consider whole-of-life assurance. The amount of insurance can remain at the same level throughout the term of the policy (**level term** assurance), or can reduce throughout the term (**decreasing term** assurance). Both of these types of policy are used to cover **mortgage loans**. Level term assurance is used to cover interest-only mortgages, as no capital is repaid during the term of the mortgage loan. Decreasing term assurance is used for capital and repayment mortgages, where the capital amount outstanding reduces over the time of the loan.

Endowment policies provide both life cover and an investment element. These policies were popular with customers who wanted to take out an interest-only mortgage because the investment element was designed to accrue sufficient to pay off the mortgage loan at the end of the term. However, poor performance in the stock market led to endowment values not reaching their projected amount and, in many cases, they proved insufficient to pay off mortgage loans. As a result, many customers claimed that the products had been mis-sold, on the grounds that the risks (of investments based on the stock exchange going down as well as up) had not been properly explained to them. A large number of customers received compensation. Many mortgage providers no longer accept endowment policies as repayment vehicles for mortgages.

9.4.2 Permanent health insurance

Permanent health insurance (PHI) is designed to provide **replacement income** in the event of an individual being unable to work due to illness, disability or an accident.

The term of a PHI policy cannot extend beyond the person's intended (or actual) retirement date, and there is a **maximum permitted benefit** level that most companies set at around 60–65 per cent of earnings, less the basic state Employment and Support Allowance (or Incapacity Benefit for those claiming before 31 January 2011). The maximum benefit rule is enforced by companies to prevent the excessive claims that would no doubt ensue if policyholders could receive more income when sick than they would if they returned to work.

Each PHI policy is subject to a **deferred period**, which is the time that must elapse after the policyholder falls ill before benefit payments can commence. The minimum deferred period is four weeks, but the policyholder can choose 13 weeks, 26 weeks, one year, or even two years.

9.4.3 Critical illness cover

Critical illness cover (CIC) benefit is payable in **one tax-free lump sum**, on the **diagnosis** of one of a specified range of illnesses and conditions. It is not necessary for the claimant to be off work, and the benefit is paid irrespective of whether the claimant subsequently recovers. This type of insurance is useful to repay a debt or to make the quality of life better for someone who is ill, for example to make alterations to their home to enable disabled access.

Each company has its own list of illnesses covered, but they normally include:

◆ most forms of cancer;

◆ heart attack;

◆ stroke;

◆ coronary artery disease requiring surgery;

◆ major organ transplants;

◆ multiple sclerosis;

◆ total and permanent disability.

Some CIC policies also include payment of the sum assured on death if death occurs before a claim has been paid for diagnosis of a specific disease.

9.4.4 General insurance

General insurance can also be known as non-life insurance or 'property and casualty' insurance. This covers all other types of product, most of which are annual contracts that need to be renewed each year.

General insurance may be subdivided in a number of ways. For personal customers these categories are:

◆ **accident and health**: personal accident and credit insurance, eg cover for monthly loan payments in the event of sickness or unemployment;

◆ **motor**: compulsory insurance for private cars and motor cycles;

◆ **property**: home insurance, including personal liability;

◆ **travel**: this can be for a single trip, multi-trip or annual cover. Many of the current account premium packages include travel cover as a benefit.

Often the majority of products are sold in packages or 'comprehensive' policies, covering a wide range of 'perils' (eg fire, earthquake, theft, liability, sickness or accidental damage). These will be segmented according to the particular customer groups. These packages may also include non-insurance services such as legal advice or breakdown assistance.

Activity

Where else can customers buy these types of general insurance products, other than from a bank or building society?

9.5 Delivery channels

The first part of this section explains the principal types of delivery channel and discusses the facilities that each provides. The section then goes on to discuss how they are used within different retail banking business models.

9.5.1 What is a channel?

A delivery channel is the means by which a bank acquires and builds its client base. It provides the basis for customers to access and operate the account that they have opened with the bank, including the ability to withdraw and deposit cash, and make payments. A branch (discussed below) is the most complete example of a channel. The principal objectives of a fully developed delivery channel are as follows:

◆ to protect and develop the existing customer base;

◆ to acquire profitable new customers;

◆ to provide service that is a critical requirement of its location; and

◆ to project and represent the brand (or sub-brand).

Clearly, there is also a need to ensure that – directly or otherwise – the institution is receiving the required return on its often considerable investment in a particular channel.

It is sometimes necessary for retail banks to offer certain types of delivery channel to their customers, irrespective of their cost, to both reflect changing consumer demands and retain a competitive position within the sector. Examples of these include the provision of banking services through the mobile phone. Such channels are also being developed in the belief that they will provide a more effective longer-term delivery framework – but the timeframe for achieving this has yet to be defined.

9.5.2 The principal delivery channels

9.5.2.1 The branch

The conventional branch provides a full range of facilities to support both the provision of customer service and the sale of bank products. It offers customers the ability to undertake a full range of transactions, including a teller service. While increasing numbers of personal customers are using self-service facilities (see below), the teller service remains important for many small business clients, such as local shopkeepers. The branch also provides the means to access products and services that are normally delivered by other parts of the bank. For example, foreign currency is not kept at every branch and must often be ordered and then delivered from a central office.

Branches may include additional facilities dedicated to specific customer groups. For example, HSBC is one of the banks that provide lounges for their higher-value customers (users of their Premier service). Lloyds Banking Group has started creating lounges at certain branches that provide dedicated facilities for its business customers.

A small number of variations on the conventional branch have been created. Some branches offer only self-service banking (see below). Royal Bank of Scotland is one of the banks that use mobile branches (in a van) as a well-established means of taking banking services to remote or rural communities, exhibitions and shows, and concentrated areas of employment. Small branches have been created to operate at specialist locations, such as in stores or at work sites, such as hospitals. These mini-branches may have both service and sales capabilities. They may offer a counter service or they may only provide self-service facilities. Branches have also been designed that are dedicated to the sale of a specific range of products, such as mortgage shops.

Overall, the branch continues to provide the most effective platform through which to acquire and develop customer relationships. A decade on from the height of the first Internet banking revolution, the branch continues to be regarded as the lead delivery channel by the majority of retail bankers. This situation exists because, for the time being, there is no complete substitute for the personal contact and local marketing that can be achieved through a branch.

9.5.2.2 Self-service

The term 'self-service' is subject to an increasing number of interpretations. These notes discuss the usual use of the term, covering a range of equipment that originated with the ubiquitous automated teller machine (ATM) or cash dispenser. Other types of self-service terminal include:

◆ automated depositories;

◆ change dispensers;

◆ statement printers;

◆ passbook printers and dispensers;

◆ chequebook printers and dispensers;

◆ bill payment kiosks; and

◆ payment card reloading terminals.

Some of this functionality can also be provided from more sophisticated ATMs. Depositories are now able to handle the rapid acceptance of notes and coins, and also take in cheques. ATMs are able to dispense notes and coins, for accounts operated by payment card or passbook. A limited number of ATMs have occasionally been set up to cash cheques. They are also capable of dispensing cheques for which the customer has entered the payee and amount.

Various combinations of terminals are deployed by banks according to the needs of the location. Self-service lobbies can offer a wide range of functionality for customer use and are often open on a 24-hour basis. Or, as mentioned above, there are an increasing number of branches that are being run on a self-service-only basis. HSBC ExpressBanking is an example of a branch-based self-service facility that also includes an online terminal for customer use, replicating the Internet home banking service provided by the bank.

The benefits derived from introducing self-service in the branch environment are largely related to process efficiency and the enhancement of the branch facilities and environment. The banks have enjoyed considerable success in migrating cash withdrawals and a range of other transactions to ATMs and other customer-activated terminals. Significant progress is now also being made in personalising self-service, and carrying out one-to-one marketing activities when a customer uses a terminal. This is achieved through linking self-service terminals to the bank's customer relationship management (CRM) systems. The CRM system recognises the customer and promotes products and services that it deduces might be appropriate.

9.5.2.3 The call centre

Call centre or telephone banking came to prominence within the British market after the launch of First Direct in 1989. The following decade saw all the principal players in the retail banking sector developing the capability to offer telephone banking services across extended hours. The most ambitious provided round-the-clock availability of a call centre agent for seven days a week.

The call centre has two principal roles within retail banking, which are:

◆ the provision of supplementary service support to the branch network – this not only includes being available to customers when the branches are closed, but may also include taking phone calls that the branches are too busy to answer;

◆ the principal delivery channel within a direct banking business model (see below).

Call centres must offer levels of service that are consistent with the overall customer proposition of the bank and the expectations that are therefore created in the minds of callers. Issues that play a significant role in building customers' perceptions of call centre service include the:

◆ time to establish contact;

◆ use or otherwise of Interactive Voice Response systems (IVR);

◆ quality of the greeting;

◆ nature and quality of the agent's language;

◆ need for hand-offs – passing the call to another colleague;

◆ manner in which any attempted cross sell is carried out;

◆ the extent to which the customer's needs are met;

◆ customer feeling, at the end of the call, that their business is valued.

Modern telephony systems can play a major role in monitoring service performance levels and identifying training needs. They not only monitor staff but can also detect erratic or stressful customer behaviour creating difficult situations for call centre agents.

9.5.2.4 The Internet

The advent of the Internet has enabled customers to access their financial agreements with banks and other financial services institutions through a user-friendly online terminal and customised, secure programs. This facility is typically made available to customers through their own computer and enables them to carry out a range of monetary and non-monetary transactions. As a result, there is no need for customers to use either branches or call centres for many types of enquiry or other service transactions. The Internet has also developed as a sales channel with many attractive Internet-only customer propositions. The low cost of Internet operations has meant that the institution has been able to offer more competitive rates than would have been viable when selling through another, more costly channel.

The development of the Internet as a banking channel has occurred in two distinct phases. The first phase, arguably, ran up to 2001 and saw an excited industry pursuing a multiplicity of strategies that included the establishment of Internet-only banks, a rapid change by some telephone-based direct banks to become Internet-led, and the development of the Internet as an alternative channel within the traditional retail banking business model. The second phase of development sees a major service role for Internet banking, evolving into a progressively more powerful sales medium. Consumers are now using the Internet as a research tool to compare products and pricing, then telephoning to find out more details and make purchases.

9.5.2.5 Mobile banking

The provision of banking functionality through a mobile handset – which should now be regarded as a portable banking terminal – has become a competitive imperative. Retail banks recognise that this channel offers both added value services within the customer proposition as well as new sales opportunities. A basic transaction set provides information about account activity and is now increasingly supplemented by the availability of functionality facilitating payments. The most sophisticated offerings also include such features as lines of credit. Early work has already established a capability that allows the mobile phone to set up transactions that are then transmitted to and fulfilled by self-service terminals.

Market experience and anecdotes suggest that the principal uses of mobile banking services include checks on account balances, the payment of bills or the transfer of funds. Other banking functionality is progressively being added. SMS alerts are offered by many banks. These can relate to an account balance or overdrawn position. Other alerts could relate to the requirement to make a bill payment, or to stock trading. They might also be used to alert the customer to potential fraud on their account. In circumstances where the bank is able to charge for providing alerts, it may be possible to create a business case for the development of the service.

Valuable opportunities for extending the service include the payments market and the remittance market. Mobile payment opportunities include point of sale, the transport sector, person-to-person transfers, vending machines, and parking. The increasing mobility of labour will be one of the drivers of a growing demand for remittance functionality.

Operators of mobile banking services are still using a range of technology platforms. These include message-based (SMS); browser-based (WAP); and an application-based approach.

9.5.3 Other delivery channels

A number of other channels are used by the banks to deliver their services to the market. **Mobile financial advisers** are usually deployed in a relationship development and sales role, but should be taken into account when building a bank's delivery channel strategy. The use of automated voice response systems that are activated by telephone handsets provides a form of self- service with functionality that includes enquiries and certain types of payment.

The **Post Office network** not only supports the development of its own banking customer base, but also provides cashier services for a number of other banks. This offers useful support to banks that have a limited branch network, or need an alternative when they close their own branch in a locality.

9.5.4 The three principal business models

The current mix of delivery channels available to retail bankers have been used within three principal business models. The first of these is the traditional, **branch-led** business model where self-service and the direct channel are used on a complementary basis. This is the business model into which the traditional banks have evolved. None of the new channels has proved to be an effective substitute for the branch, as yet. But all play a valuable role in maintaining the service levels that customers have come to expect.

The second model is the **direct telephone bank**. First Direct claims to have introduced this to the British banking market when it was launched in 1989. Customers can take advantage of a full range of retail banking facilities, which include a branch cashier service and self-service provided by the bank's parent, HSBC. In common with the many other banks of this type, First Direct has also recognised the importance of the new technology channels to its customers and has developed sophisticated e-banking services to complement its round-the-clock call centre.

The third model is the **Internet bank** with no 'high street' presence. Again, customers can enjoy a full range of banking services, which must all be operated online. The leading British example is Smile, which is operated by Co-operative Financial Services. Where customers do require the services of a cashier they may use the branches of the parent bank, or post offices. The service is also supported by a call centre and email.

Activity

> Review the functionality offered by two banks to users of their Internet banking and mobile banking services.

9.5.5 Delivery channels strategy

Of the five components of the delivery mix discussed above, the branches and call centres can be categorised as legacy channels, as can the core facilities within self-service. Branches and call centres have seen some of the transactions that they have handled taken over by customers using the Internet or mobile banking facilities. However, while the latter channels – and self-service – can undertake transactions at much lower costs, two factors have frustrated their ability to eliminate the need for branches.

Firstly, many customers still wish to retain the services of a branch as well as using the virtual channels. Indeed, it is now widely accepted that the advent of the new virtual channels has generated additional customer transactions rather than migrating significant volumes from branches. The second factor has been the inability of the new channels to replicate the income volumes generated by the branch. Nevertheless, the new channels are now necessary to sustain the credibility and competitiveness of any retail banking proposition.

The effectiveness of delivery channels is constantly changing. Examples of this include the new facilities and functionality coming on stream and variations in the local market conditions and customer needs experienced by branches. Examples of situations that must be monitored include the relationship between telephone banking and the use of Internet banking. In 2008 the number of British users of Internet banking increased to 21.5 million, while the use of telephone banking continued to decline, falling to 12.3 million (*Source:* UK Payments Administration Ltd).

Increasing numbers of banks recognise the need to develop a holistic delivery channel strategy, often managed through a dedicated team. The work of such a team includes:

◆ monitoring and sustaining the competitiveness and effectiveness of the existing channel mix;

◆ ensuring that the bank receives the required return from its channel investment;

◆ identifying and responding to trends eg telephone banking versus Internet banking;

◆ monitoring and evaluating new channel developments and concepts.

9.5.6 Delivery channels and new technology

As seen above, the consumer is provided with a number of different delivery channels, whether telephone, Internet or high street. With growing sophistication in technology and improved reliability in machinery, the march forward with new solutions for delivering banking services will continue.

PayPal has risen in popularity, primarily on the back of the online auction site eBay. It is a system that allows payments by debit and credit card online with the resulting funds credited to the seller's PayPal account. The seller can either transfer funds directly to their bank account, or use funds on their PayPal account to make other purchases.

A new method of payment uses **'contactless' technology**. Users pay for their goods by touching the card on a reader and the money is then deducted from their bank account or added to their credit card bill.

MasterCard's contactless technology system, PayPass, is already used in 19 countries, including the US, and has 16 million users overall. The UK rollout began in London in 2007, with newsagents and cafes among the first to use the technology.

PayPass uses a chip integrated into credit and debit cards, and operates in a similar way to the Oyster cards used on the London Transport system. Fraudulent use, if a PayPass is lost or stolen, would be limited as users still need to enter their PIN after a certain number of transactions. However, the card could be used up to five times, with a potential £50 being spent, before this happened.

With increased use of mobile phones, the **SMS** messaging system has provided an opportunity for banks to offer unobtrusive contact with customers. While a telephone call from a bank to a place of work was considered to cause a major embarrassment to a customer, a text message does not cause the same concern. Banks have therefore started to offer text messaging services relating to customers' accounts. For instance, if an account becomes overdrawn or the limit on an overdraft facility is exceeded, a message notifying the customer will more often than not result in the account being restored to order or prompt the customer to contact the bank. This type of service is effective and cheaper than having an adviser telephone a customer during peak telephone rate hours.

The use of **wi-fi** technology (the ability to dial into the Internet from a laptop anywhere within range of a wi-fi network) has been expanded into many areas of the country. While there are, of course, security implications with this type of technology it is possible to access account information through personal digital assistants (PDAs) and new generation mobile phones.

The supermarkets are looking at ways of automatically debiting a current account with the total amount purchased by simply placing goods in a shopping trolley. This type of facility will be advanced shortly with the move away from the barcode system to the **chip** system. This will allow the contents of a trolley to be read by passing through a radio emitter that will read all the contents at once, rather than each item having to be passed through a barcode reader individually.

'Chipped' cards, in which customers are asked to input their PIN at the point of sale (PoS), have been with us for a few years now. With the continued push to combat fraud and the need for greater security, we are already not too far away from using our thumbprints as identification rather than using a PIN. This type of **biometric** (biometrics is the technique of studying the characteristics of a person from fingerprints, hand geometry, eye structure or voice pattern) already uses recognition software in airports as an opportunity to improve security. Each passenger's iris is scanned, as the iris pattern is unique to the individual.

With new technologies come concerns regarding the security of systems and the ability of fraudsters to access and use this personal financial information. Concerns have been evidenced as to the security of websites, and 2003 saw the growth of **'phishing'** in the UK. Phishing is the act of sending an email to a user falsely claiming to be an organisation such as a bank, in an attempt to scam the user into surrendering private information that can be used for identity fraud.

For example, suppose a fraudster is targeting a particular bank. They will send out thousands of emails to any number of Internet users claiming to be that bank and instructing the user to click on a link to go to the bank's website. A false website will have been constructed to look the same as the bank's official website. The customer will be asked to input their personal details and entry codes into the website. These details will then be used to empty the account or obtain further details so a fraud can be committed. When the original email is sent out, the fraudster does not know whether any of the users bank with that bank but they are hoping that some will, and of those, some may click on the link provided (the fraudster is therefore 'fishing/phishing' for information). This type of fraud is combated only by giving clear direction to customers that once they have provided certain data, the bank will not require them to enter it again.

The investment in new technology is considerable, but necessary to maintain banking services at a level that combats fraud, protects the customer and provides a high-class service in line with customer expectations.

Review questions

The following review questions are designed so that you can check your understanding of this topic.

The answers are provided at the end of these learning materials.

1. In relation to mortgage loans, who is the mortgagor and who is the mortgagee?

2. What are the rights of a borrower when they have given a legal charge over their property?

3. Why is a lender interested in affordability when looking at a borrower's ability to service a debt?

4. What is the difference between a further advance and a second mortgage?

5. What are the main differences between the concepts of 'saving' and 'investment'?

6. What is the benefit of a pooled investment?

7. How are pensions tax efficient?

8. Why might a customer be attracted to a SIPP?

9. What are the differences between level term and decreasing term assurance?

10. List the features and benefits to customers of the three main delivery channels for financial services.

Topic 10

The opening and running of accounts

Learning objective

After studying this topic students should be able to demonstrate a knowledge and understanding of customer interactions and how they are governed by regulation in relation to account opening and running.

Introduction

This topic focuses on the opening and running of bank accounts, including the circumstances in which a customer/provider relationship can be terminated. We will return to the theme of 'know your customer' as this is highly important at account-opening stage.

We will look at some of the technical aspects of account operation in relation to how money is allocated both between a customer's accounts and within a customer's account. This is of particular interest when seeking the repayment of a debt from a customer.

Finally, we will explore how bank interest is calculated. Understanding how this is done is important to customers as it enables them to make comparisons between providers and shop around for the best deal with confidence.

10.1 Account opening and transfers

10.1.1 Account opening

The account-opening process is (computer) screen-led in most financial services providers now, whether this is at customer interview, via a call centre or over the Internet. There are immediate checks on the electoral roll and with external credit reference agencies for county court judgments (CCJs − bad debts confirmed by the court). It is an ideal opportunity for the provider to collect valuable information on which future sales can be based. The application will be credit scored against known criteria for acceptable customers and a 'suitable' account offered that matches the credit-scored result. We looked at the different types of account available in Topic 8.

The second part of the account-opening process is fairly straightforward, as providers now need to identify and verify an account holder as being the entity/person they purport to be. The officials of an entity who are acting on the entity's behalf (either by being signatories to the account or being officials of that entity) also have to be correctly identified and verified. This is to enable banks to comply with the 'Know Your Customer' (KYC) rules and adhere to money laundering regulations, as we have previously seen.

The term '**entity**' above relates to the account holder. So the entity may be one of a number of different legal persons, as discussed in Topic 1. The documents required to confirm the identity and verify the entity include the following:

◆ **John Smith**: a passport/driving licence to identify him and a utility bill or bank statement to verify that he lives where he says he does.

◆ **John Smith trading as 'Smiths' Butchers'**: a letter heading or invoice created by the sole trader showing an address. Verification could be made by a member of staff visiting the premises and seeing a sign above his door.

◆ **John Smith Ltd**: sight of the certificate of incorporation, verified by searching at Companies House, where every limited company has to be registered, to reveal the full details of the company.

◆ **John Smith Ltd Sports and Social Club**: an invoice issued by the club, or their rule book detailing who the social club committee are.

◆ **Executors/trustees of John Smith deceased**: the executors/trustees applying for the account must be identified in their personal capacity and verified by the will/trust document.

The initial identification of the entity will reveal the business owners, directors, employees, executors or trustees, and they will then in turn have to be identified and verified, much the same as John Smith in his personal capacity.

Activity

> This is not an exhaustive list, as different banks and building societies may have differing views on what is acceptable identification and verification, and what is not.
>
> Research what your organisation asks for when a customer **cannot** provide identification or verification that is on the standard list.

Obtaining the correct and appropriate documentation can make the account-opening process a long and drawn-out affair. However, banks have to be extremely careful that all the documentation is correct before allowing the account to be opened and operated. We will come back to this topic again in Topic 11.

Activity

> What is the danger of not obtaining all the correct documentation?

As part of the account-opening process, the parties to the account sign a **mandate**. This is a standard document that sets out signing instructions on the account, thereby giving the bank instructions by which to operate the account. There are slightly different mandates, depending on the types of customer opening the account. Some banks may have one type of mandate covering all instances, although some will have a separate mandate for each situation. We will look at mandates in section 10.2.

10.1.2 Account transfer

At some point after account opening the customer may wish to transfer their account elsewhere. Transferring accounts between branches of the same bank is usually quite straightforward. The customer signs an authority to make the transfer and the account details are set up at the new branch in a matter of days, using the existing data held in the computer system. The process causes little disruption to the customer and the running of their account.

However, switching the account to a new provider can be somewhat more problematic and time consuming than it should be. The most effective way for customers to switch bank accounts is to open the account with the new provider first, then give the account-switching authority to their existing banker.

The new provider will ask the existing bank to supply a list of the standing orders and direct debits on the account. They will then set up the standing orders and write to all the direct debit companies asking them to change their records to the new account details. It is this process of swapping all the payments over that takes time, in most cases around three weeks. Some providers will also supply letters for the customer to give to people, such as employers, who make regular payments into the customer's account, asking them to redirect payments to the new account. The customer will have to give back all the cheque books and cards on their existing account and confirm when they want the balances transferred to the new bank.

Activity

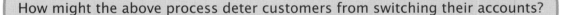

> How might the above process deter customers from switching their accounts?

There has been criticism in the past of the delays in transferring accounts between banks and how this impacts on customer service. The Banking Conduct of Business rules state that banks should 'deliver a prompt and efficient service when switching customers' accounts'. This requirement also applies to products such as cash ISAs, as well as current accounts. Many providers have introduced a dedicated switching service to make the process easier and obtain market share more quickly.

10.2 Mandates and signing instructions

A mandate (contract) is used to operate an account on behalf of a customer. As consideration for this contract, the provider will allow money into and out of the account according to the mandate form.

A provider has a duty of care to its customer to conform to whatever the customer has stipulated within their mandate form. It must pay a cheque drawn by the customer, if it is dated, signed, appears to be proper (not out of character with the account), and there are sufficient funds on the account to allow payment. It cannot debit a customer's account with a forged cheque, as it has not acted in accordance with the mandate form (it is not drawn by the customer and is not proper). Where a provider has reasonable grounds to think that a customer's funds are being misappropriated then it can refuse to debit the account until such time as it is able to settle the matter.

A further example of where a provider may breach its duty of care to its customer relates to an agent of the customer. In some cases, a mandate form may state that a third party – let's call him Jim – can sign cheques up to the value of £500 on John's account. If Jim signs a cheque for £5,000, the customer is not liable for the amount of that cheque as the provider has allowed Jim to exceed its customer's given authority, and it is negligent in allowing the transaction.

We considered the effect of mandates in Topic 1 in relation to each of the different types of account and it may be worth reviewing Topic 1 again at this point. What we will consider next is the issue of joint and several liability that applies to joint accounts, partnerships, executors and trustees' accounts.

10.2.1 Joint and several liability

A joint account with a joint account mandate establishes the principle of 'joint and several liability' for debts created on an account. This is for current accounts, as well as loan accounts. The principle means that **each party** to an account is liable for any debts created on the account in two ways. They are '**jointly liable**' – as a group, or partners, for the whole amount of the debt created on the account, and can be sued as a whole unit. They are also '**severally liable**' – each individual is liable in their personal capacity for all of the debt. So, joint and several liability means that a debt can be recovered from an individual, or the group. Either a part of the debt or all of the debt can be recovered from an individual.

Consider the situation where there is a joint account in the name of husband and wife, with either to sign. The husband has disappeared leaving the account £5,500 overdrawn. The wife has never used the bank account, doesn't have a chequebook, guarantee card or debit card on the account, has no income and lives in rented accommodation. Her husband controlled the finances, and she has only just found out about the state of the account. In these circumstances, would she be liable for the debt?

The simple answer is yes. They are both jointly and severally liable for the debt. The more difficult issue is the moral question, and would a provider make demand for repayment on this woman for the full amount of the debt? The answer to this is also yes, as the provider has a responsibility to its shareholders to use its funds wisely and recover debts when appropriate. This will, however, be a difficult time for a banker and not one that anyone would relish. It could be made easier, if at the time a joint account is opened, it is fully explained what signing a joint and several mandate can mean if anything goes wrong.

Activity

What does your organisation ask customer advisers to do at account opening to highlight this issue?

10.3 Cancellation/termination of a mandate

A mandate can be cancelled (ceasing the operation of the account) at any time by any of the parties to it, that is to say, either the provider or the customer. It is important to understand that in this instance the *customer* is the joint account, the partnership or the limited company, and not the individual parties who have signed the mandate form.

The individual parties to the mandate form can also cancel the signing arrangements on the form. For instance, assuming that the mandate is either to sign, if there is a joint personal account in the name of husband and or wife, the mandate can be cancelled by either of them. If this occurs, the mandate for this account would revert to the 'default' signing arrangement that both of the parties would have to sign in the future. This is a common situation where a marital dispute has arisen.

Activity

> Research the procedures that your organisation uses for operating accounts that are in dispute.

Practically, how the account is to be dealt with is often sorted out by the individuals concerned before the provider is made aware, and the bank can continue to pay out all of the funds on the account to either the husband or wife until funds are exhausted.

What should be made clear is that termination of the mandate, for whatever reason, does not terminate the customers' liability for any debit balances of those accounts. In practice, if the bank becomes aware that there is a **dispute** between the parties to an account then the account will be frozen until the situation can be resolved. This will then prevent the rule in Clayton's Case from applying (see section 10.5).

If the mandate form is already 'both or all to sign' a provider cannot vary the mandate until such time as it has the agreement of all the parties to the account. Any new parties signing on the account need to be identified and verified in the same way as in the account-opening process. If this is not done, it leaves the account open to fraud and is negligence on the part of the provider.

The provider's mandate to operate an account can also be terminated by:

◆ notice;

◆ death;

◆ mental illness;

◆ bankruptcy;

◆ resolution of a limited company;

◆ winding up of a limited company; and

◆ liquidation of the bank.

We will look at each of these in turn in the next section.

10.3.1 Notice

Either of the parties can give notice to terminate the relationship. Generally, if the account is in credit, it is the customer who will terminate by giving notice; if the account is in debit, it is usually the provider who gives notice. However, providers do give notice on credit accounts on occasions.

Activity

> In what situations would your organisation give notice on a credit account?

The notice period for a credit current account will normally be nil, as a provider will pay out the funds immediately when asked to do so by the customer. The notice period for a deposit account will depend on the terms of that deposit account. If the account were restricted to 90 days' notice of withdrawal then the provider would be within its rights to hold onto those funds until the 90 days' notice period has expired. In practice, providers do allow funds to be repaid immediately, although there will usually be a loss of interest, or a penalty fee to be paid.

A provider may wish to give notice to close on both personal and business accounts in credit. This could be due to concerns over the reputational risk to a provider operating an account for an undesirable person, a company working in an undesirable field, or a company not complying with a request for financial information. These types of decision will be taken at a high level, as there may be further damage to a provider's image because of adverse publicity.

Activity

> Following the economic crisis, from what areas of business has your organisation withdrawn, resulting in the closure of accounts?

If a provider terminates a credit account, then some notice has to be given to enable customers to make alternative banking arrangements. The provider, however, has a duty in law to ensure that the notice period is **appropriate** and **reasonable** in every circumstance. Normal practice suggests that this should be a minimum of 30 days.

If a provider wishes to terminate a relationship for an account in debit (an overdrawn account), then the balance of the debt becomes repayable immediately, as it is 'on demand'. The provider can commence recovery procedures straight away. If there is a loan account in existence that has a separate agreement on it, the bank will not be able to demand repayment of the loan unless it is in default.

10.3.2 Death

As we have already seen, a bank account is a contract. **Death cancels all contracts**, and in the case of personal customers the personal representatives of the deceased will (eventually) be entitled to any balance.

The mandate is only cancelled when the provider receives notice of the death. If cheques were made out by the deceased and were presented for payment before the provider became aware of the death, the cheques will be paid and the provider will not be liable to repay any of this money to the personal representatives.

In the case of a **sole** personal account, although the personal representatives will eventually be entitled to any balance on the account, they will not be able to draw directly on the funds. An executor or administrator's account will be opened and the balance on the deceased's account transferred to it when the appropriate authority is obtained. If for any reason the account is overdrawn then the personal representatives will have to account to the provider for repayment out of the deceased's estate when it is wound up. If there are no funds in the estate to make the payment then the debt will have to be written off. If there are some funds available, the provider will join with any other creditors and receive a proportion of the funds.

In the case of a **joint** personal account, if the account is in credit then the balance will be transferred to the other party and the account closed. If the account is overdrawn then the bank has to approach the surviving party regarding the repayment of the funds.

10.3.3 Mental incapacity

If the customer is mentally incapacitated and unable to manage their own affairs, the banker/customer relationship is terminated.

10.3.4 Bankruptcy

We have seen in previous topics the effect of a bankruptcy order. Once issued, the order means that all of the bankrupt's property vests in the trustee in bankruptcy who will administer their estate. On production of the appropriate certificate of appointment, the bank is able to pay away any credit balances on the account.

The mandate is terminated as soon as the bank receives notice of a bankruptcy. Bank systems are automated to advise the account-holding branch of any petitions to ensure that no money is paid away until they receive court authority to do so. This is in contrast to the late 1970s and early 1980s when branch staff physically had to review the *London Gazette* and local papers for any impending actions.

10.3.5 A company resolution

A company will have passed a resolution originally to open a bank account. This will remain in force until it is either amended by resolution, or a new resolution passed to close the account.

10.3.6 Winding up of a company

The winding up of a company can either be **voluntary** or **compulsory**. The directors confirming they no longer wish to trade will pass a voluntary resolution. A compulsory winding-up order will result from a creditor of the company presenting a petition in court to wind up the company. The provider's mandate will terminate as soon as they are made aware of the intention to pass the resolution, or at the commencement of the petition for winding up.

10.3.7 Liquidation of a bank

The mandate is terminated at the time 'when the legal personality of the body corporate ceases to exist' (in other words at winding up). The customer is then entitled to receive any credit balances. Obviously in today's financial services regime, any protection due under the Financial Services Compensation Scheme may come into play (see section 3.2).

10.4 Set-off

When operating a customer's account, providers have certain rights over the accounts where there is more than one. Providers have the **right of set-off** (or combination) of a customer's account in credit with an account that is in debit. There are a number of rules allowing the right of set-off that have been established in numerous legal cases. Detailed below are the rules that banks use.

◆ A provider can combine two or more accounts in the same name at any time.

◆ Notice of the intention to combine the accounts does not have to be given. While it may be considerate, there is no legal obligation on the bank to do this.

◆ A provider can combine two or more accounts at different branches of the same organisation. While the provider may not have an express instruction from the customer to enable this to be done, the customer is assumed in law to know the state of their accounts. When issuing a cheque/debit on an overdrawn account, the customer is giving an *implied* instruction to the provider to transfer funds from a credit balance account to cover the cheque/debit.

◆ There is no right to combine two accounts held by one person in two separate capacities, for example a personal account and a trust account. If the customer has not informed the provider that one of the accounts is a trust account then the provider is entitled to set-off the two balances should it wish.

◆ The accounts cannot be combined if there is a specific agreement *not* to.

◆ If money has been deposited for a special purpose of which the provider is aware, it cannot be combined.

◆ Where there is any doubt as to the identity of an account holder, money cannot be set off.

◆ Providers are able to combine accounts in bankruptcy. This is a legal right as long as there have been 'mutual dealings' between the two parties on both accounts.

◆ A current account and loan account cannot be set-off unless there is reasonable notice of the intention to change the arrangement or insolvency has occurred.

In practice, the right of set-off is usually only performed at the end of a banking relationship, although it can be used at any time. There may be an occasion when a cheque has been issued and presented for payment. To pay the cheque would mean the account going above an agreed facility or going overdrawn. The cheque could always be returned unpaid and the bank is within its rights to do this. However, if there are funds on a deposit account that could cover the cheque by paying the cheque, and transferring the funds across to cover, the bank is providing a service to that customer.

Activity

Research your organisation's rules in relation to the right of set-off and compare these to the rules within the Lending Code.

10.5 Appropriation of payments

Appropriation of payments is a key banking phrase in relation to the operation of accounts, and the case in law that relates to it, while old, still affects every bank current account in the UK. The case is titled and known as '*Clayton's Case*' and refers to *Devaynes v Noble* (1816). *Clayton's Case* will usually come into play at the end of a banking relationship, particularly on the death of a partner, but also on the winding up of companies, or where security for a debt has been taken. It relates to current accounts, mainly where the account is in debit (overdrawn).

Consider a current account that changes on a daily basis with credits being paid in, and debits (cheques, standing orders, direct debits, etc) coming out of it. While on most occasions a provider or customer will only need to know what the balance is on the account, there may be other occasions where it is important to determine specifically what credits have come in and what debits have been issued against those credits.

An example could be where a third party guarantees an overdraft facility for one year. On expiration of the agreed period, the bank decides not to freeze the account and the account continues to run with credits being paid in and debits coming out of it. If the provider then subsequently seeks to enforce the guarantee then there will almost certainly be a dispute about the debts covered by the guarantee. The provider will claim the full amount overdrawn, while the guarantor will argue that their liability has been reduced by credits paid in after the year end.

Clayton's Case established the 'appropriation of payments' rule that means each item paid to the credit of the customer's account is deemed to discharge the earliest debit on the account. In other words, first in, first out (or first discharged).

Following a number of cases since 1816, *Clayton's Case* has still been upheld. The following circumstances relate to those cases, and offer confirmation to a provider that when an 'event' occurs, it should immediately freeze the account to preserve any claim that it or a customer may have. However, there are cases that have also defined when *Clayton's Case* will or will not apply and these instances relating to personal accounts are detailed below:

◆ If the provider is lending on a current account against the security of a first or second mortgage and it receives notice of a further mortgage on that property, the account should be frozen to ensure that the liability is retained. Any credits received to the account after the date of receipt of the notice will have the effect of repaying the debt and any further debits create new debt that will not be covered by that security. The new debt will then only be secured by the property behind the new mortgagee and their debt. In practice, providers seek to obtain a certificate/letter of priority from the subsequent mortgagee, which will preserve their rights to an amount agreed by them and the subsequent mortgagee.

◆ As above, if a provider receives notice of a second or subsequent mortgage it can freeze the account, open a second account and continue lending or receiving credits to that account. The receipt of funds into the second account will not allow the rule in *Clayton's Case* to apply as it is considered that the new account will constitute new debt and any credits received will repay that debt. The security against the first account will be maintained.

◆ The rule does not apply when trust fund money is mixed with personal account funds. It is assumed that personal funds will be paid in and out of the account first, so protecting the trust fund money as it should be retained intact. In the normal course of events this would not arise, as trust fund money would be retained in a separate account.

◆ The rule does not apply to separate bank accounts even if they are maintained at the same bank.

◆ The rule will not apply where accounts have been stopped, as there will be no payments into or out of that account.

◆ The rule will not apply where the provider has specifically stated it will not apply the first in, first out rule. All modern guarantee forms contain a clause that *Clayton's Case* will not apply in relation to the debt and stating that the provider will not apply the first in, first out rule.

10.6 Interest – types and calculation

Another important aspect of account operation is the application of interest to the account. When people borrow money from a financial institution, they are charged a price for the use of it. That price is **interest**. Borrowers are willing to pay interest to be able to borrow money so that they pay for goods and services now rather than wait until they have earned or saved enough to pay for them from their own funds.

Conversely when customers deposit money with a provider they expect to be paid interest for the funds they are lending to the bank.

10.6.1 Calculating simple interest

Interest is quoted as a percentage rate – that is, as an amount to be paid per £100 per year. This is what is known as 'simple interest' or 'flat' rate.

Example 1

Katie pays 8 per cent interest for her bank loan of £100. This means that, for the £100 she has borrowed, she pays £8 a year in interest.

£100 x 8% = £8

To repay the loan including interest Katie must pay £108.

There are more complex ways of working out interest.

Example 2

Katie is paying back the £100 at an even rate throughout the year:

£100/12 months = £8.33 per month

It is therefore unfair to charge her £8 interest, because she owes the full £100 only before she makes the first month's payment. In the second month, she owes:

£100 − £8.33 = £91.67

In the last month, Katie owes only £8.33.

Activity

> How easy is it for Katie to work out the difference in overall cost of interest in the two examples?

Both examples could quote the flat rate of 8 per cent but the actual costs would be different. We will now go on to look at interest rates in more detail.

10.6.2 Interest rates linked to base rate

All UK interest rates are linked to base rate, some more closely than others. For example, a quarter-point fall (0.25 per cent) in base rate should lead to a fall in mortgage interest and therefore repayment levels. However it may not do so, because banks and building societies can decide not to change rates immediately. In the long term, however, they cannot ignore the change and will eventually follow base rate.

Banks and other financial institutions charge different interest rates for different types of loan, depending on the amount of money lent, the length of time of the loan (the term) and the amount of risk involved. They also pay different interest rates on different types of savings account, generally linked to how easily the saver needs to access their money. In general, the longer that money is tied up, the more interest the providers will pay.

Factors that affect the 'price' of a loan include the following:

◆ **Loss of the money**: when someone lends money to someone else, they are losing the use of that money until it is repaid. For example, they could have spent it or put it in a savings account to earn interest. So the rate that a lender charges must compensate it for its lost opportunity to invest it and earn at least the going rate of interest for savings.

◆ **Amount**: the amount that someone borrows or saves can affect the interest rate. For example, providers try to attract people to save more by offering a higher interest rate on larger balances. On the other hand, very large loans can be cheaper, because the administration cost to the provider is not much more for a large loan than for a small one.

◆ **Term**: generally, if money is lent for a long time, the lender will charge a higher rate because of the increased uncertainty of repayment and the possible change in economic circumstances.

◆ **Risk**: the borrower might be unable or unwilling to repay the loan on time – that is, there is a risk to the lender that the money might not all be repaid. The higher this risk is, the higher the interest rate must be to compensate the lender for the risk. If the risk is high, the lender may also want some form of security. A secured loan is cheaper than an unsecured loan for the same amount over the same period of time.

◆ **Term and risk together**: the relationship between term and risk can be summarised as 'the higher the risk, the higher the interest rate'; the longer the time period of a loan, the higher the risk, because outcomes become more uncertain the further they are in the future. This is why long-term loans, such as mortgage loans, are backed by security to make the interest rate more affordable for the customer and give the lender a secondary source of repayment.

Activity

> What do you think are the effects of an interest increase on the following groups of customers:
>
> ◆ Credit card holders with debt on their cards.
>
> ◆ People with mortgage loans.
>
> ◆ People with spare cash.

We mentioned in section 4.2 that banks lend money to each other and charge a rate called London Interbank Offered Rate (Libor). Banks use this rate as a reference point for larger customer deposits and for loans, mostly those made to large organisations.

10.6.3 Calculating compound interest

Fortunately the provider's computer system will manage the interest calculation process by monitoring the balance of the account on a daily basis and recording the balance at the close of business, whether it is in credit or in debit. Interest will then be paid to or debited from the customer at whatever interval is set out by the account features.

The frequency of the payment or debit of interest is important. The following simple calculations explain why this is over a period of twelve months for accounts where interest is paid annually, half yearly and quarterly, where the interest is paid to the account.

Interest paid annually on a deposit of £10,000 at 5%:

£10,000 x 5/100 x 1 (payment made once during year) = £500

Total amount of interest paid = £500

Interest paid half-yearly on a deposit of £10,000 at 5 per cent:

End of first half year:

£10,000 x 5/100 x ½ (payment made twice during year) = £250

£250 added to balance

End of second half year:

£10,250 x 5/100 x ½ (payment made twice during year) = £256.25

Total amount of interest paid = £506.25

Interest paid quarterly on a deposit of £10,000 at 5 per cent

End of quarter 1:

£10,000 x 5/100 x ¼ (payment made 4 times during year) = £125.00

£125.00 added to balance

End of quarter 2:

£10,125.00 x 5/100 x ¼ (payment made 4 times during year) = £126.56

£126.56 added to balance

End of quarter 3:

£10,251.56 x 5/100 x ¼ (payment made 4 times during year) = £128.14

£128.14 added to balance

End of quarter 4:

£10,3790.70 x 5/100 x ¼ (payment made 4 times during year) = £129.74

Total amount of interest paid = £509.44

It can be seen that over the twelve-month period the more frequently that interest is paid, the more interest is earned by the customer. For very large deposits this difference could be quite significant. Conversely, for a borrower, the less frequently that interest is applied the less interest will be paid by that customer. The effect of this frequency is termed '**compound interest**'.

Regulations specify the exact mathematics behind these calculations. All financial services providers have to use these calculations and follow the rules laid down as to when and how the figures are used. It is important that both the providers' employees and the general public understand what the various terms relating to interest calculations mean. The following sections explain what these are.

10.6.4 Annual percentage rate

Annual percentage rate (APR) is used to describe the **true cost** of money borrowed on **mortgages**, **loans and credit cards**. The calculation for APR takes into account the basic interest rate, the frequency with which it is charged, all initial fees and any other costs the customer has to pay.

All lenders calculate APR in exactly the same way, thus enabling customers to make direct cost comparisons between lending services. This means that if one provider is offering a mortgage loan at 4.5 per cent plus an arrangement fee of £750 and another is offering an interest rate of 5 per cent with a £200 fee the APR figure will show which of the two loans is the cheapest.

There are two further expressions that use APR:

◆ X per cent **APR variable**: this means that the cost is currently X per cent but the interest rate is not fixed and from time to time the rate will vary either up or down.

◆ X per cent **APR typical variable**: this is frequently used for promotions for loans. This means that the lender is not being specific about the interest rate being charged as the rates vary depending on the customers' individual credit rating and the amount they wish to borrow. The figure therefore gives customers a general idea of the rate they can expect to pay. The word 'typical' means that at least two thirds of the approved applications are offered at that rate or cheaper. When the loan offer is confirmed to the customer the paperwork will disclose the actual APR or APR variable that is being offered.

Activity

> What spread of interest rates does your organisation use when offering APR typical rates to customers?

10.6.5 Equivalent annual rate

Equivalent annual rate (EAR) is used to illustrate the full percentage cost of **overdrafts** and any type of account that can be in credit and also go overdrawn. The calculation shows the **true cost** if the overdraft facility is used. In the same way as APR calculations, EAR takes account of the basic rate of interest and when the interest is charged, plus any additional charges.

In most respects EAR and APR achieve the same thing; however, APR applies to pure lending products only whereas EAR applies to a service such as a bank current account that can be in credit or overdrawn.

Calculations for both EAR and APR always **exclude** any payment protection insurance (which covers the monthly repayments if the customer is off work due to accident, sickness or unemployment). This is because the insurance is optional and not a condition of the lending.

10.6.6 Annual equivalent rate

Annual equivalent rate (AER) is only used in relation to **savings** and **interest-based investments**. It shows the **true rate** of interest that a customer will receive by the end of the year taking into account the frequency with which interest is added to the account. The AER calculation also removes the effect of any **promotional offers**, which are used to attract new customers by placing products at the top of 'best buy' tables but are withdrawn after a few months.

Activity

> Why is it important for customers to know the interest rate after promotional offers have been removed?

Review questions

The following review questions are designed so that you can check your understanding of this topic.

The answers to the questions are provided at the end of these learning materials.

1. List the various different 'entities' that may open a bank account.

2. What is the principle of 'joint and several liability'?

3. How might a mandate be terminated?

4. When a customer dies leaving a sole personal current account overdrawn, how does a bank go about recovering this money? How would the process be different if the account was joint?

5. In what circumstance can a bank exercise its 'right of set-off'?

6. When is the rule in *Clayton's Case* likely to come into effect?

7. What factors affect the price of a loan?

8. Why is a secured loan cheaper than an unsecured loan?

9. How does the frequency with which interest is paid/debited affect the interest rate applied to accounts?

10. What is the difference between APR and EAR?

Topic 11
Payments and payment systems

Learning objective

After studying this topic students should be able to demonstrate a knowledge and understanding of customer interactions and how they are governed by regulation in relation to payments and payment systems.

Introduction

This topic looks in more detail at payments and payment systems, access to which is one of the main reasons why people open a bank or building society account. The most established form of payment is the paper-based cheque; however, advances in technology and electronic systems have led to more sophisticated forms of payment such as standing orders, direct debits, direct credits, CHAPS and the Faster Payments system. Many of these are covered by the Payment Services Regulations covered in section 5.11.

Cheque usage has been in sharp decline, with a 40 per cent fall between 2005 and 2009 (*source:* Payments Council). The Payments Council has announced that cheques will be withdrawn on 31 October 2018. Nevertheless, while cheques remain a method of payment it is important to understand the law and conventions surrounding their use. In this topic we will look at the law relating to bills of exchange and the concept of negotiability. We will also consider how the practice of crossing cheques affects negotiability and how the use of cheques has changed as a result.

11.1 Negotiability

The most common form of **negotiable instrument** seen today is the cheque. Negotiable instruments are transferable documents that have an obligation on the part of one person to pay money to another. In the case of a cheque it evidences an obligation on the part of one person (the drawer) to pay money to another person (the payee). The obligation is fulfilled by directing an institution such as a bank or building society to make payment on the presentation of the cheque. However, the essence of a negotiable instrument is that if the payee does not want to receive the funds, they can 'negotiate' the instrument to another person. Providing this other person receives it in good faith and for value (there must be something given in exchange for the cheque), they take it free from any defects in title.

The rules of negotiability were adopted as part of the common law from the practices and usages of merchants and their use of **bills of exchange**. Bills of exchange developed during the Middle Ages as a means of transferring funds and making payments over long distances without physically moving bulky quantities of precious metals such as gold in payment. In the hands of thirteenth-century Italian merchants, bankers and foreign exchange dealers, the bill of exchange evolved into a powerful financial tool, accommodating short-term credit transactions as well as enabling foreign exchange transactions.

The invention of the bill of exchange greatly helped foreign trade. The mechanics of this can be seen in the following example.

Assume that a trader in Holland sold goods to an Italian merchant. He accepted in payment a bill of exchange drawn on the Italian merchant, promising to pay an agent of the Dutch trader in Milan at a certain date in the future, and in a certain currency. The bill of exchange allowed the Italian merchant to accept delivery on the goods from Holland, sell them, and take the proceeds to redeem the bill of exchange in Milan, probably in Italian currency.

The common law rules in respect of negotiable instruments were adopted in the **Bills of Exchange Act 1882**. A negotiable instrument is actually transferred by mere delivery (an instrument payable to a bearer is transferred by handing it to the transferee). The delivery of the document must be accompanied by the intention to transfer title. Bills of exchange are still used for international trade today and usually accompany letters of credit.

The transferee of a negotiable instrument takes it free from any defects in title as a '**holder in due course**', unless the instrument is tainted by fraud, duress or illegality. Even then, the holder can still enforce the instrument if they can prove that it was taken in good faith and that they gave a good value for it. However, a forged or unauthorised signature renders the instrument invalid, even to a holder in due course.

A cheque, as mentioned above, is a negotiable instrument and the Bills of Exchange Act 1882 defines a cheque as a bill of exchange drawn on a banker payable on demand. Section 3(1) goes on to state that:

> 'a bill of exchange is an unconditional order in writing, addressed by one person to another, signed by the person giving it, requiring the person to whom it is addressed to pay on demand, or at a fixed or determinable future time, a sum certain in money to or to the order of a specified person or to bearer.'

You will note that the definition does not require a date to be entered, although, in practice, cheques are always dated to ensure that they remain 'current' (banks and building societies will usually only pay out on a cheque that is less than six months old). However, there are certain aspects of the definition that require further explanation.

◆ **An unconditional order in writing**: the cheque must be unconditional, as it would prejudice the validity of the cheque if it had conditions that would mean the holder had to enquire whether the conditions had been met.

◆ **Pay on demand**: it must be an instruction to a bank requiring it to make payment. A post-dated cheque (a cheque that has a date in the future on it) is still a valid instrument even though banks actively discourage customers from using them.

◆ **A sum certain**: a cheque can be drawn for any sum of money but it must be for a sum certain (ie a specified amount). It cannot say 'pay John Smith after deducting what he owes me'.

◆ **To a specified person or bearer**: where a cheque is not payable to a specific named person, it can only be made out to the bearer if it is to remain a bill of exchange. A cheque being made out to cash and subsequently handed to a third party is not a bill of exchange. A drawer of a cheque (the account holder) can, however, make a cheque out to cash if they are withdrawing funds from their account.

A cheque may be used to pay a third party (the payee) by a customer (the drawer) who has purchased goods. The cheque is either sent in the post or delivered personally. The cheque is an instruction to the paying bank to credit the payee's account with the amount of the cheque. Payment by the paying bank will discharge the drawer of the debt. However, the payment to the payee will also discharge the paying bank's liability to its customer for the credit balance held, providing the bank acts in accordance with the mandate.

However, as a cheque is a bill of exchange and therefore a negotiable instrument, the payee may wish to use it to pay another person, Mr Jones. The cheque can be endorsed (signed on the back) by the payee and sent or delivered to Mr Jones, who will then have title to it. The cheque has now been negotiated. The new holder, Mr Jones, now becomes a 'holder in due course' and can sue the original drawer for the amount of the cheque should it be unpaid.

11.2   Crossed cheques

Although cheques are negotiable instruments, they are rarely presented in this format. They are usually presented by the payee to their bank for collection and are rarely endorsed in favour of a third party. You will see on looking at modern cheques that there is a 'crossing' already printed on them with the words 'account payee' or 'account payee only'. These can only be accepted for the credit of the named payee.

Crossed cheques first originated in the late eighteenth or early nineteenth century in the banker's clearing house where cheques were collected to be distributed to the paying bank. Clerks working for the banks in the clearing house established a practice of writing the names of their employers across the cheques in order to allow payment to be made. The crossing of cheques by the drawer was a later development.

The purpose of a crossing is to **reduce the risk** of the cheque being misappropriated and funds going to the wrong person, especially when a cheque is delivered by post. If the drawee bank acts contrary to the mandate given in the crossing, it is liable to the drawer for breach of contract and cannot debit the drawer's account.

The Bills of Exchange Act 1882 recognises two basic crossings – the **general** crossing and the **special** crossing: in practice, the special crossing is obsolete. A cheque may be crossed generally by placing two transverse lines across its face. As mentioned above, cheques come with these two lines pre-printed on them, and may be accompanied by the words 'not negotiable' or 'account payee', which have assumed an important status since the Cheques Act 1992.

Activity

> What crossings do the cheques issued by your organisation have?

11.2.1 'Not negotiable'

Section 81 of the Bills of Exchange Act 1882 provides for the 'not negotiable' crossing. The words do not have to appear within the crossing itself, although they do have to be detailed on the face of the cheque.

The effect of the crossing is to restrict the negotiability of the cheque but not its **transferability**. As this means that the cheque crossed in this manner is not now a bill of exchange, a person who takes the cheque cannot obtain a better title (rights in ownership) than that of the transferor and they, in turn, can only confer a limited title to a subsequent transferee. Consequently, although a transferee can be a 'holder for value', they cannot be a 'holder in due course'. A third party taking a cheque crossed in this manner therefore takes the risk that the person from whom they have taken it has no title to the cheque in the first place and therefore they cannot pass valid title to the third party.

11.2.2 'Account payee'

The Bills of Exchange Act 1882 gave provision for the use of the 'account payee' crossing, although the use of this crossing caused confusion as to what it actually achieved. The confusion related to whether 'account payee' made the cheque non-transferable or not ie could it be used to pay one individual only. Although the general understanding was that such a crossing would make it non-transferable, there have been a number of cases in law that did not confirm this. Not until the Cheques Act 1992 was it clearly laid out in statute what the crossing actually meant:

> '...where a cheque is crossed and bears across its face the words 'account payee', either with or without the word 'only', the cheque shall not be transferable, but shall only be valid as between the parties thereto.'

11.3   Collection of cheques

The relationship between a financial services provider and its customer when the provider pays a cheque drawn by the customer is in essence that of an agent and principal. An agent is someone that an individual can appoint to act on their behalf. Agents can create or continue contracts and undertake certain activities on behalf of their principal. The principal will delegate tasks to the agent but does not in fact delegate away responsibility. In this instance the provider is acting as an agent on the customer's instruction to pay money from their account.

The provider must conform to the strict terms of the instruction given to it by the customer: the written cheque being the instruction to make payment. If the provider makes payment contrary to that instruction, it cannot debit the customer's account. A paying bank may find it has acted without an instruction where:

◆ a cheque has been stolen and the drawer's signature is forged;

◆ there is an unauthorised alteration to the cheque (eg where the holder has changed the amount of the cheque);

◆ an agent for the customer has acted in excess of their authority in drawing the cheque (eg where they are only authorised to draw cheques up to £100 and a cheque is drawn for, say, £500);

◆ it makes payment on a cheque that has been countermanded (stopped);

◆ payment is made against a cheque where the endorsement is forged (less likely nowadays as a result of the use of cheques crossed 'account payee only', as described above).

The provider may be able to counterclaim against the customer where they have made the fraud possible, or have misled the provider into believing that the cheques are valid. Where a provider acts in breach of the customer's instruction, it may find that it is liable for the breach of the instruction but also in breach of common law for **conversion**. A provider is said to have 'converted' a cheque if it is made payable to Mr Smith and the provider allows it to go into the account of someone else, for example Mr Smithers.

Consider the following example.

Miss Jones banks with Multinational Bank. She writes out a cheque to her uncle, Mr Manners, and posts it to him.

The cheque is intercepted in the post by Mr Mannering. Mr Mannering pays it into an account with Conglomerate Bank. Conglomerate Bank collects the money from Multinational Bank.

This is 'conversion', because Mr Mannering (deliberately) and Conglomerate Bank (innocently) have committed the legal wrong of 'converting' the cheque by allowing it to be paid into the account of someone it was not intended for.

How does Mr Manners stand? Once the original cheque has gone through, Miss Jones will not want to pay her uncle a second time. There is little chance of Mr Manners getting the money back from Mr Mannering, even if he can be found. Can Mr Manners get the money back from Conglomerate Bank (which collected payment of the cheque) or Multinational Bank (which paid the cheque)?

Mr Manners is not a customer of either bank. He cannot take action against Multinational Bank (the paying bank), but he can take action against Conglomerate Bank — if he is what the law calls the 'true owner', or 'the person entitled to immediate possession', of the cheque.

Financial services providers have been given statutory protection against the action of conversion, firstly in Section 82 of the Bills of Exchange Act 1882 and subsequently in Section 4 of the Cheques Act 1957. This is because in the normal course of business providers are dealing with the collection of large numbers of cheques, and it is difficult for them to verify title to those cheques in every instance.

In order to obtain protection against conversion under Section 4 of the Cheques Act 1957 a provider has to satisfy the requirements that it:

◆ acted for a customer in collecting the cheque;

◆ must have received payment for the customer, or collected the cheque for itself where it has already credited the customer's account;

◆ must have acted in good faith;

◆ must have acted without negligence.

There are two important points here. Firstly, even if a customer has no title (legal ownership) or a defective title to the cheque (if, for instance, it is stolen), a provider will be protected against conversion. Secondly, 'without negligence' is an area open to debate in what constitutes good practice when accepting a cheque for collection. What may have been acceptable in the early twentieth century with low volumes of cheques may not be acceptable in the twenty-first century with substantial volumes passing through the system.

While it is not possible to give a full list of circumstances that would allow protection under the Section 4 of the Cheques Act, the following provide examples where acts or omissions will amount to negligence.

◆ Poor precautions taken when opening an account – anyone having stolen a cheque could pay it into a new account in the name of the payee quite easily. This is why there is a real need to identify and verify new customers and wait until this has been done before accepting any cheques from them.

◆ Collection of cheques payable to officials, companies or firms.

◆ Collection of cheques in favour of employers or principals for the account of an employee.

◆ Collection of cheques drawn by known employees in their favour on the account of the employer or principal.

◆ Collection of employer's cheques in favour of third parties for the account of the employee.

◆ The degree of scrutiny of an endorsement or order cheque.

◆ Account payee cheques collected for someone other than the named payee.

11.4   Clearing systems

The clearing system is a method providers use to **obtain payment** for items paid into their customers' accounts, and to **pay out** money where their customers have issued cheques or debits. It is an exchange of money or funds between the different providers.

All items (cheques and electronic debits), with the exception of cash, have to go through the process, which takes some time to complete. Historically this is due to the requirement physically to move cheques from one provider to another. The time element involved will determine whether an item is **cleared** or **uncleared**. Figure 11.1 shows how the clearing cycle works.

Figure 11.1 The clearing cycle

Day 0	Day 1	Day 2	Day 3	Day 4
Cheque paid in at payee's account with Bank A	Cheque arrives at 'clearing' processing centre for Bank A	Cheque is debited from payer's account at Bank B	Bank B could still decide to return cheque for lack of funds	
Payee does not have access to funds	Payee still does not have access to funds	Payee can earn interest on funds but cannot access them	Still no access to funds	Payee can now have access to their funds

By day 6, the payee will be certain that the cheque will not be returned. This is known as the 2–4–6 rule.

The principle behind a clearing system is that, rather than each bank branch presenting its cheques separately to every other bank branch for payment, each bank collects all its cheques together centrally and presents, **in bulk**, cheques drawn on each other member bank for payment. Settlement of the amounts due between banks can then be made on a net basis of all cheques presented, rather than with reference to individual cheques. In the case of the English and Welsh clearing system, settlement is made via the account of the member banks at the Bank of England.

The origins of the clearing system can be traced back to a coffee shop in the City of London in around 1770, where the first exchange of cheques took place. The membership of the clearing house/system was, for many years, restricted to the major clearing banks but, in recent years and with increasing competition in the financial services industry, the membership has increased. Other banks, and some building societies that require payment systems but do not have their own clearing service, have to establish an **agency** arrangement with one of the clearing banks.

The **UK Payments Administration** (UKPA) is the successor to APACS, which was set up in 1985, and is the umbrella organisation for the payments industry. Its function is to manage the development of payment clearing services and to oversee the process of money transmission in the UK. We considered UKPA in section 7.6.1.

There are three individual companies that operate the two main functions of the clearing system, ie paper clearing – the clearing of cheques and paper-based credits – and electronic clearing, covering automated and electronic transactions such as direct debits:

◆ **Cheque and Credit Clearing Company (C&CCC)**: this organisation manages the process of clearing the 8 million or so cheques that are written every day in England and Wales. Cheque clearing operates on a three-day cycle (although some banks are considering the possibility of moving to a two-day clearing cycle).

◆ **Bankers Automated Clearing Services (Bacs)**: deals with bulk electronic clearing of direct debits, standing orders and automated credits. Settlement takes place through the settlement accounts held at the Bank of England.

◆ **Clearing House Automated Payments System (CHAPS)**: operates same-day clearing for interbank electronic transfers of payments of £5,000 and over.

11.4.1 Payment/non-payment of cheques

When a cheque arrives for presentation at the drawee's bank on day 3, following processing via the clearing system, it needs to be examined to ensure that it is in order and properly drawn, so that the customer's account can be debited. The following checks will be made.

◆ Are there **sufficient funds** to pay the cheque? Are the funds all cleared? In practice, individual cheques are not monitored manually, but a computer printout, produced daily, identifies those cheques that are creating unsatisfactory debit situations.

◆ Is the cheque **signed** in accordance with the mandate? The signature on the cheque should conform to the specimen held by the bank and the appropriate person(s) should have signed the cheque in accordance with the mandate held.

◆ Is the cheque **post-dated**? Cheques with a date sometime in the future cannot be debited to the customer's account.

◆ Is the cheque **in date**? Cheques that are over six months old are considered to be out of date.

◆ Do the **words and figures** on the cheque differ? If so, this could suggest that there has been an attempt to fraudulently alter the cheque, leading to the customer's account being debited with more than is due.

◆ Is the cheque **mutilated**? If the cheque has been ripped it could suggest that it was the customer's intention to destroy the cheque and, again, that someone is fraudulently trying to obtain funds.

◆ Are there any **other alterations** on the cheque? If an alteration has been made on a cheque, it needs to have been confirmed by the drawer adding their signature.

◆ Has the cheque been **stopped** by the drawer?

In practice, many providers do not now scrutinise every single cheque due to the high volumes. They may look at those over a certain limit, eg £5,000. Should a problem occur later with a cheque, the provider will take appropriate action and may be willing to accept a small loss.

If the above examination of a cheque identifies a **problem**, the cheque cannot be debited to the account and needs to be returned to the collecting banker (the bank at which the cheque was paid in). The following procedure needs to be adopted.

◆ The cheque is deleted from the provider's computer system so that the account is not debited.

◆ The cheque is returned by first-class post to the collecting banker.

◆ As the cheque has been processed via the clearing system, a payment has been made between the banks in respect of this cheque. However, as it is not to be paid, the drawee's bank needs to claim the money back from the collecting bank by a claim for the unpaid item which is done via an interbank settlement account.

All the above checks should take place on the day the cheque is presented and, where appropriate, the cheque should be returned to the collecting bank on the same day. However, the **inadvertence rule** gives a drawee's bank longer time to return a cheque if it overlooks any of the irregularities on the day of presentation. As we saw above, a cheque can be returned on the next working day after presentation, providing that a telephone call is made to the collecting bank before 12 noon if the cheque is above £500. The accounting entries are the same as above, apart from the need to credit the customer's account rather than delete the cheque from the computer, as it will already have been debited. It should be noted that not all providers hold over cheques to day 4.

Activity

Does your bank hold cheques over to day 4?

If so, what is the benefit to customers?

Automation of the dishonour process is currently being reviewed. The electronic notification of dishonour of a cheque would negate the need to use the postal system. This would reduce the clearance time, after which withdrawal is allowed, by up to one day. Such a decision would naturally be at the discretion of individual banks and building societies.

Activity

Research the reasons for return your organisation uses and what 'reply' is written on the top of the cheque.

What fees are levied to the customer in each of these instances?

11.4.2 Stopped cheques (orders not to pay)

A customer has the right to **countermand payment** of a cheque – in other words, stop it. The customer has this right up to the moment when the provider pays the cheque. Customers may telephone their providers with details of the stopped cheque but the request must be **confirmed in writing**. It is vitally important that this written confirmation is received, as this will confirm categorically the request for the stop and the particular cheque to which it refers.

The provider must be very careful to stop the correct cheque as it may potentially be liable for heavy losses if:

◆ the provider pays the stopped cheque – the customer must be refunded;

◆ the provider stops an incorrect cheque, which may result in it being sued for breach of contract.

The bank will require all the information about the stopped cheque, including the payee's name, date and, most importantly, the cheque number, which is unique to that particular cheque. Hence, it is vital that customers keep a full record of the cheques that they issue. It is also useful to take a note of the details of a replacement cheque if it is being issued. Banks normally make a charge for stopping a cheque.

11.4.3 Truncation

The clearing system is somewhat cumbersome, the volume of cheques passing through it is enormous and although there has been a drop in cheque transactions owing to electronic alternatives, it is likely to remain a principal money transmission system. It is enormously costly to operate – UKPA calculates that over £1.5bn is spent by member banks each year on paper clearings.

One method of reducing the movement of paper throughout the system is truncation, whereby **cheques stay at the collecting bank**. This system, which is used to a very limited extent in the UK, is widely used in other European countries, particularly in Germany, Belgium and Denmark.

Truncation refers to a method of processing a cheque, whereby it is not returned (presented) to the drawee bank, but rather is retained by the collecting bank. The drawer's cheque is debited on the basis of the payment information incorporated within the cheque, and is electronically transmitted from a collecting bank to the paying/drawee's bank.

Currently, in the UK, the use of truncation is limited to cheques encashed by providers for customers of their branches under open credit arrangements (where a branch maintaining the main account has specifically authorised another branch or provider to cash funds up to a specified amount and to specific persons) and those guaranteed by cheque cards. It is a difficulty of the truncation system that a collecting bank would not always have access to information at the drawee's bank to confirm the suitability of paying the cheque, ie records of specimen signatures and access to the balances of the accounts.

Nevertheless, UK providers have decided, in principle, to proceed towards a system of truncation of cheques. This will involve 'stopping' the cheque at some point in the clearing cycle, which is currently foreseen to be at the clearing centre of the paying/drawee's bank.

However, a clause of the Bills of Exchange Act 1882 required cheques to be presented at the address on which they are drawn, and this for many years precluded the development of truncation. After many years of lobbying by UKPA, the government passed the Deregulation (Bills of Exchange) Order in 1996, which will allow the movement towards full truncation. Presently, cheques are being retained at a central point within paying banks (the bank upon which the cheque is drawn), and the debit applied electronically to the branch account. At some future time, the point may come when providers do not physically transfer cheques at all but debit accounts electronically.

Following criticism that providers are effectively earning interest on these moneys 'in transit', the Office of Fair Trading undertook research in 2006 and concluded that, for the time being, there was no case for providers to invest at the levels required to build a new central cheque-processing system in order to speed up clearing times (and in fact, as we have seen, cheques are to be withdrawn in 2018). However, there was agreement that funds paid into an account by cheque start to earn interest two days after deposit, are available for withdrawal after four days and cannot be taken back out of the account six days after deposit (unless the payee is a knowing party to the fraud) (see section 11.4 for further explanation of the 2–4–6 process).

11.5 Standing orders, direct debits and customer credits

As previously mentioned, there are three main agencies for the clearing system. Standing orders and direct debits operate through Bacs, which provides an automated clearing house service covering the whole of the UK. In 2010 almost 5.7bn UK payments were made via Bacs (source: www.bacs.co.uk), and it is the world's largest single automated clearing house.

Transaction instructions are originated by Bacs members themselves or by others sponsored by them to use the service. Currently there are in excess of 35,000 of these sponsored service providers, many of which use computer bureaux to prepare and input their data. These payment instructions are accepted from members or sponsored customers, on magnetic media or via telecommunication links.

Three types of payment are processed by Bacs.

1. **Standing orders**: these are fixed-sum, regular-date payments initiated by a provider on behalf of and at the instruction of its **customer**.

2. **Direct debits**: these are similar to standing orders in that they are regular payments from customer accounts and the customer has given instructions to allow them to be passed. However, it is the **beneficiary** who originates them, and the money is taken from the payer's account. Most input instructions in this respect come directly from companies sponsored by Bacs members. This type of payment, owing to its flexibility, is becoming increasingly popular and is replacing standing orders.

3. **Customer credits**: these are originated by sponsored companies and enable them to make direct payments to a beneficiary's account, consisting largely of wage and salary payments, pension and state benefits. Some 90 per cent of the UK working population is now paid through the customer credit system.

While the number of standing order transactions processed is enormous, it is interesting to note that they were on a declining trend during the 1990s. This can be explained by the increasing usage of direct debits, which are more flexible, both for the customer and the beneficiary. However, since the late 1990s there has been an uplift in the use of standing orders, which can be explained by two factors:

◆ **the launch of supermarket banks**: customers establish standing orders to pay money from their main account into subsidiary accounts;

◆ **the increase in telephone banking**: when customers pay bills over the telephone, the payment is actually made by the telephone bank via the standing order system.

The payment from the customer's account is processed by computer via Bacs, and is received to the beneficiary's account on the **third working day** inclusive after the debiting of the account, ie if the standing order payment is made on Monday 20 January it will be received in the beneficiary's account on Wednesday 22 January. Some providers now undertake same-day crediting and debiting between branches of their own bank, and some treat them as Faster Payments (see section 11.5.1).

Bacs is responsible for:

◆ the routing of the payment to the beneficiary bank and branch;

◆ the settlement of funds between the banks, ie when a Barclays' customer pays a standing order to a Lloyds' customer, funds have to be transferred between the banks to facilitate the transfer. While the actual accounts of the banks are held at the Bank of England and the actual interbank transfers take place there, Bacs, in processing the payments, will provide the details.

The major benefit to customers of paying bills by standing order is **convenience**. Once a customer has established a standing order it will be paid regularly on the due date without their doing anything further. On the other hand, should the customer decide to pay by another method, such as by posting a cheque or by paying by cash over the counter, they will be penalised in terms of cost, time and convenience.

Also, by paying via standing order, the customer will **not forget to make the payment**, while a customer paying by cheque or cash may find it difficult to remember. Should they forget, they may incur additional costs, as well as potential embarrassment.

The payment of the standing order will appear on the customer's statement and will provide a **proof of payment**. Many customers also feel that the payment of bills by standing order helps them to **budget** and, in other cases, reconcile their bank statements.

The direct debit system, which is used for the payment of regular bills such as mortgages, life and other insurance and assurance premiums, club, society and charity subscriptions, and the payment of utility bills, has become increasingly popular over recent years as a result of its advantages over standing orders for both the payer and the beneficiary.

Activity

> List the similarities between standing orders and direct debits.

Direct debits differ quite significantly from a standing order in the following ways:

◆ The payment is **originated by the beneficiary** and taken from the account of the payer. The customer has to sign an authority to approve the direct debit. With a standing order the payment is made by the customer's provider and the customer has total control. The opposite situation prevails with the direct debit, with the beneficiary having control.

◆ The payment is much more **flexible**. Providing the customer has signed the direct debit instruction, the amount, date and frequency of the direct debit can be changed. Accordingly, building society mortgage repayments are increasingly being paid by direct debit to assist with the administrative burden incurred both by customers and mortgage providers when interest rates change. In recent years the introduction of direct debits has also allowed credit card companies to have their bills settled this way, as the amounts will naturally change each month. Most utilities, eg telephone, water and electric companies provide an incentive, often by giving a small discount for their customers to pay by direct debit.

◆ The debiting of the payer's account takes place on the **same day** as the beneficiary account is credited.

If a customer complains that a direct debt has been **wrongly drawn**, the provider must put it right, even if the fault was not the provider's, ie it could have been the originator's. The originator, however, has signed an indemnity to confirm that it will put all incorrect payments right immediately. If it was found that the originator was not abiding by the terms of this indemnity then they can be withdrawn from the direct debiting system. This is a very powerful tool to be used against any originator.

A customer can **cancel** a direct debit at any time by writing to their provider and requesting cancellation. Normally this can be done at any time up to the payment of the direct debit.

In a similar way to standing orders, providers are only obliged to pay direct debits from customers' accounts if there are **sufficient funds** to meet them. If there are insufficient funds then the payment need not be made. Most banks and building societies advise their customers of this on the first occasion, advising them that any subsequent return of the direct debit will result in its cancellation. The charge for returning a direct debit or standing order unpaid is similar to that of a cheque.

11.5.1 Faster Payments Scheme

The Faster Payments scheme was introduced because the UK banking industry felt that a low-value, high-volume, twenty-four hours a day, seven days a week, real-time payment system would become an important part of the economy of the twenty-first century. As the world we live in increasingly becomes '24/7', an electronic payment system that reflects that speed and availability is important. By introducing this payment system, providers should gain income directly from payment charges and indirectly by making the UK an attractive place to do business and so gaining from a growing economy.

A secondary reason is that providers will use the new payment system to replace those payments that incurred '**float**'. Float is where paying customers are debited on day 1 but the beneficiary is not credited with the payment until day 3; providers thereby earn two days interest on the payment. Float is a legacy of the older Bacs payment systems for interbank payments and is now expressly prohibited by the Payment Services Regulations.

The Faster Payments scheme is a sterling-only system, which means that payments can only be made in sterling to and from UK bank accounts. The scheme has been designed to be easily extendable to other currencies in the future and hopefully to be useful within the Single European Payments Area. By the end of 2008 around two thirds of telephone and Internet payments were processed in this way.

The following types of payment can be processed through the Faster Payments scheme:

◆ **Single immediate payments** are typically those made when the customer sends the instruction to their provider via phone or through their Internet banking service, and requests the transaction to be made straight away. These types of payment can be made all day, every day.

◆ **Forward-dated payments** are individual, one-off payments set up by a customer to be made at a future date. For example, some people will arrange to pay all their bills at the beginning of the month, setting the payments up in advance, but having the money debited on a specified date in the future. Unlike standing orders, it may be possible to make this type of payment on 'non-working days', depending on the service offered by the provider.

◆ **Standing orders** are regular payments made on a specific date for the same amount, to the same person or beneficiary. These payments will continue to be made on 'working days' only.

Banks and building societies have made a phased launch of this system depending on their own timescales, and it does not involve the direct debit or cheque-clearing systems. Faster Payment has led to a major improvement in customer service: the near-real-time nature of the payments means that customers can seek near-real-time feedback on whether the payment has successfully reached the beneficiary account, hence eliminating lots of 'where is my payment?' queries. The payments are irrevocable (unable to be recalled), thus reducing the work associated with payment recalls.

11.5.2 Card payments

We have looked at credit cards in section 8.4.1 and we will return to them again in Topic 13. However, it is worth mentioning here that they provide the seller with an electronic settlement in three days via the **electronic funds transfer at point of sale (EFTPOS)** system. This gives the retailer access to their funds after three days without the worry of the payment being unpaid, which gives a distinct advantage over payments by cheque. There is, therefore, certainty of payment as long as the card has been accepted in accordance with the credit card company's rules. The retailer pays the credit card company a commission, typically around 2 per cent of the transaction amount, for the certainty and ease of payment.

Resources

http://www.ukpayments.org.uk

Review questions

The following review questions are designed so that you can check your understanding of this topic.

The answers are provided at the end of these learning materials.

1.   What is the effect of endorsing a cheque?

2.   What is the purpose of crossing a cheque?

3.   What is the effect of the 'not negotiable' crossing?

4.   Explain how a bank may be guilty of conversion.

5.   If a bank or building society does not have its own clearing system how does it make payments for customers?

6.   What checks will a bank make to a cheque that is presented for payment from a customer's account?

7.   What is the purpose of 'truncation'?

8.   What are the three types of payment made via the Bacs system?

9.   If a customer complains to their bank that a direct debit has been incorrectly taken from their account, what must the bank do?

10. Explain the concept of 'float'.

Topic 12
Dealing with debt

> **Learning objective**
>
> After studying this topic students should be able to demonstrate a knowledge and understanding of customer interactions and how they are governed by regulation in relation to issues surrounding problem lending situations.

Introduction

In this topic we shall look at some important areas in relation to customers and how they get into debt. One of the first areas to be considered, however, is the actual credit agreement itself as this sets out all the information about the borrowing. In the event of default the agreement will be an essential document.

Connected lenders, as we shall see, become involved in disputes between the customer and their suppliers. Part of a connected lender's agreement with a customer is to refund moneys in the event of a complaint with a supplier not being satisfied. This is great benefit to customers who may find themselves disadvantaged through no fault of their own. It is likely that many customers do not know about this benefit and could find themselves in debt due to a purchase that has gone wrong, without actually needing to be.

Finally in this topic we shall explore how customers get into debt, usually through a negative life-cycle event. This will be a difficult time for the customer, who may approach a debt counselling service (section 3.3) for help and advice rather than the lender. In this instance the lender will have to rely on its management information for clues that the customer is in difficulty. We shall see what these clues are.

12.1 Credit agreements

In section 7.4 we considered the Consumer Credit Acts (CCAs) and other consumer credit regulations. We will now look specifically at the regulations relating to agreements. When a customer first takes out a credit agreement with their credit card or loan provider, they should be issued with a true, legible copy for their records. All the text in the agreement should be given equal prominence so that important details are not lost in the 'small print'.

The form and content of regulated consumer credit agreements should:

◆ have information presented in a clear and concise manner, where 'clear' includes a requirement that the wording, apart from any signature, is to be easily legible and in a colour which is easily distinguishable from the background medium upon which the information is displayed;

◆ contain statements of the protection and remedies available to debtors under the Act;

◆ contain details of any security provided in relation to the regulated agreement by the debtor;

◆ contain details of any underlying insurance contracts whose premiums are included in the loan covering:

– accident;

– sickness;

– unemployment;

at any time before the credit has been repaid.

The credit agreement is a legally binding document and is governed by the CCAs. The 1974 Act was originally created to protect the general public from unscrupulous lenders. It laid down requirements that had to be complied with for a credit card or credit loan agreement, known as a credit agreement, to be enforceable. Under the Acts, the credit agreement must contain the prescribed terms above, which clearly define all the conditions of the loan and to which both the lender and the borrower must adhere.

Recently, it has come to light that a number of credit agreements signed before April 2007 may be flawed. It would appear that many lenders have inadvertently not met the requirements of the Act, thus rendering some credit agreements unenforceable. This means that the lender cannot force the borrower to pay back the outstanding balance of their loan or credit card. Some customers have therefore sought to have their credit agreement set aside, leaving the provider to write-off the debt.

With effect from April 2008, the CCA 2006 gave the courts discretionary power to enforce all invalidly executed agreements, thus preventing borrowers from avoiding repayment of their debts on a technicality.

Activity

> How does your organisation ensure that credit agreements are completed correctly?

Credit agreements are important to ensure that both parties are clear what amounts have been borrowed and how these will be paid back. There are two types of contract: those that are for **restricted** use – for example, for the provision of goods and services – and those that are for **unrestricted** use, for example loans made in cash that can be used for any purpose. If a dispute arises later or the customer has difficulty repaying the debt, the parties need to understand what their rights and responsibilities are. We shall now go on to look at what happens in a variety of situations where there are either disputes or difficulties.

12.2   Connected lender liability and dispute

A **connected lender** is a credit card company that lends money on credit cards it has issued to customers. Credit card companies become involved in a wide variety of disputes arising between cardholders and suppliers, whether those suppliers are located at home or abroad. Such involvement can be via face-to-face transactions, transactions effected over the Internet, by mail or telephone orders.

The most common types of complaint relate to goods/services that:

◆ have been supplied but are of the wrong description (this is known as misrepresentation);

◆ are damaged/faulty/incomplete – such as double-glazed windows that do not open properly;

◆ are delivered late or not at all – such as a holiday that does not happen as a result of the holiday company getting into financial difficulty.

While cardholders will generally try to resolve the matter with the supplier direct, they will often at the same time approach their **card issuer**. This is because the card issuer can also be held liable for the amount of the claim, as we will see below. Sometimes the card issuer will be the customer's first resort. The two main card schemes, VISA International and MasterCard International, operate under detailed and complex rules. Part of this framework deals with the resolution of disputes between the card issuer, its cardholders and the supplier (and the parties that have provided goods/services to the supplier).

The majority of complaints received by a card issuer can be handled satisfactorily by reference to the card scheme rules. When a complaint is received, the card issuer will ask for evidence from the cardholder to support the claim. If the required evidence is produced (and this will vary according to the nature of the claim), then in certain circumstances the card issuer will have a limited period (normally 180 days from the original transaction date) to charge back the value of the disputed transaction to the supplier.

Activity

> Why do you think it is important to be able to obtain refunds for customers in this way?

The supplier, in turn, through its contractual arrangements with whoever it obtained the goods/services from, will have the ability to recover that sum. Of course, if the provider of the goods/services has become insolvent in the interim then the liability rests with the supplier.

If such a **chargeback** does not conform with the card scheme rules, then the card issuer has to decide whether to enforce payment against the cardholder under the card agreement or to absorb the loss. If there is some doubt as to the validity of the chargeback then the matter may be referred to the relevant card scheme body for an arbitration to take place between the card issuer and the supplier.

If a cardholder has been promised a refund by the supplier and, for whatever reason, the supplier defaults on the promise, then the cardholder can obtain a refund, on submission of the relevant proof, from their card issuer. The card issuer will then attempt to recover that sum from the supplier under the card scheme rules. These procedures apply to all card transactions, whether domestic or cross border.

As a consequence of the joint and several liability provision, the cardholder could choose to sue the card issuer alone, even if the supplier is still trading. The card issuer will, of course, have no firsthand knowledge of the facts of the dispute and will in such circumstances be forced to join the supplier in the legal action.

More commonly the cardholder will issue proceedings against supplier and card issuer. In these circumstances the card issuer will have little or nothing to add to the debate. However the card issuer has a right of indemnity against the supplier, whereby the supplier agrees to pay the card issuer for losses incurred, including any reasonable costs spent defending the action.

Activity

> Who do you think the customer should approach first — the supplier or the card issuer?

12.3 Dealing with debt

Customers can get into debt in a number of ways, not just through poor financial management or unwillingness to pay. As we have seen in section 12.1, credit agreements are regulated by the CCAs and the recovery of debts is also regulated. This has particular relevance for lenders who resort to legal action to recover a debt from a customer. There is a **process** that the lender should follow to ensure that the consumer is given the **full information** about the amount of the debt. There are also**timescales** to which the lender must adhere to ensure that customers are treated fairly. The customer should be given a **reasonable opportunity** to make proposals for repayment before the matter is referred to the courts.

Customers can get into debt for a variety of reasons. In Topic 2we looked at the typical customer life cycle and people's attitude to risk and debt. As well as the positive life events such as, say, leaving university, starting a new job, getting married and starting a family, there are also life events that are negative and can lead to financial hardship.

In the customer adviser role it is important to understand what these events are and how they impact on the customer and their needs. Firstly, this is because it is an FSA requirement to treat customers in difficulty **sympathetically and positively**. Lenders have been criticised for failing to deal with customers in this way, since such failings have an impact on consumer confidence in the financial services sector as a whole, not to mention the reputational risk for the provider concerned. The following case study shows how the FSA handles organisations that do not treat customers fairly.

> **Treating customers fairly over mortgage arrears**
>
> The Financial Services Authority (FSA) has today set out the rules which will ensure there are proper protections in place for vulnerable customers in arrears on their mortgage.

Today's announcement demonstrates the FSA's commitment to intensive and intrusive supervision to ensure firms treat their customers fairly. It forms part of crucial next steps following the FSA's Mortgage Market Review launched last October.

It defines the standards firms must follow on arrears handling, to provide customers with greater protection from 30 June 2010.

The FSA has also confirmed its plans to make all mortgage advisers and those who arrange non-advised sales personally accountable. They will be required to demonstrate they are 'fit and proper', helping to clamp down on mortgage fraud and enabling the FSA to monitor individuals in the mortgage market.

Customers in arrears must be treated fairly by firms and the following key areas have been confirmed:

◆ Firms must not apply a monthly arrears charge where an agreement is already in place to repay the arrears.

◆ Payments by customers in financial difficulties must first be allocated to clearing the missed monthly payments, rather than to arrears charges, which can be repaid later.

◆ Firms must consider all options for borrowers. Repossessions should always be the last resort.

A new rule has also been introduced requiring firms to record all arrears-handling telephone calls and to keep the records for three years.

Lesley Titcomb, FSA director responsible for the mortgage sector, said: 'We think it is wrong that arrears charges should be taken from customers already in difficult circumstances and trying to get their finances back on track. Today's rules make absolutely clear the standards we expect of firms, and we have already taken tough action against some of the worst offenders. Not being treated fairly or having all the facts can be a source of real distress for people in already difficult circumstances.'

Source: Adapted from www.fsa.gov.uk/pages/Library/Communication/PR/2010/106.shtmll, June 2010

The Lending Code and the Banking Conduct of Business rules (introduced in section 3.2.3 and section 7.2.6) support the Treating Customers Fairly requirements.

The second reason why it is important to understand how **life-cycle events** can impact upon customers is that it makes it easier to spot opportunities to help customers protect themselves against a problem before it occurs. An example might be highlighting the need for life cover that would repay a loan in the event of the death of the main earner of the family, so protecting the welfare of the dependants.

The following points give the main reasons for customers getting into financial difficulty.

◆ **Redundancy**: loss of employment is a major and obvious factor in financial hardship. In an economic downturn this will be an all-too-common occurrence, and the chances of finding a new job quickly could be diminished. Some redundancy packages give cash lump sums to leavers, although the amounts vary according to length of service, with employees with under two years' service entitled to very little. Whatever amount is received, it will probably have to be spent on day-to-day living expenses and finding a new job.

Activity

> Research how much people are able to claim under Jobseeker's Allowance. How long is this payment available to them?
>
> If you were made redundant how helpful would this be to you?

If a customer is made redundant or leaves their job for some other reason, then ideally they should inform their bank as soon as possible. This enables a discussion about how to deal with any debts; a plan can be agreed that will help the customer over what it is hoped will be a temporary problem. From a provider's perspective, seeing the income on an account dry up and debt levels rise without an explanation rings alarm bells, and an adversarial situation could ensue.

◆ **Ill-health**: this is another reason why a customer may become unable to maintain their level of earnings, and the extent to which it is a problem will depend on their type of employment. People in a salaried role will be paid for some time under their contract of employment; if their illness is prolonged, the period for which they are paid will depend on their individual circumstances. Those on a wage are more likely to be paid only for the hours they work, so a period of long illness could be quite difficult for them to cope with. People who are self-employed rely on themselves to provide their goods or services; their income will be severely affected if they become unwell, unless they are able to employ someone to act on their behalf.

A report completed by the NHS Institute for Innovation and Improvement in March 2008 showed that, although the self-employed reported higher levels of work-related health problems than the employed – 45 per cent compared with 33 per cent – they actually took far fewer days off sick. For example, a one-person enterprise took off an average of 2.5 days per year compared with a worker within a large enterprise, who took off on average 7.4 days. This report and its findings led to the concept of the doctor's 'fit note', which identifies what people are capable of doing, instead of indicating they are unfit to work at all . When a lender encounters a customer with health issues, it is important that their employment type is considered.

◆ **Mental incapacity and powers of attorney**: as we saw in section 10.3, mental incapacity terminates the bank–customer relationship. However, in section 2.1 we also saw that people with debts can have mental health problems. There could be a situation in which a customer is having debt problems that are being made worse by a condition such as depression. While it is not for the customer adviser to provide counselling for depression, it is worthwhile noting that people who have debt problems may not be able to cope with the situation particularly well and there can be underlying problems that are not at first apparent.

If someone is deemed to be incapable of making decisions through a mental impairment they can appoint an agent (or someone can be appointed for them) to undertake tasks on their behalf. **Lasting powers of attorney (LPA)** can be set up that will enable a third party to act on behalf of the customer and deal with their financial affairs. If a financial services provider is asked to accept an

LPA on a customer's account, they should check that the LPA has been executed properly and that signatures have been verified, so that the 'donees' have the authority to act on behalf of the customer.

In addition, if the provider is asked to lend money on the customer's account, it should check if there are joint donees, whether the powers are joint or several, and that the LPA is currently in force. If the LPA only comes into force on some particular event happening (for example, the customer being sectioned under the Mental Health Act) then the provider must ensure that that event has actually taken place.

Activity

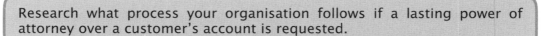

Research what process your organisation follows if a lasting power of attorney over a customer's account is requested.

◆ **Relationship breakdown – divorce and separation**: marital breakdown can cause financial hardship, partly because the stress of the situation may distract people from the handling of day-to-day financial affairs. There may be disputes over the debts and ownership of assets. The household income could be reduced, particularly if one spouse is responsible for most of the childcare, say, and so does not have their own income. There may be an additional mortgage or rent to be paid if one of the parties has moved out. Data from the Office for National Statistics for 2009 indicate that 23 per cent of couples who married in 1999 had divorced before reaching their tenth wedding anniversary, making relationship breakdown a relatively common potential cause of financial hardship.

This will be a difficult situation for the parties to deal with. Some couples will be able to sort out their financial affairs and the only indication the bank will have of the situation will be that the joint account is closed. Others will not be so amicable, perhaps with one party taking the funds from the joint account and even running up a debt without the other party knowing about it. We have already looked at how joint and several liability makes both parties liable for the debt irrespective of how it has been incurred.

◆ **Death**: again as we saw in section 10.3, death terminates the relationship with the bank. However, the death will have an impact on the surviving relatives and it is in everyone's interests for a lender to adopt a sensitive approach. The relatives will be both distressed and anxious and may be worried about the future, especially if the deceased has left debts. Surviving partners would benefit from advice and guidance on any joint mortgage loans or personal loans outstanding, and other financial affairs, such as budgeting and managing money. If an adequate life cover policy has been taken out, then these outstanding loans will be repaid; if this is not the case, there will be cause for concern. The time taken to sort out the estate of the deceased can mean that interest can accrue, and it may be that the personal representatives can make payments from the estate to meet these costs until matters have been finalised.

If the account was in arrears at the time of death and action was being taken by the lender to recover the moneys, then it would be sensible to suspend interest accruing. It would be insensitive to the survivors and may prove unnecessary once the affairs of the estate have been finalised. It would be quite rare for a lender to litigate against the estate of a deceased borrower except as a last resort.

◆ **Bankruptcy and individual voluntary arrangements**: as we have seen in section 7.5, these are a last resort for customers to enable them to start afresh. If another party starts proceedings to make a customer bankrupt the lender has a variety of options.

  ◆ If the lending is a secured loan and the value of the security exceeds the loan, then the lender is best to rely on their security and sit tight. There would be little point in surrendering the security, joining the other creditors and being in a worse position.

  ◆ Where the security does not exceed the value of the debt, then the lender should asses the shortfall and be in a position to claim for it.

  ◆ The lender could sell the asset held as security and claim for any shortfall in the bankruptcy, although practically this may be difficult to do within the timeframe of the bankruptcy proceedings.

  ◆ If there is no security then the lender has to join the other creditors and hope there will be some repayment of at least part of the debt.

Lenders tend not to favour making customers bankrupt as it does not necessarily achieve the best outcome for the lender. The customer's assets become available to other creditors and therefore the lender is not really likely to achieve any greater repayment amount.

12.3.1 Identifying other extenuating circumstances

In an ideal world the lender would hope to have a relationship with the customer whereby the customer could contact the lender to explain their situation and work out a plan together. However, many individuals who are in financial difficulty do not feel fully in control and are likely to be defensive and unwilling to discuss their situation openly. This is why customers will often approach organisations such as **Citizens Advice** and other agencies (see section 3.3) when they have a problem, as these organisations are seen as impartial and fair.

Lenders are able to **monitor** accounts to identify if a customer is experiencing financial difficulty. They need to ensure that the borrowing is within the customer's ability to repay and be able to observe any **adverse trends** that might indicate a problem. It would be unrealistic for a lender to monitor every account manually so computerised systems monitor the accounts and produce reports for 'out of order' accounts. These might show:

◆ excesses above agreed overdraft limits;

◆ unarranged overdrafts;

◆ arrears of loan repayments; and

◆ behavioural scores.

The monitoring system also collects historical information on every account, thereby building up an account profile upon which future lending decisions can be based.

These monitoring systems have a variety of early warning signals. If the lender can identify signs of strain in repayment patterns, it provides an opportunity to open the dialogue with the customer before the situation becomes unmanageable. Typically, management information systems will show:

◆ balance trends and unauthorised excesses over the limit;

◆ evidence of overdraft balances or credit card balances that do not return to credit after salary or wages payments have been received each month (this type of debt is known as 'structural' or 'hardcore' debt);

◆ monthly debit turnover of the account and whether this is increasing or decreasing in relation to any credits paid in;

◆ monthly credits to the account and whether these have dried up;

◆ failure to adhere to the agreed conditions, such as an overdraft not being repaid by an agreed date;

◆ overdrawn accounts that have become dormant altogether without contact from the customer, suggesting that the customer is ignoring the problem – this could be linked to letters and statements being returned from the customer's address because they have left the area;

◆ dormant accounts that have suddenly become active and overdrawn – this situation could suggest that the customer is in difficulty and is searching for any available credit facilities to make ends meet;

◆ evidence of regular cross-firing, where the customer withdraws funds on uncleared cheques, often between several accounts, which could indicate a customer who is continually moving funds around to hide a bigger problem.

If any of the issues outlined above are identified, the lender will usually send a letter to the customer asking for an explanation. The more responsible customer will approach their lender for help and in some ways these customers are easier to deal with because they have acknowledged that they have to deal with their problem.

Activity

In your organisation, what management information is generated to indicate a problem to those responsible for lending control?

Resources

www.fsa.gov.uk

Review questions

The following review questions are designed so that you can check your understanding of this topic.

The answers are provided at the end of these learning materials.

1. Why is it important to complete the credit agreement accurately and fully?

2. What is a connected lender?

3. If a customer has used their credit card to purchase goods that subsequently turn out to be faulty, whom can they approach for a refund?

4. What is the FSA's stance on the way that customers who are in arrears should be treated?

5. What are the main reasons for customers getting into debt?

6. What is the purpose of a lasting power of attorney?

7. What is 'hardcore' debt?

8. How might a dormant account indicate a customer having financial difficulty?

Topic 13
Lending products

Introduction

This topic builds on Topic 8 and goes into more detail about lending products. We shall explore the range of unsecured and secured borrowing that is available to personal customers. We shall see that while the decision to take security may be determined centrally in an organisation by the credit risk committee, it will be influenced by the amount required, the complexity of the proposition and the potential risk to the lender.

'Revolving credit' is the term for unsecured borrowing on overdraft and by credit card. As the name implies it does not have a fixed repayment date and is therefore fairly simple and straightforward to arrange and use. However, secured borrowing, such as that for property purchase, where the lender has some additional comfort by taking a charge over an asset, does have a defined repayment schedule and date. These types of loan can be more complex and costly to arrange. Indeed, for many people, buying their own home is the biggest financial commitment they will ever make.

As we shall see, there are a variety of specialist mortgages and other loans for specific customer circumstances. This type of borrowing is made more attractive to customers by having the option of different interest rate schemes.

Business customers have similar requirements for overdrafts to finance short-term cash flows, credit cards for convenience and loans for business development. Business owners may also be required to charge either assets of the business or their personal assets to secure the borrowing. We shall however, in this topic, be focusing mainly on the requirements of the personal consumer.

13.1   Unsecured borrowing

Where the lender does not take security, the borrowing is described as 'unsecured'. In effect the lender relies on the borrower's **promise to repay** and nothing more, although the lender may have to resort to **legal action** in the event of default. In 'secured' lending, as we shall see later, the borrower gives some additional form of assurance of repayment, usually by **pledging assets**, such as their house, to the lender. This means that in the event of default the lender can claim these assets, or rights to enforce a recovery, so giving the lender a **secondary route** to repayment.

In unsecured borrowing situations the lender's risk is clearly rather higher: the prospects of repayment depend entirely on the borrower's **ability** and **intention** to repay. It is usual (and very good discipline) for providers to use a **structured approach** when assessing propositions, to make sure that as much relevant information as possible about the borrower has been obtained on which to make a sound decision.

The provider should have a standard format for loan assessments, and there may well be some **automated filter**, such as computer-based assessment, statistical analysis or credit-scoring (which we shall look at later in section 14.1.3), to remove the subjective, human element from the decision-making process. The manner in which applications are handled these days is often very different from the personal approach traditionally used around twenty years ago. Volumes of lending have increased dramatically, and for many lenders the vast majority of applications for unsecured loans are processed and assessed automatically.

The most common types of unsecured personal lending that we shall look at include overdrafts (both authorised and unauthorised), credit cards and personal loans.

13.1.1 Overdrafts

An overdraft is a facility offered by a provider that allows a customer to make withdrawals (debit card payments, draw cash, etc) when there are **insufficient funds** in the account to cover them. Overdrafts are lines of credit generally provided to cover **short-term** needs and as such are repayable '**on demand**' facilities, which means the lender does not need to give any notice to request repayment. They are intended to cover borrowing of a **temporary** nature that will be repaid on the receipt of expected funds.

Activity

> What expenses might customers require temporary overdraft facilities for?

The amount lent is usually equivalent to one month's salary and any requests for much more may well be better taken in the form of a loan account. If a borrowing request is not for short-term borrowing requirements then the facility would also be best provided in the form of a loan.

Activity

> What are your organisation's guidelines for maximum amounts that can be agreed on overdraft for customers?

Providers have no obligation to let customers overdraw their accounts, but they may do so by either:

◆ an '**authorised overdraft**' — which is a prior arrangement; or

◆ an '**unauthorised overdraft**' — where there is no prior arrangement; for example, if a customer makes a payment that would take their account overdrawn, this may be seen as a request for an overdraft.

Interest is charged on the overdrawn account; in addition, an **arrangement fee** for the overdraft facility may be charged. The interest rate may depend on whether the overdraft is authorised or unauthorised. The interest rate on an unauthorised overdraft facility is usually substantially higher than for an agreed overdraft.

A provider would be justified in refusing to allow an unauthorised overdraft — for example, by returning unpaid direct debits on the customer's account. It may, however, in light of its relationship with the customer, allow the direct debits to be paid and the account to go overdrawn. Where an overdraft has been agreed with a provider, the borrower may still incur **penalty rates** of interest and charges if they borrow more than the pre-agreed limit.

If no formal agreement is in place, the lender does not technically have a common law right to apply interest (or any other) charges; in practice, it establishes this right for authorised overdrafts by way of its written terms and conditions. In any case, a provider's right to charge interest would most likely be justified on the grounds that this is common industry practice; and, after the interest has been applied, through the customer's implicit acceptance of the terms.

An overdraft can sometimes indicate that a customer is under some financial strain, albeit perhaps only in the short term. As the higher interest rates and administration charges associated with unarranged overdrafts can make matters worse, customers are best advised to agree overdrafts before incurring them. Overdraft interest is usually charged at variable rates linked to the base rate. This can make **budgeting** difficult for customers. Where certainty is needed, some more structured form of borrowing may be more appropriate.

An overdraft is nonetheless a form of credit that lets people cope with short-term difficulties arising from **uneven cashflows**. Early repayment of some structured loans can incur penalties, whereas an overdraft is more flexible.

The most obvious risk to the lender is that of **non-repayment**. This is mainly mitigated through a constant review of the lender's processes for new lending assessment and the monitoring of existing accounts.

A further risk that can arise from overdraft offerings is that of **mispricing** of the interest rate (ie the mismanagement of the interest rate spread between moneys deposited by customers and moneys lent out to customers). This tends not to be so great a problem as it would be with, for example, fixed-rate personal loans, because overdraft interest is usually levied at a margin over base rate. Therefore, the rate can be automatically adjusted to reflect fluctuations in market rates and thereby protect the lender's margin.

The term '**revolving credit**' applies to any line of credit that is restored as the borrower pays off what is owed, such as an overdraft facility. Revolving credit may become '**structural**', that is, permanently in use; this is a risk to the lender as the borrower may become '**over-borrowed**' and be unable to repay the debt. Lenders generally remain on the lookout for this: sophisticated computer systems can monitor account trends and warn of a potential dependence on a revolving credit facility. If this does happen, the lender may agree with the borrower to

consolidate the borrowing into a loan account to provide a structured repayment plan. This loan may also include borrowing with other providers.

13.1.2 Credit cards

Credit cards are another form of **short-term, unsecured, revolving credit** and combine two elements:

◆ a credit account on which the customer can draw up to a pre-agreed sum (the 'credit limit'); and

◆ a plastic card, which can be used as the payment mechanism.

The credit card limit will be determined initially from a **credit score** of the customer information on application. Then, as a pattern of card usage by the customer develops, **behavioural scoring** might automatically increase the limit. Account **statements** or 'bills' are sent monthly, detailing the transactions that have taken place in the period, the interest applied and the end balance. The borrower can either:

◆ repay the whole amount outstanding; or

◆ repay only part of it; a certain minimum amount will, however, be payable each month.

Credit card users who have a continuous stream of repayments and new transactions that keep their balance high are known as '**revolvers**' or, occasionally, '**transactors**' . Such card users rarely reduce their balance to nil but rather, each month, pay down an amount and at the same time spend more on the card, thereby running their balance back up to, or near, their borrowing limit.

Not all users choose to use their cards in this way. Borrowers can repay some or all of their outstanding balances and incur new borrowings each month (up to their credit limit). They need not consult the card issuer every time they want to borrow more; the supply of available credit is constantly renewed as they pay off outstanding balances. Many customers see credit cards as a useful alternative for **short-term liquidity needs**, rather than arranging an overdraft with the provider of their current account.

Credit cards are a **flexible** way to borrow; if the full balance is repaid each month, they can also provide cheap finance (most cards offer an interest-free period provided full repayment is made by the due date). If the balance is repaid within a set time after the statement date the customer is provided with a short **interest-free** period. The period from statement date to payment-due date is perhaps a week or so and, given that statements are issued monthly, this means that a person could, by timing their purchases carefully and repaying in full on the due date, borrow interest-free for four to six weeks – depending on the terms offered by the issuer. Otherwise, a payment of at least a **set minimum** is required by the 'due date' – generally 3 per cent of the total balance. The remainder is carried forward as an outstanding balance, with interest. The interest rate charged on outstanding balances tends to be higher than that of a current account overdraft.

Credit cards can be used for many transactions: at retailers, over the telephone or Internet (by quoting the card account number) and, if used in conjunction with a personal identification number (PIN), to obtain cash at automated teller machines (ATMs).

Card issuers make their money in two ways:

◆ by charging interest; and

◆ in some cases, by levying fees.

Not all issuers levy fees, but some have an annual fee to cover their administrative costs, such as monthly statements. Where cards are used to obtain **cash advances**, there may also be a charge of around 1.5 per cent of the advance; alternatively, interest may be levied on the balance from the day of the advance (ie without the interest-free period discussed earlier).

Credit card accounts are not generally suitable, however, for large amounts borrowed for a longer term. In these cases structured finance such as a personal loan, with a disciplined repayment schedule and most probably a lower rate of interest, is more appropriate. Nevertheless, as appetite for credit continues unabated, competition in this market is fierce and there are now many different brands on the market. In 2009 credit and charge cards were used to make two billion purchases in the UK, to a value of £139bn. This figure is projected to reach £196bn in 2019 and shows the value of the business to credit card providers (*source*: www.theukcardsassociation.org.uk).

The major **risk** with this type of lending is similar to that of overdraft facilities, in that the **borrowing may not be repaid**. Another danger, particularly with credit cards, is that the borrower arranges such facilities with **a number of lenders**.

Activity

> How much do you think credit card companies are to blame for people getting into debt with multiple credit cards?

It can be easy for such borrowing to get out of hand and much harder for any one lender to establish the borrower's total outstanding debt. Regular monitoring of customers' spending patterns coupled with an annual review of their facilities, perhaps supported by occasional credit checks, can limit these risks.

The **automatic increase of limits** mentioned above, while good for the lender in that it reduces administration, can leave a lender exposed to a greater loss if the customer's circumstances suddenly change. This is potentially another reason why interest charges on credit cards (where the interest-free period is not utilised) tend to be higher than overdrafts.

Activity

> Make a list of the similarities between credit cards and overdrafts and their differences.

13.1.3 Personal and term loans

Most high-street providers offer personal loans, which are assessed via automated credit scoring, credit reference and fraud agency search. We will look at the assessment process in section 14.1. Loans provide a more **disciplined** form of borrowing than overdrafts, which has both advantages and disadvantages for the borrower. They are generally for a **fixed amount**, and the terms will cover the:

◆ rate of interest – which is likely to be fixed;

◆ amount and frequency of repayments – these usually consist of a fixed monthly repayment made up of both interest and a portion of the capital;

◆ repayment date – which is therefore predetermined.

Personal loans are therefore ideal where, for example, the borrowing is for:

◆ a specific purpose – a holiday, a car or some other one-off purchase, such as a domestic appliance;

◆ rescheduling earlier borrowings that may have got out of control. Multiple loans, credit card debts and so on can be consolidated into a single personal loan so as to provide an orderly repayment framework.

In the latter case lenders will sometimes use a variable interest rate – for example base-rate linked. This may enable the lender to offer the borrower a preferential rate of interest.

This form of 'term' or 'ordinary' loan may be more appropriate where:

◆ the amount of the loan is in excess of the personal loan limit or the purpose does not qualify;

◆ equal monthly repayments are not appropriate, for example where the customer will be able to make regular lump sum reductions from bonuses;

◆ loans are to high-value customers, where competitive pressures indicate a finer interest rate;

◆ the customer has been granted a capital repayment holiday, usually of no more than twelve months.

Activity

> Research the differences in interest rates offered by your organisation for an ordinary personal loan and a loan for consolidation of borrowing.
>
> Why are there these differences?

The risks associated with personal loans and term loans are largely similar to those associated with other forms of unsecured lending, except that where a substantial part of the lender's business is made up of fixed-term, fixed-interest loans there can be a greater exposure to the risk of **mispricing** of interest rates. Lenders can manage, and mitigate, this risk through appropriate lending book management, ie ensuring that they have sound policies in place to ensure that they do not end up with an asset/liability pricing mismatch.

Activity

> Undertake some research to establish the difference between typical interest rates for overdrafts, credit cards and personal loans.

13.2 Secured borrowing

In general, to 'secure' lending means to give the lender some **assurance** – security – of repayment. It is achieved by arranging that if the borrower defaults on their borrowing, the lender can claim legal rights to specific assets or rights to enforce a recovery, so limiting their exposure to loss. This may result in full or partial repayment of the debt.

The benefits of taking security are twofold. Firstly, it provides a **safety net** in the event that the borrower defaults and the lender has to take steps to recoup the money it has lent. There is, however, a second and very important benefit: the effect on the **borrower's attitude**. Where the asset over which the lender has taken security represents something of value to the borrower, the prospect of potentially losing it may increase their financial self-discipline and therefore the likelihood of their keeping up repayments.

Where security is available, it clearly plays a role in reducing the lender's risk associated with a particular loan, so we may regard a secured loan as generally being **less risky** than an unsecured one. Security is not all the same; different forms of security can vary considerably both in terms of:

◆ how robust their values are at the point when they need to be sold; and

◆ how easy it is actually to gain control and possession of them (enforceability).

This latter factor will be determined not only by the nature of the security itself, but also by whether the lender has the systems, procedures and knowledge actually to enforce the particular type of security in question.

There are different **processes for taking security**: the process for taking security over, say, stocks and shares differs from that required for a residential property. For instance, the requirements for valuation are different: stocks and shares can easily be valued from the financial press, but property has to be valued by a qualified professional who carries the relevant professional liability insurance, in case of a later dispute.

Lenders therefore take into account the **availability** and **nature** of any security when assessing loans. This assessment will determine not only whether they decide to proceed, but also, quite possibly, how much they **charge** for the loan (both in terms of interest rates and for any charges specifically relating to the security). However it should be clear that a lender may be inclined to regard an unsecured loan as riskier than a secured one, and, accordingly, to expect a **greater reward** for the risk taken in granting it, if indeed it decides to proceed at all.

Activity

What secured lending can be agreed within your organisation by branch staff?

13.2.1 Mortgages for property purchase

A loan made to a customer who requires funds to purchase their own home is known as a **mortgage loan**, and the loan is secured by a **charge** over the borrower's property. It is usually a long-term commitment over a twenty- and sometimes a thirty-year period, tied into the customer's expected retirement date. There are two elements to be repaid:

◆ the loan capital;

◆ the interest element.

Mortgage loan repayments are generally made **monthly**, although many mortgage loans allow lump sum reductions should the customer wish to make such payments.

Mortgages can be divided into the following types:

◆ **Repayment mortgages**: these provide for the repayment of both interest and capital throughout the life of the mortgage. They suit borrowers who want **certainty** that if they keep up regular monthly repayments, the whole debt will be paid off at the end of the mortgage term. Repayment mortgages are sometimes also referred to as 'capital and interest mortgages' or 'principal and interest' mortgages.

Each month, the borrower makes a payment, part of which is interest and part representing capital. Initially, when the capital outstanding is at its highest, most of each monthly payment comprises interest but as time passes and the loan reduces, interest is being calculated on an ever-decreasing capital sum. Rather than the monthly repayments falling because of this, they are kept at the same level and so later monthly payments are made up mostly of capital. The lender will advise the borrower to purchase **life assurance** that mirrors the term of the loan, so that if the borrower dies during the mortgage term the loan will be repaid by the insurance policy.

◆ **Interest-only mortgages**: with this type of mortgage only **interest** is repaid during the life of the mortgage, with the capital being repaid at the end of the term. Interest-only mortgages may be divided into the following groups:

– Interest-only offerings that rely on an **investment vehicle**, so that while only interest is repaid during the mortgage term, the investment (such as a pension or ISA) is intended to repay the capital balance at the end. The mortgagor will pay interest every month, and at the same time contribute to the monthly savings vehicle. Such mortgages are generally described in terms of the investment repayment vehicle associated with them (for example, pension mortgage, ISA mortgage) but they are all kinds of interest-only mortgage. It is worth noting here that if the investment performs well, there may be some **surplus** left at the end, but the converse is also true; there may be a risk of a **shortfall** if returns are poor.

– Mortgage products that require interest payments only, with the borrower relying on some completely *independent* source of money to provide the capital repayment, for example an **expected inheritance** or **external investment programme**. These are what some lenders regard as true interest-only mortgage offerings. They are much less common than the former type, but some private banks offer them to customers who expect to come into capital sums to repay their loans, perhaps by way of inheritance.

The FSA **regulates** mortgage providers and the sale of mortgage loans. It is also important to remember that where an interest-only mortgage is coupled with a separate repayment vehicle, that vehicle may itself be an investment product, and advice in connection with it may constitute the giving of investment advice, which is 'investment business' and therefore a regulated activity. As we have seen examples include pensions and ISAs (and, less commonly now, endowment policies), all of which may be linked with an interest-only mortgage.

13.3   Types of interest rate

We looked at interest rates and how they are calculated in section 10.6. As we have seen in earlier sections of this topic, overdrafts and credit cards tend to have variable rates that move broadly in line with the Bank of England base rate, and personal loans have fixed rates that stay the same for the term of the loan.

There are several other ways in which interest can be levied on a mortgage loan. There is a variable rate, known as the **standard variable rate**, which is the default rate to which any mortgage that is not on a 'special deal' reverts. There are also at any given time a number of **fixed-rate** deals from which customers can choose, which will be, for example, between one and five years in duration. These often carry **arrangement fees** to set up and **penalty fees** for early repayment.

In addition to variable and fixed interest rates, other options are available to them.

◆ **Discounted-rate mortgages**: these generally offer a reduced rate for an initial period only. After this the mortgage loan rate will revert back to the lender's standard variable rate. The discount period can be from six months to several years. Lenders often offer these rates to people whom they consider to be attractive long-term customers – perhaps those who are unable to afford current standard rates but whose prospects are expected to improve, such as young professionals. Such deals can be used as a marketing tool, with lenders building in application fees and penalties for early repayment during the discount period to offset some of the costs.

◆ **Capped and collared mortgages**: these are variable-rate mortgages with an upper limit, or **cap**, above which the rate cannot go, and a lower limit, or **collar**, below which the rate cannot fall. Say, for example, that a customer has a mortgage with a cap of 6 per cent. If variable rates rise above 6 per cent they would still continue to pay 6 per cent. However, if they have a collar of 3 per cent and rates fall below 3 per cent, they would still have to pay the higher interest rate of 3 per cent. This arrangement protects the customer against very high interest rates and the lender against making a loss when rates are very low. Again, there will be an application fee and early repayment penalties.

◆ **Base-rate tracker**: the name might be a bit esoteric, but a base-rate tracker is actually just an interest rate that is directly related to the Bank of England's base lending rate. These deals can last for an agreed period, reverting to the lender's standard variable rate after that, or they can be for the whole mortgage term and known as a **lifetime tracker**. An example is where the interest rate is set at base rate plus 0.25 per cent for two years, or base plus 0.75 per cent for life. Most lenders set their standard variable rate at about 2 per cent over base rate, so effectively this is a type of discount deal. Every time the Bank of England changes its base rate, the interest rate will change by exactly the same amount.

There is one other type of mortgage loan that has specialist interest arrangements: the **offset mortgage**. The provider allows the customer to 'offset' savings balances against their mortgage debt and, by giving up earning interest on the savings, they pay less interest on their mortgage loan. Over a 25-year mortgage this could save a substantial amount as well as being tax efficient (because no tax is paid on the savings interest that the customer would have otherwise earned).

Some offset arrangements allow the customer to link current accounts and savings balances to the mortgage, while others just use a savings pot. They can be described in different ways, but essentially both work the same.

In the simplest type of offset, deposits are kept in separate accounts or 'pots', but linked for the purposes of interest calculation. If the customer puts more money on deposit the balance for interest calculation reduces; if money is withdrawn from the deposit the balance for interest calculation increases, thus affecting the amount of interest paid on the mortgage loan.

The first offset mortgages launched in the UK were **current account mortgages** (CAMs), linking a homeowner's current account with the mortgage. With CAMs, the bank account and mortgage were combined so customers viewed just one statement and saw one balance. For example, if there is £3,000 in the current account and the mortgage is £90,000, the customer's balance will register £87,000 overdrawn.

Again, the balance is calculated daily and the customer pays interest only on the balance. CAMs offer the same services as an ordinary bank account. Customers can also add any **savings** into the CAM account to reduce the debt balance. Any **other debts**, such as personal loans or credit card balances, can be transferred to the account. With both types of offset, borrowers usually make a regular monthly repayment, though this may not be strictly necessary. For repayment mortgages, this guarantees that the mortgage will be repaid at some future point, regardless of the offset.

The amount of choice can seem confusing for customers and they will need specialist advice to ensure they take the option that is most suitable for them.

Activity

> What mortgage interest rate deals are available to customers of your organisation at the present time?
>
> When do they expire?

13.4 Security

Security for loans can be taken over a variety of assets, the most typical being:

◆ land and property;

◆ certain kinds of investment such as stocks and bonds, equities, collective investment schemes, National Savings products;

◆ life assurance policies;

◆ cash.

The asset over which security is taken may not belong to the borrower (although it often does). As an alternative, loans can be secured by way of **guarantees** and **third-party security** (rights over assets owned by someone other than the borrower). An example would be where a parent guarantees the borrowing of their child – for example, where the son or daughter wishes to buy their first home and the lender wants some additional comfort. The lender may also insist on taking a charge over the home owned by the parents to support the guarantee.

Activity

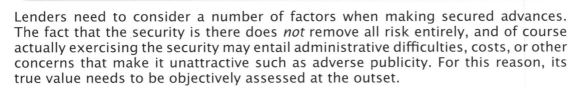
What types of asset does your organisation accept as security?

Lenders need to consider a number of factors when making secured advances. The fact that the security is there does *not* remove all risk entirely, and of course actually exercising the security may entail administrative difficulties, costs, or other concerns that make it unattractive such as adverse publicity. For this reason, its true value needs to be objectively assessed at the outset.

This often means that rather than lending 100 per cent of the value of the security, a lender will make a loan of a lesser amount – a sum adjusted down by an amount known as a '**margin**'.

Activity

When lending to a customer using their home as security, what margin does your organisation apply to the valuation?

Who undertakes the valuation of the customer's home?

The following are the main concerns to be borne in mind when considering what margin to apply:

◆ **Fluctuations in the asset's price**: most asset classes, property, stocks and shares, can go down as well as up in price, and between the date the loan is made and the date the security is realised that security could fall in value. Ultimately it may fail to cover the loan.

◆ **Expenses incurred in realising the asset**: these may include estate agent's fees and legal fees, depending on the nature of the asset.

◆ **Time taken to realise the asset**: the point here is that, once the lender has decided to take legal action and enforce its security, it may be some time before it can actually realise (sell) the security. This is particularly so in the case of property. During this period the capital amount of the loan may have been frozen; however, the lender may or may not decide to suspend interest charges. If interest continues to accumulate, the total amount owing may increase substantially before the sale proceeds of the security can be applied.

The offer of security itself should not influence a lender to make a loan that it would otherwise consider to be an unsound proposition. Taking security is costly and time consuming; lenders take it in the hope that they will not be forced to exercise it. The lender should be conscious of the amount to be taken, as it is not worthwhile for small sums or over assets that are difficult to control, such as jewellery or antiques.

However, security does provide valuable support should the borrower be unable or unwilling to keep up repayments. If the asset taken as security is of personal importance to the borrower, then they are more likely to try hard to maintain the loan repayments. This is especially so if the security is over the borrower's home and they run the risk of losing their home.

It is worth summarising briefly the circumstances in which security may be taken:

◆ Where the loan is to buy a **specific asset**, that asset itself may be used as security for the loan. An example is a mortgage loan to fund a property purchase.

◆ Where loan repayment is intended from the **proceeds** of a specific asset, that asset may be used as security for the loan. An example is where a bank lends money to a client against the security of an investment that will mature in the future, so that the eventual proceeds of the investment will repay the loan.

◆ Where the risks and consequences of the expected source of repayment failing are significant, it is necessary to have a clearly defined **alternative source**. For example, parents may be asked to guarantee a loan taken by one of their children because the child's income is only just sufficient to cover the loan repayments.

This third situation is the most difficult for the lender to assess and the assessment will be split into two areas: risk and consequences.

13.4.1 Risk

The assessment of the possibility of repayment failure will be determined by:

◆ the **margin** between income and commitments – how comfortably can the customer repay the borrowing from disposable income?

◆ the possibility of **major changes** in personal circumstances and life-cycle events, for instance, death, sickness, redundancy – can these risks be reduced by insurance?

◆ the **term of the lending**, as the risk of adverse changes is greater over the longer term than the shorter term.

13.4.2 Consequences

While the risks relate to the borrower's income and expenditure, when considering consequences it is the customer's assets and liabilities that are more important. In the absence of income it is the surplus of assets over liabilities that will provide repayment. We should therefore consider the following points.

◆ The size of the **surplus** in relation to the borrowing: a good margin is usually required. Valuation of assets should be on a '**forced sale basis**' and the lender should take into account any joint ownership, such as the matrimonial home, which obviously does not belong to just one party.

◆ The **speed** with which assets can be realised: a share portfolio containing a high proportion of publicly quoted companies is much easier to realise quickly than the matrimonial home.

◆ The borrower's likely **attitude** in adversity: will the customer be willing to dispose of the assets to satisfy debts?

In situations where the possibilities of repayment failure are significant and obtaining repayment from any alternative source looks difficult, serious consideration must be given to not lending at all. If the decision to go ahead is made then it should be made on a secured basis only.

Review questions

The following review questions are designed so that you can check your understanding of this topic.

The answers are provided at the end of these learning materials.

1. When a lender makes an unsecured borrowing facility available to a customer, what does it rely on for repayment?

2. What are the features of an overdraft?

3. How might a lender deal with a customer who has become over-borrowed?

4. Why are credit cards unsuitable for larger purchases over the longer term?

5. What are the features of a personal loan?

6. What are the benefits to a lender of taking security from a customer?

7. Which is the least risky for a customer — a repayment or an interest-only mortgage?

8. How does a customer benefit from a capped and collared mortgage?

9. What factors affect the margin applied to assets held as security?

10. When would a lender be most likely to take security?

Topic 14
Making credit decisions

Learning objective

After studying this topic students should be able to demonstrate a knowledge and understanding of the key principles of lending in relation to making credit decisions and post-drawdown events.

Introduction

There are five stages in any lending proposition.

1. **Introduction of the customer**: this is often covered by the account-opening process and the requirement to 'know your customer'.

2. **The application by the customer**: by a paper- or screen-based set of questions or a customer interview with an adviser.

3. **Review of the application**: this is to ensure that the information supplied is accurate and up to date and may involve double checking against other information — for example, the salary figures stated may be checked against salary slips from the customer's employer.

4. **Evaluation and assessment of the application**: an appraisal of the risks and the customer's ability to repay.

5. **Monitoring and control**: usually via the lender's computerised systems to ensure that repayment is going according to plan and any deviations from this are highlighted.

In this topic we are going to consider stages 4 and 5 and any changes that could affect the lending agreement, such as the addition of a new party to the lending agreement. We will also consider what happens if the customer defaults on the lending agreement and how a lender may seek to recover the debt.

14.1 Credit assessment

Credit assessment is the term given to how lenders **analyse** a request from a customer to lend money. There are various ways of doing this and in a retail banking context it tends to be technology led, with underwriters only looking at marginal propositions or those that fall outside the normal lending criteria. This approach applies to both personal customers and small businesses. However, applications from larger businesses with more complex requirements will require assessment by a lending manager and possibly the lender's credit committee; such applications are outside the scope of retail banking for our purposes.

Before examining the different techniques for credit assessment it is worth considering briefly the **credit culture** of the organisation, as this is the context in which lending decisions are made.

14.1.1 Credit culture

Credit culture is the **attitude** of the organisation to all matters relating to its management of its **credit risk**. Credit risk, put simply, is the risk of not being repaid. The skill of the lender is to ensure that money it has lent *is* repaid safely, along with an appropriate reward for the risk involved, which as we have seen earlier is a profitable interest charge. This risk must be managed well across the whole customer portfolio and for the different types of lending products. If an organisation is to manage its credit risk portfolio well it must fulfil the following criteria:

◆ It must have a credit culture that fits with the overall business and organisation of the lender and delivers a service that customers require. Sometimes it can be seen that the marketing section of the lender wants to sell a high volume of loans; however, in order to do so the lending department is asked to accept a higher credit risk by relaxing the lending criteria. The organisation may decide that it is acceptable to incur more losses in order to attain a higher profit and thus may pursue this as an agreed marketing strategy.

◆ It must have a credit assessment framework that is championed by the top management of the organisation. To avoid a conflict between the commercial aspects of the business and the management of losses, senior management have to be clear and be ready to back up the criteria set down for credit assessment.

◆ The type and level of risk the organisation is prepared to take must be set out clearly, together with the reward it expects to earn for given levels of risk, both at the individual lending and the portfolio level.

◆ It must establish the relative status and authority of the credit risk department and its relationship with those parts of the organisation focused on developing the business through making sales, perhaps at the expense of non-repayment.

◆ It must be willing to pay the cost of maintaining the culture, whether through training, computer systems or educating customers.

◆ It must be strong enough to withstand downturns in economic cycles. It has been evident in the recent economic cycle that a good proportion of lenders' credit culture could not withstand a downturn.

14.1.2 Credit assessment by underwriters

Assessment by underwriters is the traditional way in which all lending used to be assessed, following a face-to-face interview with the customer. It enabled the lender to use **experience and judgement** to assess a customer and perhaps pick up additional information that would not be available from a standard set of questions.

Review of the application would usually take the form of a lending **mnemonic**, which is effectively a checklist for the lender. Each bank has its own preferred list, which covers the canons (or rules) of lending. One of the most popular ones is **CAMPARI**, which covers the following factors.

◆ **Character**: it is not easy to assess a customer's character after an initial meeting, which is why a customer with a good track record would be preferred over one with no track record. There are some indicators that a lender can use to help assess the character of an individual:

— Has there been any previous borrowing and if so was it repaid satisfactorily?

— How reliable is the customer's word relating to the detail of the proposition?

— What does their employment record tell us about them?

◆ **Ability**: this relates to the borrower's ability to manage their financial affairs. Further questions a lender would seek to ask are:

— Does the customer make exaggerated or over-optimistic claims that seem out of line with the rest of the information given?

— If the customer is new, can we see bank statements from previous providers?

— What is the customer's net worth ie assets less liabilities? In the absence of income it is this figure that will provide repayment.

◆ **Margin**: this relates to the interest rate charged, commission and other relevant fees/costs. The interest rate charged will be a reflection of the risk involved in the lending, and the commission and other fees will reflect the amount of administration work involved. The more risky the proposition from the lender's perspective the higher the interest margin that will be charged. Many lenders have their own internal guidelines on this, depending on the organisational appetite for different types of borrowing.

◆ **Purpose**: the lender will seek to ensure that the purpose is acceptable. It may be that the customer is taking on a project that is too ambitious and could easily fail. It may therefore be in the customer's best interests if the lending is declined, with the lender putting forward a logical explanation of its reasons for rejecting the application. The term of the loan should also match the purpose for which it is required ie the term of a loan for a car should not really exceed the expected useful lifetime of the car where it has some value – most lenders would say five years in this instance.

◆ **Amount**: this should be in proportion to the customer's own resources and contribution. A reasonable contribution shows commitment and provides a buffer to the lender should problems occur. The lender should consider whether the customer is requesting too much or too little. By asking for too little the customer may have to approach the lender again later to increase the loan, incurring further costs, rather than asking for a larger amount in the first instance. The customer needs to allow for contingencies in the amount they request, especially in building-related projects.

◆ **Repayment**: this is where the main risk for the lender lies. It is important that the source of repayment is clear to the lender, and also the likelihood that the funds will be forthcoming. For example, if the funds are to come from the sale of a property, how likely is the sale to proceed at the amount the customer says and within the anticipated timescale? Where the source of repayment is from income the lender will need to see proof of income, especially where this is made up of bonuses or commissions. Often a lender will require a customer to undertake an income and expenditure budget planner to ensure that the customer's perception of the surplus funds available is an accurate one. The term of the loan should also match the repayment source – for example, a person looking for a mortgage loan should not really expect to be paying the loan after their retirement date, when their income is substantially reduced. We shall look at this aspect again in section 14.3.

◆ **Insurance (security)**: ideally the proposition should be viable without the need for security. However, for larger loans – and to ensure that the customer is committed to repayment – security is necessary, just in case repayment fails to materialise. The security taken for the loan should be commensurate with the proposition; asking for too much security, for example, could damage the relationship with the customer as well as causing unnecessary additional cost.

It is important that the customer understands the consequences of charging the asset to the lender. It is equally important that no advances of funds are made to the customer until all the security procedures have been completed. This would leave the lender in a position where the borrowing was unsecured and its rights to realise the asset diminished.

Once the above evaluation has been undertaken the lender will be in a position to weigh up the 'pros and cons' and decide whether to support the customer. The main factors are the assessment of the customer's ability to make repayment and an appreciation of what could go wrong, how likely that would be and how it would affect the lender's position.

At this point the lender may have a number of supplementary questions to clarify the proposition further. It may be that the proposition has to be 're-engineered' into a more acceptable format – for example a larger deposit from the customer or an extension of the term – and the lender would seek the customer's assistance in doing this. The lender should then be in a position to make an offer to the customer, outlining the terms and conditions. These terms and conditions may also include cross sales which have been identified during the evaluation process.

Activity

> Research the lending mnemonic that is used in your organisation.
>
> What types of lending application would an underwriter use it for?

14.1.3 Credit scoring

Credit scoring evolved in retail banking in the 1980s to help lenders assess high volumes of information about large numbers of customers applying for credit. It combines two elements, a '**scorecard**' of questions and the **statistical analysis** of certain responses to those questions.

The scorecard itself consists of a table of questions (known as characteristics) along with a list of potential answers for each one (known as attributes). Each of the attributes has a different value (or score) associated with it. The scorecard questions have been found to be relevant to an individual's likelihood of repayment and the total scorecard gives a statistical indication of the debt being repaid. Within the sample group there will be strong indicators that vary with factors such as age and demographics. The questions include a variety of things such as home ownership, length of time in employment and an automatic check with an external credit reference agency for any historical debt problems. Some of the questions may not seem relevant to the ability to repay; however, experience has shown that they do relate to a person's creditworthiness even if they are not an existing customer.

Activity

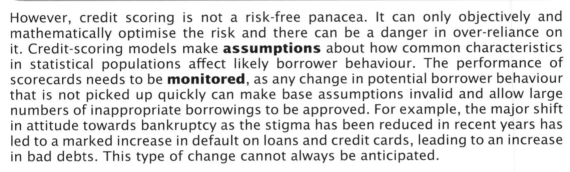

Research the questions used in your organisation's scorecard.

Which of these relate directly to a customer's financial situation?

However, credit scoring is not a risk-free panacea. It can only objectively and mathematically optimise the risk and there can be a danger in over-reliance on it. Credit-scoring models make **assumptions** about how common characteristics in statistical populations affect likely borrower behaviour. The performance of scorecards needs to be **monitored**, as any change in potential borrower behaviour that is not picked up quickly can make base assumptions invalid and allow large numbers of inappropriate borrowings to be approved. For example, the major shift in attitude towards bankruptcy as the stigma has been reduced in recent years has led to a marked increase in default on loans and credit cards, leading to an increase in bad debts. This type of change cannot always be anticipated.

Credit-scoring models need a large and broadly similar statistical base to work effectively: this means many borrowers with similar characteristics who can be readily compared with one another and for whom common conclusions can be deduced. It might be thought that for a personal borrower the most valuable indicator of propensity to repay would be disposable income. However, this has not proved to be the case, because customers can interpret the term in different ways and this makes it subjective. On the other hand, factual data, such as having a telephone line, is more objective and it can be checked easily. It is evidence of relatively permanent residence as well as regular financial obligation in the form of telephone bills. Having a fixed telephone line has proved a good indicator for credit-scoring models.

Credit scoring therefore has advantages and disadvantages. The advantages include the following:

◆ Credit scoring **removes the subjective human element** of the assessment process. Thus an individual lending manager cannot be swayed in their judgement by personal factors.

◆ Through the use of **technology** the lender gains the **ability to process many applications fast** – a key factor in borrower satisfaction. It could be said that this is even more critical in the case of rejected applications, where a swift rejection is better than one preceded by a lengthy wait.

◆ It **brings costs down** because it is automated and does not require lengthy manual credit assessment by skilled staff.

◆ Lending institutions can apply and change **a standard set of lending criteria** across their branch and other delivery networks quickly through the centralised computer programme.

◆ Credit-scoring models are always being **improved**, enhancing the robustness of their assessment of potential borrowers.

◆ The applicant does **not need to have a track record** with the lender on which the scorecard is based.

However, disadvantages can include the following:

◆ Individuals whose applications are rejected can feel **aggrieved**, and this may made worse because there is no single identifiable reason; their total score based on an average total of different factors may simply be insufficient and no letter of explanation is sent.

◆ There may also be a perception that they have been **rejected** by a 'mere computer'.

◆ Credit scoring can be seen as **inflexible** and is inappropriate to some specialist lending situations; however, the counter argument to this is that applicants who are 'borderline failures' can receive a response quickly and be rerouted to a lending underwriter who can look more closely at their special circumstances.

◆ The **Data Protection Act 1998** gives 'data subjects' certain rights, including the **right to object to automatic processing** of decisions relating to them. Few individuals have objected to credit scoring using this right, but that may be because of a lack of awareness of the terms and conditions of their application.

◆ Some customers could become skilled in anticipating the 'right answers' to achieve a satisfactory score; consequently some form of **validation** or outside check is also necessary to back up the results produced by a credit-scoring system.

The final disadvantage listed above may be an argument for using credit-scoring techniques as a method of screening in potentially viable applicants, rather than the definitive method of screening out unviable ones. Credit scoring is only as good as the analysis and monitoring techniques used to ensure it is working effectively and its continued relevance to the population group. We can see that it is not infallible, but it does help lending institutions to improve their balance between increased lending volume and limiting bad debts.

14.1.4 Behavioural scoring

Credit scoring can be a useful tool for assessing applicant risk before business is taken on; but technology-based screening need not stop at the application stage, and such tools can also be highly effective for risk management of an existing loan portfolio.

One such tool is 'behavioural scoring'. Behavioural scoring uses information on live, operational accounts to support risk management decisions on existing accounts. This clearly has some parallels with credit scoring, but has some further advantages, including the following:

◆ Information is available at first hand, derived directly from the lender's own database. It gives objective analysis based on experience and as such it is therefore possibly more **reliable** than that obtained from external sources.

◆ The information is as **up to date** as the sources from which it is pulled: given that these are in-house information systems, this should mean very up to date.

Several types of model are directly involved in assessing the ability to repay, including:

◆ **general account management**: which can highlight developing problems, support the annual account review process and assist in setting or changing credit limits and making authorisation decisions;

◆ **usage**: used in connection with plastic cards, these analyse current spending patterns in order to predict likely future patterns.

They can also be used for a variety of other management aims, depending on the lender's risk management strategy and the information available. For example:

◆ **attrition**: this model assesses the likelihood of accounts becoming inactive and closing;

◆ **recoveries**: this is used when an account is already in default; it can be used to help select the repayment schedule to which the customer is most likely to adhere.

Activity

What does your organisation use behavioural scoring for?

Behavioural scorecards help management to use the available information to achieve two potentially conflicting aims:

◆ minimising account risk; and

◆ optimising the lending balances advanced to good, non-defaulting borrowers.

In short, they help managers to achieve the optimum balance for profitability.

They can also identify **cross-selling opportunities**, helping a provider to further improve the profitability of its customer base by tailoring and targeting offerings appropriately. By demonstrating to its borrowers that it has a good understanding of their needs, a lender can improve customer satisfaction, retention and profitability.

14.2   The role of credit reference agencies

A credit bureau – also known as a credit reference agency – collects information about individuals and companies, and organises, stores and supplies this information to customers. Credit bureaux can be used as a **source of information** in their own right, or **to verify information** provided by a third party. The most commonly used in the UK are Equifax, Experian and Call Credit.

Credit bureaux are a commonly used resource in assessing the **ability of a potential borrower to repay** and they form an automatic part of the credit-scoring process. They can provide an invaluable resource for assessing the accuracy of applicant details and for identifying potentially fraudulent or non-creditworthy applications.

Credit bureaux get their information from a variety of sources, including:

◆ information in the public domain:

◆ electoral rolls;

◆ county court judgment records (CCJs).

Other sources include:

◆ information supplied by lenders;

◆ searches made by other potential lenders in the past six months that could suggest debt elsewhere;

◆ shared industry information databases covering material such as fraud and 'gone-aways';

◆ databases supplying geodemographic information.

The results of such enquiries may show that the applicant for credit has a poor credit history, owing, for example, to:

◆ late mortgage, rent or credit payments;

◆ county court judgments (CCJs), which are records of unpaid debts;

◆ individual voluntary arrangements (IVAs); or

◆ bankruptcy.

The term used for such cases is '**adverse credit**' or impaired credit; it does not necessarily mean that an individual will be unable to borrow, but they will be regarded with great care and avoided by some lenders. Others specialise in this area and structure products to the needs of the adverse credit market; for example, there are specialist mortgage packages aimed at such borrowers.

Under the provisions of the Data Protection Act 1998, individuals have a right of access to data held on them by credit bureaux. However, this only covers enquiries about individuals in their personal capacity.

Activity

> Visit www.equifax.co.uk, www.experian.co.uk or www.callcreditcheck.com and note what information individuals can find about their credit rating and how they can go about obtaining this.

14.3   Serviceability and budgeting

The repayment of an overdraft or loan, particularly a mortgage loan, will depend on a customer's ability to **service** that borrowing; in other words, their ability to make repayments when they are due. For a customer and the lender to ensure that this can be done, a budget for the customer will need to be prepared.

The need to budget underpins all forms of financial planning. At its simplest, it reflects the need to have sufficient funds to purchase the necessities of daily living.

It also encompasses the need to determine how much can be spent on other items: on capital purchases; on leisure pursuits and holidays; on provision for a secure retirement.

Budgeting is the process of planning future **income** and **expenditure**. In other words, a budget predicts the income on which the customer might be able to rely in the future and where it might be spent. This is also known as '**cash flow analysis**', because it looks at what cash is coming in, what is going out and the net effect.

If a budget has more income than expenditure, it is in **surplus** – that is, extra money. If there is no surplus and the customer is just making ends meet, the budget is **balanced**. If the customer is spending more than they have coming in, then one of two things is happening: they are either using savings or they are using debt. Either way, the budget is running a **deficit**.

If someone finds that they are spending more than they have coming in, they may need to make changes. There are two options:

◆ obtain more income; or

◆ spend less.

Many savings products can be used to help budget for future capital and income needs, but advisers must be careful not to put pressure on the client's current and future income when selling products paid for out of that income. An increase in mortgage interest rates, for example, could push a family's expenditure beyond its means. It might be argued that the need to balance the budget on a weekly/monthly basis is not as great as it once was, as a result of the easy availability of credit, but all borrowing must be repaid at some point, and advisers should exercise caution when considering clients' likely future income and expenditure levels.

The customer will be required to prepare a budget as part of a mortgage lending application form. From this the mortgage adviser can see what surplus is available (or not) to meet the mortgage repayment amount. Lenders have certain criteria that they will accept – usually the mortgage repayment should be no more than 35–40 per cent of the customer's monthly income after tax. The adviser is checking the **affordability** of the repayments against the income the customer has. If the customer has a special deal for the first few years of the mortgage that keeps the repayments lower than if the mortgage loan was at the standard variable rate, the adviser will advise the customer of the amount of the repayments when the special deal expires (assuming base rate remains the same). This should ensure that the customer is fully aware of the costs of the mortgage and can build this into their long-term plans.

Activity

> Research the items that are used in income and expenditure budgets for customers applying for mortgages with your organisation.
>
> What mortgage affordability ratio is used to access serviceability?

14.4 Credit limit management

Credit limit management is a way of monitoring customer accounts and, where appropriate, offering increased credit limits without the customer needing to apply for them. In a similar way to the behavioural scoring described above, the computerised system makes a **regular review** of the transactions on customer accounts, linked to checks with a credit reference agency. The account history directly influences the value of customer card limits so those customers who pay promptly have higher limits than those that have a poor payment history. The same system will be used to identify the overdue accounts and generate letters to customers requesting payment.

This computerised system helps to reduce costs for the credit card company and increases business to those customers with a good track record. It should also assist in monitoring those accounts where the situation is deteriorating.

14.5 Early repayment

Once a loan has been made there are many reasons why customers may decide to repay borrowing early. They may have a large bonus or be the beneficiaries of an inheritance. If it is a mortgage loan they may move house and make new borrowing arrangements with a new provider.

When a mortgage is repaid it is known as **redemption** and the borrower is said to have '**vacated**' the mortgage (or, in Scotland, 'discharged'). When borrowers are considering repaying any debt they will have to pay any outstanding interest. If they have had a fixed or other special rate deal, such as a discounted rate, they must also pay any penalties due.

In the same way, partial repayment can be made but may be subject to conditions. The lender should advise them of these conditions at the time the loan is taken. Partial repayment can mean that:

◆ payments continue at the same level but the term is reduced;

◆ the term is kept the same but the monthly repayments are reduced.

14.6 Other changes in the lending relationship

There are a variety of other events that can change the lending relationship after a customer has drawn down borrowing from a lender. We covered a number of these in section 12.3 and they are:

◆ third-party operation of the account;

◆ powers of attorney being granted;

◆ bankruptcy and insolvency;

◆ death of the borrower;

◆ mental incapacity;

◆ removal of parties from an account, perhaps through divorce or separation.

However, there can also be other changes:

◆ **Changes to the terms and conditions of the borrowing**: these will most commonly be changes to the interest rates. Lenders commit to advising customers of such changes either by press advertisements or, more usually, by letter advising of the new monthly repayment amount. There may be other changes – for example, to fees and charges – that lenders advise as soon as practically possible, or, for mortgages, within the annual statement of account.

◆ **Addition of parties to an account**: this is particularly relevant in mortgage lending where the new party's income will be taken into consideration within the serviceability of the loan. The lender will wish to verify the identity of the new party and their credit status, so the checks that are made are similar to those made at the opening of an account. The lender may also wish to revalue the property, as market conditions may have changed since the property was purchased, and take the opportunity of asking for additional security to protect its position.

Arrears and default are the most frequent change and we will consider these in the next section.

14.7 Debt and arrears

As we saw in section 12.3, there may well be a simple explanation for a problem on a customer's account. However, this may only be the tip of the iceberg and the customer may have a number of other debts in the background. The action taken will depend on whether the account is in **excess**, ie over an agreed limit, or whether there are **arrears**, ie missed loan repayments. The period over which the situation has existed – whether this is 30, 60, 90 or 120 days – is also relevant. The longer the time that has elapsed, the greater the problem is considered to be.

The first step to be taken when a problem becomes apparent is to **contact the customer** by letter or telephone. This will be a request for funds to correct the position or for contact from the customer so that the situation can be discussed. A reasonable time should be given for the customer to respond, say, two weeks.

If no response is received, **firmer action** will be required, which should follow a strict timetable and adopt a logical approach. The second contact will therefore take the form of a stronger letter or a further attempt at telephone contact: the latter option, if feasible, is likely to have a better result.

The refusal of the customer to respond to the first letter is a warning signal in itself and the lender should consider tougher action, which for a current account could be:

◆ returning cheques, if the lender has not already done so;

◆ cancelling standing order and direct debit mandates;

◆ cancelling any unadvised internal limits on the account;

◆ requesting the return of the customer's cheque book and cheque/debit card;

◆ cancelling debit cards so the customer is unable to use them at retail outlets or in ATMs;

◆ searching with a credit reference agency in case there are problems elsewhere.

Activity

> What action does your organisation take if a customer ignores letters regarding unauthorised borrowing?

The lender needs to avoid sending a steady stream of threatening letters and then doing nothing. Often, one of the actions above will prompt the customer into contact; however, a persistently defaulting debtor will be used to this sort of treatment and find it easy to ignore.

Once contact has been made with the customer, it is important to establish an understanding and **show empathy** towards them. After checking that the contact details are correct, the lender should give support that will help the customer to **correct the position** or **establish a realistic repayment programme**. This may mean helping the customer to prioritise their payments and essential expenses. If the customer does not feel this is possible then the lender needs to establish why this is the case. The customer will need to be informed, in a polite way, of the consequences of not being able to meet the lender's request. Care should be taken that the customer does not perceive this as harassment. Any promises to pay need to be **monitored** to ensure that the agreement is honoured.

14.7.1 Collections and recoveries

Where an account is already performing poorly, it has become '**delinquent**'. This will be typified by arrears, ie the borrower has missed making repayments according to the loan agreement, and/or excesses, where their borrowings are repeatedly above their approved credit limit.

Solutions to delinquent debt generally involve the account administration team calling in specialist support colleagues to assist in dealing with the situation. Many lenders employ a team who step in and take over when warning signals are spotted. This has the twin advantages of:

◆ allowing difficult cases to be handled by those with expertise;

◆ letting the rest of the team concentrate on their core competencies, whether these be assessing loan propositions or handling the ongoing administration of such loans.

Most larger lenders are highly organised about how they handle delinquent accounts. Arrears are categorised in terms of magnitude and/or term, with short-term loans arrears typically being seen as those between one and three payments overdue. Their processes often follow the steps set out below.

14.7.2 The collections team

The collections team handles those accounts that are as yet **not seriously in arrears**. Their main aim is to achieve a return to acceptable account performance without escalating matters to the next stage. They aim to collect the maximum amount while helping the customer return to a normal payment pattern, and without souring relations. A skilled collections team can actually enhance long-term relationships with a customer, rather than alienating them.

They will undertake a full **reappraisal** of the creditworthiness of the borrower and their prospects for repaying the loan. Any security held will be examined promptly to ensure that there are no deficiencies in the way it has been taken, and that it has not deteriorated in value.

From this assessment of the current and likely future position an action plan will be agreed, which is likely to include encouraging the borrower to 'manage for cash'. This means taking actions that will i**mprove their cash flow** generally and hence their ability to service the debt.

The action plan may also include a recommendation to the credit committee that the loan be **repriced**, either upwards (to reflect the increasing risk) or outwards (spread over a longer period so as to reduce monthly payments to a more manageable level).

It might also include a recommendation for a **refinancing** package. This referral to the credit committee may not be practical for high volumes of lending, where individual discretion may be allowed up to certain limits.

Refinancing takes the form of a **consolidation loan** to pay off the existing loan with the provider and other loans that the borrower has outstanding, so as to bring all the borrowings under one roof. The team will make a direct payment to the other lenders so as to minimise the danger of funds being diverted for other uses. The borrower then has the advantage of a single consolidated loan to one lender, with whom they can work out a single, realistic repayment package. The team has the certainty of some control over the situation and (provided the borrower does not immediately go out and arrange further borrowings with new lenders) knows the borrower's overall status. This arrangement can also **protect the long-term relationship** with the borrower, who may grow into a valuable customer over time and with the benefit of a fresh start.

Where no refinancing package can be arranged, and the borrower's prospects of repaying the loan appear limited, the team may recommend **removing the loan** from the lender's portfolio. This can mean, for example, that the lender may encourage a borrower whose account is not yet seriously delinquent, but who is exhibiting warning signs (late payments, cross-firing), to take their borrowings to another lender. This assumes that the story is not yet so bad that no other borrower would take the customer on. Alternatively, the next stage is action for recovery, and prompt action is required.

14.7.3 The recoveries team

The recoveries team takes over from the collections team once it is apparent that an ongoing solution cannot be achieved and that the customer is not going to be profitable in the long term. They aim to recover as much as is possible and thereafter to **sever the relationship**. This is the stage of the process at which a **default notice** is served on the customer and the need for **legal action** arises. The recoveries process frequently involves the need to trace absconded debtors, recover cards and maybe outsource to a **debt recovery agency**.

Where a borrower has moved, the lender may be able to track down some information as to their location through the Gone Away Information Network (GAIN) database. It can be used in the context of defaults, because the database contains the new addresses of those 'gone aways' who are successfully tracked down.

Review questions

The following review questions are designed so that you can check your understanding of this topic.

The answers are provided at the end of these learning materials.

1. What is 'credit risk'?

2. What does the mnemonic CAMPARI stand for?

3. Why has credit scoring become a popular way of assessing lending propositions?

4. How does behavioural scoring differ from credit scoring?

5. From where do credit bureaux collect their information?

6. What is 'adverse' credit?

7. What is a budget? Why is it important?

8. If the customer does not respond to a letter from their lender requesting contact to discuss an unauthorised overdraft, what stronger action can a lender take to control the debt?

9. How does a collections team handle a delinquent debt?

10. What is the purpose of the recoveries team?

© *ifs* School of Finance 2011

Topic 15
Customer service

Learning objective

After studying this topic students should be able to demonstrate a knowledge and understanding of the importance of delivering high standards of customer service.

Introduction

We can all think of examples of good and bad customer service and the impact that it has. The service we receive can be through a variety of media, whether this is face to face, on the phone or via the Internet. Each of these delivery channels has its own challenges and opportunities in the way customers perceive that service and, as we shall see, what one customer may think is excellent service may be considered less than average by another.

There are some issues that financial services providers have to face in meeting customer expectations and measuring satisfaction levels. This has to be achieved while making profitable customer sales, on which income is based, in a way that is ethical and within the rules set down by the regulators.

Sometimes there will be a breakdown in the service delivered and customers will wish to make complaints. There is a set process that financial service providers should follow to ensure that customers are dealt with promptly and efficiently. In section 3.2 and section 7.3 we looked at what happens if customers are not satisfied with the outcome of the provider's investigation procedure and at the role of the Financial Ombudsman Service. If a provider can deal with a complaint promptly, efficiently and to the customer's satisfaction this will enhance the customer service experience. As such, complaints from customers, while they are not ideal, should be viewed as an opportunity to build customer relationships.

15.1 What is customer service?

Customer service is the provision of **service** to customers before, during and after a purchase. We will go on to look at the characteristics of service as these differ from those of a product that the customer can see and touch.

Service can be said to part of the overall **customer value proposition**. It is a series of activities designed to enhance the level of customer satisfaction – that is, the feeling that a product or service has met the customer expectation. However, customer expectations are all different depending on their prior experiences and personal values.

Activity

> Make a list of the features of what you believe to be good service.
>
> Ask your colleagues what they believe to be good service.
>
> What are the similarities and differences?
>
> What are the implications for your organisation?

Customer service may be provided face to face, for example in the branch, or on the telephone by a customer adviser, or by automated means over the Internet, which is **self-service**.

Other factors that form part of the customer value proposition are the price paid, the products used and the brand image. For financial services providers, whose business is largely based on service, the quality of customer service plays an important role in an organisation's ability to generate income and revenue and to retain and attract customers.

15.2 Financial services characteristics and how this impacts on service delivery

Like other services, the financial services sector has characteristics that pose a number of challenges for creating successful customer relationships. The characteristics are **intangibility**, **inseparability**, **heterogeneity** and **perishability**. The following sections will evaluate these characteristics in relation to financial services.

15.2.1 Intangibility

This is the most fundamental difference between a product and a service. Services are actions, processes or performances that are based on your **experience** of them rather than being assessed using physical senses, such as sight, sound, smell and touch. A prospective purchaser of a product such as a television can examine it for physical integrity, appearance, sound and visual quality. Many advertising claims relating to these tangible properties can be verified by inspection prior to purchase. On the other hand, services have **few tangible properties** that can be evaluated prior to purchase. This means they are **difficult to evaluate**.

There are two particular aspects associated with intangibility for financial services:

◆ In making the product difficult to grasp mentally, it compounds the already complex consumer decision-making process when purchasing.

◆ Products cannot be displayed or demonstrated to customers, requiring creativity in the advertising and trial of products.

To overcome this issue the organisation can incorporate tangible features in its service offerings. Many financial services, for example, contain **tangible elements** on which the service can be judged or evaluated, such as the branches, ATMs, account statements and promotional literature. If the financial services provider wishes to convey the idea that its services are quick and efficient, it could concentrate on a bright, clutter-free interior in its branches. Office equipment, such as computers, desks and staff uniforms, should look modern. The bank's advertisements and other communications should suggest efficiency, with clean and simple designs and carefully chosen words that communicate the bank's positioning. If these factors create the **impression** for the consumer that they are receiving a service that is reliable, professional and efficient, then the chances of creating a long-term relationship with customers increase.

The decision to market financial services on the Internet poses a different challenge because the facilities described above are unavailable for consumer evaluation. In this instance the provider can concentrate on creating and maintaining a website that is easy to use, aesthetically appealing, informative and that conveys the brand values.

Activity

How does your organisation use tangible features to highlight characteristics of the service offering?

15.2.2 Inseparability

Inseparability results from services being processes or experiences. The service becomes a performance in 'real time' in which the consumer co-operates with the provider. With financial services it may be argued that advice is produced and consumed simultaneously. If you receive advice about investing in a pension scheme, the results of the advice will not be known until the point of maturity several years later. This can make **consumer evaluation difficult**, especially with complex financial products such as pensions and investments.

Inseparability adds to the **difficulty of consistent quality control** because service production and consumption take place simultaneously. Customer satisfaction will be highly dependent on what happens in 'real time', including actions of employees and the interactions of employees and customers. This underlines the need for care in staff selection, training and evaluation.

Activity

What does your organisation do to monitor the quality of staff interactions with customers?

15.2.3 Heterogeneity

Heterogeneity means 'diversity in character'. Some services have greater potential than others for this diversity, from **highly customised** to **highly standardised** services. There has been a tendency to view the variations in quality or the inability to apply a consistent performance over time as a problem. The greater the human involvement, the greater potential for variation in service quality.

Financial services providers are predominantly people-based institutions; traditionally, most customers would interact with staff either face to face in branches, or over the telephone. Yet technology has enabled the service offering to become more standardised through the use of ATMs, automated-telephone and online banking.

While this standardisation through technology may be of benefit from the customer's perspective, **variations** in service quality and inconsistent performance will only **increase the risk** associated with purchase. Even though it may be possible to stardardise the marketing and delivery of, for example, an investment product, the final outcome may still be uncertain as a result of factors outside the control of the financial provider. For example, two people may invest the same sum of money in the same pension for the same length of time, but because they started the pension at different times they may be affected by different economic conditions, so the returns may be different for each investor. A customer experiencing a good return may be satisfied with the quality of the investment. Conversely, the person experiencing a poor return will conclude that the investment was a poor product and may decline to purchase other services from the company.

Potential problems associated with this factor can be avoided by maintaining **clear communication** with the consumer to keep them notified of the product's performance. This is why care should also be taken to determine the consumer's **attitude to risk** before making an investment. In cases where investments are performing badly, several financial institutions have been warning their investors about the need either to top up their investments or seek alternative funds.

15.2.4 Perishability

Services differ from goods in that they **cannot be stored**. A producer of cars that is unable to sell all its stocks can store cars for future sale. While this may not be an ideal situation, the issue of perishability for the service supplier is that it presents an inability to build and maintain stocks. It is argued that fluctuations in demand cannot be accommodated in the same way as for goods. This was evident when the launch of Intelligent Finance, the new Halifax bank, was delayed as the bank's senior managers predicted that their IT systems would be unable to cope with the demand for its services. Rather than disappoint customers, the bank postponed the launch until it could be confident of no embarrassing hitches. When demand exceeds capacity, customers are likely to be sent away disappointed, since there will be no stock levels available for back up. It is an important task for the provider to find ways of smoothing demand levels to match capacity.

Demand forecasting and creative planning are therefore important and challenging decision areas. The fact that services cannot be returned or resold also implies a need for strong **recovery strategies** when things go wrong.

When demand rises, service providers have the options to:

◆ work with larger groups so that more customers can be serviced simultaneously (for example, a pop concert can cater for a larger audience if it is held in an open-air venue instead of a concert hall);

◆ work faster;

◆ train staff to perform tasks and utilise time more efficiently;

◆ add more resources, for example, through the use of call centres, which try to build flexibility into work patterns to cope with demand;

◆ use alternative delivery channels, such as the Internet.

Activity

> What does your organisation do in response to problems associated with perishability?

15.3 Impact of online delivery for service concepts

We have mentioned that online delivery allows customers to **self-serve**. This is a cheaper alternative for the provider as it takes mundane transaction work away from staff, who are then available to spend time advising customers and making sales. However, online customers may have raised expectations due to the immediacy of the media. They expect higher standards in terms of convenience, speed of delivery, competitive prices and choice. They also want, indeed expect, to be in control, secure and safe.

As financial services products are essentially intangible and information based, they can be delivered directly online and do not necessarily need to be supplemented with traditional service delivery outlets. In many ways technology and, specifically, the Internet have minimised the issues stemming from the unique characteristics of the service product, particularly when these products can easily be commoditised. Specific areas where online services can be perceived as superior to traditional delivery include the following:

◆ **Reduced time dependence**: 24/7 access to websites reduces the service provider's need to have extended opening hours and allows the consumer to make first contact (website/email) at their leisure, rather than within a set time frame, as is required for phone or direct contact.

◆ **Consistent service delivery**: websites can provide a consistent performance in customer transactions.

◆ **Consistent imagery and branding**: careful selection of a site design can be instrumental in creating effective branding. The provision of a well-organised website can enhance consumer loyalty, in much the same way as a clean, attractively decorated bank branch with friendly staff.

◆ **Customer-led customisation**: consumers can work within the elements of a website that represent most value and significance to their own interests, for example, identifying which investment product suits their needs.

◆ **Consumer empowerment**: this has arisen from the range of choice for service delivery across the Internet. When buying financial services products, for example, it is much easier for consumers to compare and contrast competitors simply by visiting the different websites from the convenience of their homes.

◆ **Effective separation of production and consumption**: the producer of a service is able to upload information about their product or service that can be consumed in their absence.

Activity

> What might be the downsides of online delivery of services?

15.4 The importance of service quality in retail banking

It is true that online self-service has provided customers with improved convenience and removed the need to queue in the branch every week to undertake mundane transactions. However, this and other changes to delivery channels have **distanced customers from their providers**. It has become more difficult for providers to engage with customers, so improving sales and therefore increasing profits. The more successful providers will have been able to maximise the customer service experience whatever channel the customer chooses to use.

In order to improve the service quality, there are a number of steps that providers could undertake.

◆ Ensure top management commitment to whatever customer service programme is in place: senior level endorsement is critical to getting buy-in and making customer service a priority throughout the organisation.

◆ Have documented service standards that cover all aspects of the customer interaction, whether this is in relation to staff uniforms or how to handle a customer complaint.

◆ Provide training (and ongoing coaching) so staff understand what service quality means for them and their role in the organisation. Adjust staff appraisal systems to reflect the standards required.

◆ Put in place a complaints-handling system that encourages the logging of complaints and enable employees to take primary responsibility for handling those complaints.

◆ Run internal satisfaction surveys to ensure that all back-office functions support the frontline employees in delivering service quality.

◆ Have a customer satisfaction reporting system that collects regular data on which action can be taken and training put in place for employees.

◆ Celebrate success to reward employees for delivering sales and service quality.

Activity

> In what other ways does your organisation seek to improve service quality?

The advantage of undertaking all this activity is that if customers are happy with the service they receive, they are likely to be more loyal, have a greater likelihood to buy again and be less likely to defect to another provider. It is also likely that they will be less price sensitive to increases in costs of the service.

A superior service that the competition cannot match provides consumers with a reason for choosing the provider and staying with them. This does presuppose, however, that it is going to be a level of service that is not easily copied by competitors. Enhanced service quality leads to enhanced loyalty, retention of customers and therefore improved business performance (we will consider loyalty in more depth in Topic 16). It is important that service is delivered **consistently** across all the channels and that each channel is equally **reliable**: if a customer visits a branch, they are served by a cashier within a few minutes, if they ring the call centre they are not kept waiting in a queue, and if they use the website to view their account transactions it is available at whatever time they choose.

15.5 Ethics and social responsibility

An organisation's stance on ethics and social responsibility will be evident in the delivery of service and sales. The Cambridge Dictionary defines ethics as '*a system of accepted beliefs which control behaviour, especially such a system based on morals*'. The way in which an organisation **interacts** with its customers and society will reflect the ethics of the organisation. The interaction can take place in brand and corporate messages, advertising, sales literature and product descriptions, channel management, the customer contract, customer service or the handling of customer complaints and feedback.

Activity

> The list below suggests a number of ethical commandments.
>
> How would you rate your organisation's behaviour against each commandment?
>
> Are there any other commandments you would add to the list?
>
> Thou shalt:
>
> — not mislead customers for the sake of a sale;
>
> — be honest at all times about your service and what it does;
>
> — not lie about competitors;
>
> — not supply a second-best product because it provides a better margin;
>
> — treat all customers as equal;
>
> — endeavour to explain complex terms rather than use them as a cover for profit-taking;

> — not sell one thing and provide another;
>
> — not do something 'under orders' that you know breaks one of the above rules.

Customers today are familiar with pressured sales techniques. The technique of trying to pressurise people into purchasing a product should have no place in financial services, where there is an obvious requirement for serious consideration of, say, the details of an insurance policy or savings plan and for the establishment of trust over a long period of time with the seller. The technique is not in itself illegal; however, trying to hurry a customer into buying a product is unethical. To employ **aggressive sales tactics** will lead to loss of confidence and trust in an organisation; and ultimately to poor sales and a possible fine from the regulator.

Even when a provider has a published code of ethics, staff can still breach the terms of the code. The organisation needs to create an ethical approach to its way of dealing with customers – again, this process starts with senior management buy-in and support. One approach could be to ensure the marketing department has senior management approval for sales campaigns, and similar approval from the compliance officer and the ethics officer. The marketing team should have training on what is considered ethical within the company and this should also be communicated to the service and sales staff. These staff should be monitored for ethical behaviour and given the opportunity to feed back about marketing tactics that they feel will have a negative impact on achieving service and sales targets. The supervision of staff should include the monitoring of ethical standards. This should then feed into the overall customer experience and service levels given.

15.5.1 Corporate social responsibility

Corporate social responsibility (CSR) policy should function as a built-in, self-regulating mechanism whereby businesses monitor and ensure their adherence to law, ethical standards and international norms. Organisations embrace responsibility for the impact of their activities on the environment, consumers, employees, communities and stakeholders. Furthermore, businesses should proactively promote the public interest by encouraging community growth and development, and voluntarily eliminating practices that are harmful to the community, regardless of legality. Essentially, CSR is the **deliberate inclusion of public interest** into corporate mission, values and decision-making.

In July 2002, the UK financial services industry published a voluntary guidance on CSR. This guidance, which was produced by the FORGE Group (2002), was the first of its kind to be developed in the UK. The FORGE Group is a consortium of financial institutions and involves the British Bankers' Association and the Association of British Insurers. It follows the increasing pressure faced by the industry to demonstrate a positive response to managing its societal impact. Notably, the UK financial services industry has faced criticism over a number of issues relating to the management and delivery of its products and services, such as the mis-selling of pensions, closure of bank branches and the findings of an official review of retail banking that were published in the Cruickshank report in 2000.

More recently, banks have faced mounting criticism over bank charges and poor service. Banks have been responding to complaints about overcharging by giving compensation to a large number of customers. Customers and the regulators are becoming increasingly concerned about the behaviour of some of the large financial organisations, especially in the light of the economic crisis. There has been criticism of the handling of arrears, and lenders are more prepared to be lenient with customers in difficulty. This is an example where financial services providers have taken their corporate social responsibility seriously. However, this should not be a one-off, as CSR applies to a wide range of areas.

The voluntary **FORGE guidelines** were developed by an external stakeholder process and incorporated comments from a wide range of consultees, including the industry's trade associations, the government, mutual and investor-owned financial institutions, non-governmental organisations and special interest groups. The guidelines attempt to provide a definition of CSR that is 'appropriate' for the industry and to lay the foundations for the development of a demonstrable CSR agenda by financial services firms. The discussion of CSR in this guidance focuses on CSR values and the issues that are identified to be most relevant to the UK financial services sector.

The FORGE guidance identifies four areas of impact for CSR issues in the financial services industry, which are:

◆ the community;

◆ the marketplace;

◆ the workplace;

◆ the environment.

Figure 15.1 shows the areas in more detail.

Figure 15.1   The four FORGE areas of impact for CSR issues

While the FORGE guidance does not clearly define the parameters of these categories, it is implied that each has **key stakeholder groups**. Employees are the key concern in the workplace, while concerns about natural resources and surroundings and replenishing these resources come under the environment category. The marketplace is a key interface between business and society and the societal impact is made up of what a firm produces and how it buys and sells. The key stakeholder groups are customers, suppliers and competitors. The community largely relates to a broad conceptualisation of 'the neighbour' and to relationships of the firm with social structures and organisations.

An organisation with a good record of CSR will have a focus on employees in the workplace and customers in the marketplace. Both of these factors will affect the customer service delivered and the overall customer satisfaction.

Activity

> Visit www.bba.org.uk to review the FORGE guidance framework on Managing Climate Change in Financial Services.

15.5.1.1 Cultural awareness

Community is one of the four main topic areas in the FORGE model. At organisational level cultural awareness is a way that a business can respond to the needs of the community in which it operates. This will also enhance customer service at a local level. We covered how a financial services provider may do this in Topic 2 so for revision purposes it may be worth revisiting section 2.5.

Activity

> Research what your organisation does locally as part of its CSR activities.
>
> How do you think this impacts on how customers and the local community view your organisation?

15.6 Service standards and measurement

One of the challenges of setting and measuring service standards is the absence of absolute standards of service excellence; that is, one customer's idea of a disappointing service may be another's idea of service excellence. For instance, an infrequent traveller who has won a first-class air ticket may consider all aspects of the service to exceed their expectations, while a regular business traveller with higher expectations may express dissatisfaction if they feel that the check-in procedures are slow and the cabin crew inattentive.

In order to try to deliver good customer service across the organisation, there will be internal **service level agreements** between departments so that external-facing metrics can be met. These measures may include customer satisfaction levels, complaint volumes and measures of profitability.

As service quality is essential for successful customer relationships, we shall consider ways to overcome issues in setting and measuring service standards and suggest methods for implementing service quality systems in financial organisations.

15.6.1 Researching service quality

One of the main reasons for financial services organisations performing poorly is lack of awareness about customer expectations. The absence of well-defined tangible cues makes this understanding more difficult than it would be in the case of goods. This can be resolved through the use of marketing research that elicits information about customers' expectations and perceptions of services.

The first step in this process is for service organisations to ask the following key questions:

◆ What do customers consider the important features of the service to be?

◆ What level of service of these features do they expect?

◆ How do customers perceive or want service delivery?

Activity

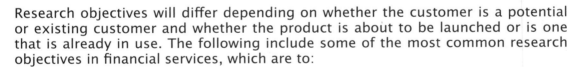

What service standards does your organisation have in place?

How were these standards formulated?

Research objectives will differ depending on whether the customer is a potential or existing customer and whether the product is about to be launched or is one that is already in use. The following include some of the most common research objectives in financial services, which are to:

◆ discover customer requirements or expectations of service;

◆ monitor and track service performance;

◆ assess gaps between customer expectations and perception;

◆ gauge effectiveness of changes in service delivery;

◆ identify dissatisfied customers, so that service recovery can be attempted;

◆ determine customer expectations for a new service – these could be a function of price, service levels or method of delivery;

◆ monitor changing customer expectations in an industry.

Whatever objectives are chosen, there should be a desire for the organisation continually to improve its service to customers.

15.6.2 Research methods

Some of the most useful methods of research are outlined below.

◆ **Regular customer surveys**: customers frequently receive surveys from service providers asking for their opinion about the level of service provided.

Typical applications include being asked to fill in a questionnaire after purchasing a service. Recipients are usually asked to relate any complaints that they may have about the services provided, along with suggestions for improvements. The results of these surveys may not always be accurate because, due to the timing of the survey, the respondents give hurried and ill-considered responses.

◆ **Customer panels**: these are used to provide a continuous source of information on customer expectations. Groups of customers who are frequent users are brought together by an organisation on a regular basis to study their opinions about the quality of service provided. On other occasions, they may be employed to monitor the introduction of a new or revised service. For example, a panel could be brought together by a building society following the successful introduction of a website format. This research method offers organisations a means of anticipating problems and an early warning system for emerging problems. The value of this research is directly related to how well the panel represents the rest of the consumers. Careful selection should be undertaken to ensure the panel matches the social, demographic and economic profile of the consumers being analysed.

◆ **Transaction analysis**: this involves tracking the satisfaction of individuals during recent transactions to enable the management to judge current performance, particularly customers' satisfaction with the contact personnel, as well as their overall satisfaction with the service. The research method normally involves issuing a questionnaire to individual customers immediately after a transaction has been completed. Call centres can use automated post-call surveys. Building societies invite customers who have just used their mortgage services to express their views on the service received via a structured questionnaire. An additional benefit of this research is its capability to associate service quality performance with individual staff members and link it to reward systems.

◆ **Mystery shoppers**: in this form of research, organisations hire outside research companies to send people into service outlets and experience the service as if they were customers. This enables managers to monitor the quality of staff performance when they are delivering the service. A major difficulty in ensuring service quality is overcoming the non-performance of staff in complying with service guidelines. Customers often complain about services when staff are unable or unwilling to perform the service at the desired level. An important function of mystery shopper surveys, therefore, is to monitor the extent to which specified quality standards are being met by staff. The mystery shoppers are trained assessors who visit the organisation, pretend to be a customer and then prepare a report on how well or badly the service personnel did their job. When applied correctly, this can provide a powerful technique for revealing how customers perceive the service.

Activity

> What methods does your organisation use to research service quality?

15.6.3 Continuous improvement

There is a need, having done the above research and obtained feedback from customers, for a programme of improvement – otherwise the research will have just been a paper exercise.

Once standards have been set and measurement is in place then regular reports need to be produced, perhaps weekly and monthly. These reports need to identify individual branches – and in some cases individual staff (such as with mystery shopper interactions) – so that feedback and support can be given to make the necessary improvements.

It is important that all managers, from the top down, view the reports, and that the results are incorporated into business targets and employee incentive schemes.

Activity

> Why do you think it is important to include results from customer feedback on service in employee incentive schemes?

Most organisations will have a **customer satisfaction index** so that they can track changes in customer service covering a range of measures over a period of time. The index results can be linked to employee appraisal and performance-related pay where appropriate. Not only will financial services providers be interested in their own comparative performance but also their performance compared with their competitors. This **benchmarking** will give an indication of performance against organisations in the marketplace and may suggest reasons why they may or may not be successful at attracting and retaining customers. Benchmarking done by third parties such as *Which?* will be considered to be quite influential in helping customers decide the right provider for them.

15.7 Complaints

However good the service may be, sometimes there will be complaints. The nature of customer complaints and how these are dealt with will be a useful tool for the organisation to **identify problem areas** and where, potentially, the service is failing. For customers, too, how the complaint is dealt with will be a major factor in their loyalty to the organisation (we will consider this aspect in Topic 16).

Financial services providers are required to follow a **set procedure** for those products that are regulated by the FSA in the Dispute Resolution (DISP) Handbook. We saw in Topic 5 those products that are regulated and you may wish to remind yourself of these by reviewing section 3.2.2. Complaints about non-regulated products do not have to follow the same procedure, although in practice there is little actual difference. All frontline employees have to undergo regular complaints-management training to ensure that they are dealing with complaints in an appropriate way.

It is important to accept that each organisation will have its own complaints processes and requirements. What we can do here is outline a 'generic' process that will summarise the basis of most firms' procedures. The structure of how the complaint is dealt with is outlined below and includes the requirements for a complaint regarding a regulated product. However, the FSA has undertaken a review of the complaints process and students should ensure that they keep up to date with any changes in this area.

15.7.1 The investigation cycle

Although commonly referred to as a 'cycle', the investigation process is, in fact, linear. In general terms, the procedure will look like Figure 15.2. The results of the complaint process should be used to improve service given, whether this is through revised service procedures or amendments to product features.

Figure 15.2 The investigation process

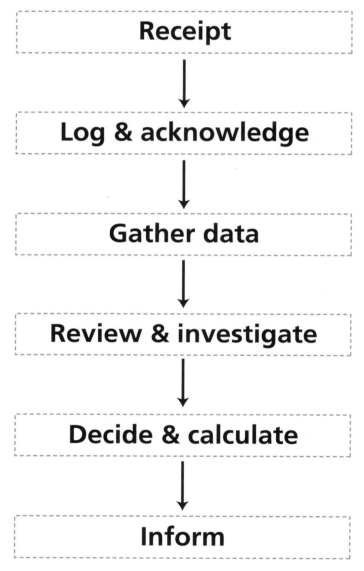

15.7.2 Receipt

Verbal and written complaints carry equal status in the eyes of the regulator. A complaint is any **expression of dissatisfaction** from an eligible person. Such dissatisfaction may relate to the provision of, or failure to provide, a financial service where the complainant feels they have suffered a financial loss, material distress or inconvenience. There will be occasions on which an expression of dissatisfaction is given during a telephone conversation but the caller is not really making a complaint – they just want something sorted out and it can be done quickly. For example, they might want:

◆ an apology for the fact that the company got something wrong, without necessarily gaining an admission of guilt or offer of compensation;

◆ a demonstration that the firm feels they are important and understands what they want;

◆ assurance that this sort of mistake will not happen again.

The DISP rules do not apply to a complaint that is **resolved** by the close of business on the business day following its receipt.

Providers with a good reputation for complaints handling are also likely to **empower** staff to make decisions informally at the start of the process, which may resolve the problem without its becoming protracted. Examples would be:

◆ immediate refunds of charges taken in error;

◆ refunds of charges taken when the customer mistakenly missed a payment deadline by a day or two and contacted the provider to explain the situation and complain about the 'unfair' charge.

Unless this type of minor complaint can be dealt with quickly, it will enter the formal complaints process and clog up progress of more serious cases.

> How much authority do frontline staff have in your organisation to deal with the initial stages of a complaint?
>
> How many expressions of dissatisfaction do not go on to become real complaints as a result?

All staff in an organisation must be able to deal with the initial stages of a complaint. It should not be permissible for an individual to claim that they do not deal with complaints and then ask the customer to ring someone else or to write in instead. It is acceptable to transfer the call to an appropriate person or department, as long as that person or department is available.

15.7.3 Log and acknowledge

When a complaint is received, the person taking the call or receiving the letter must log the complaint immediately. Again, each company will have specific guidelines about how and where a complaint should be logged.

It is important to remember that the regulatory 'clock' starts ticking when the complaint is received; the firm must acknowledge the complaint promptly and, under normal circumstances, has a total of eight weeks within which to resolve it. If administrative delays mean that complaints are not logged promptly, it will hinder the organisation's efforts to resolve them within the resolution deadline.

15.7.4 Gather data

Some letters of complaint are very detailed and provide much useful information, while others may not. The next phase in the process is to build up a case file, which will contain all of the relevant information required to resolve the dispute. The file is likely to consist of:

◆ the original complaint letter or notes of a verbal complaint;

◆ information about the customer and their dealings with the firm;

◆ any standard questionnaires used for complaints, such as a mortgage endowment questionnaire;

◆ a report from the adviser, if appropriate, explaining their recollections and thoughts regarding the complaint;

◆ sales documentation – factfind, key facts illustration, suitability letter, other correspondence;

◆ a record of any conversations with the customer to clarify points regarding the complaint or to gather extra information (it may be necessary to contact the customer in order to clarify details of the complaint);

◆ any other information or documentation that might be relevant.

It is probably better to adopt a proactive approach to gathering the data and deal with this promptly. Ringing the customer to ask for information is quicker and more personal than writing, although it is usually a good idea to follow it up in writing if the customer is expected to provide a written response. It is also an opportunity to check the customer's response and to keep him or her informed of progress. It is important to keep on top of requests for information or reports; some people need follow-up calls to remind them of the need to provide what was asked for.

In many companies, information gathering is carried out by administrative staff rather than the reviewers who, after all, are required to perform a skilled job under considerable pressure. Using other staff in this way maximises the use of resources.

15.7.5 Review and investigate

Once all of the required information has been gathered, the reviewer can start the process of looking at the case in detail. The reviewer (who should be independent from the complaint and competent to investigate) will consider all of the evidence available, looking for details that will support or contradict the basis of the complaint. It is quite likely that they will require further information or clarification of some points and will need help in collecting the information. The review will consider the following points:

◆ The 'know your customer' documentation (factfind) – is there evidence that the customer's needs, objectives and attitude to risk were taken into account and/or addressed by the advice given? In many cases, particularly where the advice was given some years ago, the evidence can be sketchy, or even missing, because factfind completion has improved dramatically in recent years.

◆ Other sales documentation:

– Does the suitability letter giving the recommendation match the factfind? Does it explain why the advice was given? A well-written suitability letter (previously called the 'reason why' letter) will complement the factfind and give a clear picture of the customer's needs and objectives and why the advice given was suitable.

– Does the key facts/features documentation shed any light on the case?

◆ Is there anything in the history of the firm's dealings with the customer that might shed light on the complaint? This might be seen in a record of previous conversations, a history of similar purchases and so on. For example, if a customer has an investment track record and the complaint relates to investment, what does the previous record indicate? A customer with a history of adventurous investments might have difficulty claiming that they are a cautious investor and did not understand the risks, although this does not mean the firm can assume they were *not* badly advised.

◆ Some firms use standard questionnaires for the more common areas of complaint, designed to enable the facts (from the customer's perspective) to be collected in a consistent way. Mortgage endowment complaints are very often the subject of such questionnaires, because the vast majority of these complaints are similar in nature and the required information can, to an extent, be predicted.

◆ The adviser must be given the opportunity to give their recollections of the advice and the reasons behind it. This is clearly required on the grounds of fairness, but it also allows them to provide other evidence where available, and to explain points that may not be clear from the documentation.

◆ Was the customer contacted to ask for further information on the case? If so, how does the information given affect other evidence available?

Looking at all the information described will allow the reviewer to gain a good picture of the situation and reach a reasoned conclusion. Of course, the more information the reviewer has, the better the quality of the decision. Where information is limited, or contradictory, the reviewer may have little choice but to decide in favour of the customer, on the basis of treating the customer fairly and giving the customer the benefit of the doubt.

15.7.6 Decide and calculate

Once the evidence has been reviewed, a decision must be made. Many companies use an internal third party, often known as 'quality assurance', to double check the case and ratify the decision. Others use senior reviewers to check others' cases.

Once a decision has been reached, the firm must work out the best way to satisfy the customer. In the case of financial loss, this is relatively easy: it involves a calculation to put the customer back into the position in which they would have been had the advice not been given, or had appropriate advice been given. In the case of less tangible 'damage', the firm will work out the best way to resolve the situation. There have been many cases where an apology and flowers have been perfectly acceptable.

15.7.7 Inform

Once the decision has been made, a 'decision' letter should be drafted to explain the firm's response to the customer. The letter should be written in terms that the customer can understand, avoiding jargon and explaining any technical issues as simply as possible. The principle of 'less is more' would be a prudent approach to adopt, because the letter should inform without confusing. A short, concise letter that covers all the points of the complaint is likely to be more effective than a long, rambling explanation.

Most firms require decision letters to be checked by another person, often a member of the quality assurance team, to ensure that it is accurate and covers all of the required details.

Letters should be sensitive to the needs and feelings of the customer. Even where the decision is that the firm had acted entirely properly and there are no grounds to uphold the complaint, the tone of the letter should be conciliatory.

Where the firm does not resolve the complaint in favour of the customer, deciding instead that the firm was not to blame, the customer has the right to refer the complaint to an ombudsman, whose role is to resolve such situations. We looked at the role of the Ombudsman in section 3.2.2 and section 7.3.

Resources

www.bba.org.uk

Review questions

The following review questions are designed so that you can check your understanding of this topic.

The answers are provided at the end of these learning materials.

1. What are the problems associated with defining a 'good' level of service for customers?

2. What are the benefits of online service delivery?

3. How can organisations improve their service quality?

4. What sales activities could be considered to be unethical?

5. What areas do the FORGE guidelines outline as having the greatest impact on the financial services industry?

6. How might an organisation research its service quality with its customers?

7. Why might an organisation be interested in benchmarking its service levels?

8. What is the process for dealing with complaints?

9. What are the timescales for dealing with a complaint?

10. If an organisation decides to find in favour of a customer following a complaint, what compensation should they give to the customer?

Topic 16

Customer retention

Learning objective

After studying this topic students should be able to demonstrate a knowledge and understanding of customer retention and its value to the organisation.

Introduction

In this topic we shall consider customer retention and its importance to the organisation. Banks used to be able to rely on customer 'inertia' to keep their customers. Moving an account to a new bank used to be time consuming and disruptive. However, increased competition, a focus on improving service, and Internet banking – which has encouraged people to shop around – have led to far more customers switching their accounts.

We will look at what banks can do to help retain customers, but also the factors that make customers want to switch. This could be through branch closure, competitor activity or dissatisfaction with service and having had cause to complain. We shall look at how best to deal with customers who complain. If an adviser can use their personal skills to turn a complaint around and solve the customer's problem, then this is an excellent way of strengthening the relationship. It is a key way in which individual advisers can help directly with customer retention.

Customer retention is important as it increases the profitability of individual customers, positively affects the brand image, removes the cost and effort of replacing lost customers, and adds to the overall profitability of the organisation.

16.1   What is customer retention?

Retaining profitable customers is an imperative in modern business; primarily, the aim is to prevent customers from defecting to alternative brands, thereby retaining their revenue stream.

Studies across a number of industries have revealed that the cost of retaining an existing customer is only about 10 per cent of the cost of acquiring a new one, so customer retention makes powerful economic sense. Customer retention is the driving force behind customer relationship management (CRM), relationship marketing and loyalty marketing.

Putting in place a customer retention strategy increases customer **profitability**: acquisition costs only occur at the taking of a new product, so the longer the relationship, the lower the cost over time. Account maintenance costs decline as a percentage of total costs (or as a percentage of revenue); long-term customers tend to be less inclined to switch and also tend to be less price-sensitive. Long-term customers may introduce new customers via verbal referral and they are more likely to purchase additional products, as advisers find it easier to cross sell and up-sell services.

Established customers tend to be less expensive to service because they are familiar with the process, require less 'education', and are consistent in their buying behaviour. The increased customer retention and customer loyalty makes the employees' jobs easier and more satisfying. In turn, satisfied employees feed back into better customer service in a virtuous circle.

Customer retention is an important issue for all businesses and especially for financial services. This is because the building and maintenance of a long-term customer relationship is central to improved business performance.

Activity

> What is the retention rate for customers of your organisation?

Losing customers is called **attrition**. **Churn rate** is a measure of customer attrition, and is defined as the number of customers who discontinue a service during a specified time period, divided by the average total number of customers over that same time period. Churn rate has been an ongoing concern of telephone and mobile phone services, for example, in areas where several companies compete and make it easy to transfer from one service to another.

Historically, churn was not a problem for financial services. In fact, it used to be said that someone was statistically more likely to change their wife than their bank. Research by Group 1 Software in 2006, however, revealed that twice as many customers were switching their bank accounts as were switching four years earlier (Murden, 2006). The survey showed that 17.5 per cent of customers changed their bank every year, about twice as many as in 2003 and equating to 8.7m customers changing their current account – a record number for the industry. These customers were worth £700m in profits to the industry. Thus the issue of customer churn represents a serious challenge to the financial services sector.

Understanding how and why customer churn occurs is critical. A key requirement is **identification** of the areas of the **consumer experience** that are to blame. Churn events are sudden moments of clarity when customers' perceptions of their service change. Customer satisfaction surveys often fail to catch enough customers who have experienced disappointment because the customers have already left.

16.1.1 Activities that help to retain customers

Providers undertake a number of activities to help to retain customers, including the following:

◆ The commitment of senior management to service quality, ensuring that the organisation offers a superior service that the competition cannot match and giving customers a reason for staying with their provider. Service quality can provide the basis for enhanced loyalty and retention, and improved business performance.

◆ A customer-focused culture, supported by internal marketing campaigns that enhance the employees' perceptions of the organisation and its brand.

◆ Targeted marketing campaigns giving clear information about products and services, provided in a medium that suits the customer. For example, if a customer uses the Internet to access their accounts, then pop-ups on the website are going to be more appropriate than a direct mail shot.

◆ Barriers to switching, such as penalties for withdrawing from fixed-rate mortgage loans or notice deposit accounts.

◆ Seeking to improve employee performance and satisfaction, as those employees who stay with the organisation build better relationships with customers.

Activity

> What specific activities does your organisation undertake to retain customers?

Individual customer advisers can help to retain customers by:

◆ displaying good interpersonal skills;

◆ keeping promises;

◆ being willing to help, so making it easy for customers to do business with them;

◆ inspiring confidence;

◆ treating customers as individuals;

◆ ensuring the physical aspects of the product or service (such as the office, its contents, documentation and staff uniforms) give a favourable impression.

16.2   Why customers switch

Switching is where customers defect to another provider. A pioneering study by Keaveney, in 1995, created a model that contained eight main reasons for switching. In overview these can be described as follows.

◆ **Pricing**: including high prices, price increases, unfair pricing practices and deceptive pricing practices.

◆ **Inconvenience**: this could be in terms of location, opening hours and waiting too long either for an appointment or for delivery.

◆ **Core service failures**: including mistakes, billing errors and service catastrophes.

◆ **Service encounter failures**: where staff are uncaring, impolite, unresponsive or lacking in knowledge.

◆ **Employee responses to service failures**: where staff are reluctant to respond, fail to respond or are plainly negative in their responses.

◆ **Attraction by competitors**: consumers focus on the pluses of the service provider they switch *to*, rather than on the negatives relating to the service provider they switched *from*.

◆ **Ethical problems**: this could relate to dishonest behaviour, intimidating behaviour, unsafe or unhealthy practices or conflicts of interest.

◆ **Involuntary switching and seldom-mentioned incidents**: this category subdivides into switching because the service provider or customer has shifted location (say, through branch closure) or because the service provider has changed alliance.

Pricing, **service failures** and **inconvenience** appear to be the dominant types of incident that influence consumers to switch financial provider.

Unfortunately, many customers choose not to approach the provider's staff to discuss the underlying matters prior to switching. The reason why they choose to remain silent is attributable to their belief that they would be wasting their own time if they voiced their concerns. Certain changes in provider policy, such as decisions to close particular branches or to introduce a higher fee structure, may encourage people to take this view. These policy decisions are made at the highest level; individuals or groups of individuals may feel that they have insufficient influence to persuade senior executives to reverse their earlier decisions. The setting-up of a scheme that seeks feedback from discontented customers may be beneficial to providers wishing to retain a proportion of those customers who would otherwise have defected.

Activity

> What are the main reasons that customers close accounts with your organisation and switch to another provider?
>
> With regard to the accounts you would like to keep, what could have been done to stop them switching?

Marketing research provides an extremely useful means for highlighting actual or potential problems that may force customers to defect. The feedback from research is meaningless, however, unless it is accompanied by actions that are tailored to provide customer satisfaction.

The analysis of customer complaint feedback provides valuable information about customer perceptions of the company and its products. It is widely acknowledged that for every customer who complains, there are probably ten others who did not voice their complaint but felt the same way. Such customers may leave the organisation, offering no reason for defection. The negative word of mouth that can damage the reputation of the organisation compounds this problem.

While complaints can be upsetting for staff within the organisation if they are not properly trained, they can provide valuable information about product and service aspects that require improvement.

16.3 Dealing with customers making complaints

In the last topic we looked at the process for dealing with customer complaints. We are now going to look at the **skills** required to deal with customers who are making complaints, and with potentially difficult situations. If a complaint is dealt with well, it is more likely that the provider will keep the customer's business. It could be seen as an opportunity to **strengthen the relationship** rather than weaken it. Often, customers will judge the way an adviser deals with their complaint to be as important as the situation being resolved to their satisfaction.

The bulk of work relating to complaints will be undertaken 'behind the scenes', away from the customer. Initial contact may, however, be through a telephone call and, in many cases, the complainant may need to be contacted to ask for additional information or to clarify points.

All staff come across customers who are unable to keep calm: it may be someone who will not listen to what they are saying, who may even shout when they fail to hear what they want to hear. Regardless of the level of experience of the individual dealing with the customer, it is not a pleasant experience and presents a challenge. In many cases, it can knock the confidence of the staff member. This text is not the place to go into great detail about how to deal with difficult customers; we can only look at some general points that will help.

The secret of dealing with such customers is part mental attitude and part skill.

◆ **Mental attitude**: there is no getting away from the fact that customers get annoyed from time to time. Someone has to deal with them. It is also important to understand that the problem is usually not with the customer adviser – the customer's anger is usually aimed at the organisation, which they feel has let them down in some way.

◆ **Skill development**: certain essential skills are needed for handling customers successfully. The more often advisers are able to practise those skills by dealing with awkward customers, the more effective they will become. Many people look at each interaction as a challenge to be relished. We will look at the key skills below (section 16.3.2 onwards).

Employees who deal well with difficult customers tend to share common characteristics. In general, they:

◆ are reasonable, flexible and thoughtful;

◆ realise that something must have caused the behaviour;

◆ are good at assessing people's needs and concerns quickly;

◆ pick up quickly on the mood of the customer and are able to empathise;

◆ are calm and collected;

◆ see customers who are annoyed as those who need help to separate feelings from facts.

Activity

> Think about your last successful interaction with a difficult customer. What did you do that enabled you to deal with them in an effective way?

16.3.1 Why do people complain?

Part of dealing with a customer who is complaining is to understand why they are doing so. People complain for a variety of reasons, including that:

◆ they have not received the service or goods they expected;

◆ something has gone wrong;

◆ they feel that the organisation has let them down;

◆ they perceive an injustice has occurred.

Activity

> From your experience can you add any other reasons to this list?

Few people are angry or difficult when they first make contact to complain. In fact, many are nervous, because complaining does not come naturally to many people and they will be dealing with a large organisation. Something usually makes them angry or difficult. Reasons include:

◆ the length of time it has taken to speak to someone;

◆ the way in which the conversation is first dealt with;

◆ they feel they are not being heard;

◆ the other person does not seem to care;

◆ they are unable to express themselves;

◆ they feel the company is trying to avoid responsibility.

Activity

> How many of these reasons are the fault of the customer?

It is useful, therefore, to minimise these factors as much as possible.

However, we also need to appreciate that other factors may influence how the customer feels when making a complaint. For example, the customer might:

◆ be having an awful day;

◆ be one of those people who habitually respond negatively;

◆ be under pressure from other sources;

◆ have just finished an argument;

◆ have just received some bad news.

In these situations – and we have all felt the same way – the customer is already in a bad mood before they speak to the adviser. In some cases, they may feel ready for a fight and will be keen to vent their frustration. Behaviour such as this must be addressed early in the interaction.

16.3.2 Starting the conversation

In many ways, the key to dealing with any customer who wants to make a complaint is to start the conversation well by appearing confident, knowledgeable and sympathetic, and by stressing the desire to help. It is important to identify the problem as early as possible and manage the customer's expectations from the beginning. Important information to establish includes the following:

◆ **The nature of the problem**: it may not be necessary to go into detail at this stage, because you want only to identify what you might be able to do and the best way to approach the rest of the conversation.

◆ **What the customer is looking for to put things right**: it is better to identify what the customer is expecting at the early stage of the process. Again, this will help you to work out the best way to approach the rest of the conversation. If the customer is asking for action that is not realistic, their expectations need to be managed from this point.

◆ **Your role in the process**: what you will and will not be able to do, and whether you might have to refer the complaint to a more senior person.

◆ **What can the customer expect now**: this will include the regulatory timescales and communications, and what will happen next in the process. Be cautious in relation to timescales – it is better to set realistic expectations and then delight the customer by beating them.

16.3.3 During the conversation

Once the conversation is in flow, there are several other points to focus on.

◆ **Gather as much information as you can to analyse the real problem**: having started the conversation with a brief outline of the problem, it is important to find out as much as possible before attempting to resolve it. We will look at questioning skills in section 17.2.5.

◆ **Identify how aggressive the customer is being**: plan a strategy to deal with them.

◆ **Make the customer feel part of the solution**: co-operation is a far more effective way to resolve disputes. If the customer feels that they have contributed to the solution, they will be happier and may even be prepared to settle for less than demanded initially. This may mean asking the customer what they would like to happen.

◆ **Adopt positive words and a constructive approach**: if the customer feels faced with a negative and obstructive attitude, frustration will exaggerate their behaviour.

◆ **Respect the rights of others and compromise if necessary**: many disputes are solved by a degree of compromise, in which both parties move their position towards each other.

Your own behaviour and reactions will also have a bearing on the situation.

◆ **Be aware of your own emotional response**: it is easy to be sucked into a negative approach or to become defensive. It is also important to remember that the customer's anger or frustration is not likely to be directed at you personally; do not take it personally and become defensive or aggressive in response.

◆ **Avoidance tactics are a short-term measure**: the problem will not go away. Passing the customer on to someone else or making promises that you cannot keep may relieve the immediate pressure but will probably lead to more problems later.

◆ **Listen to others if you want to be listened to yourself**: it is vital to listen carefully to the customer, both to gather information and to show that you are trying to help.

Advisers may achieve results faster by changing their own behaviour rather than expecting the customer to change, since *how* you communicate is as important as *what* you communicate. It is also important to be able to recognise a stalemate situation and signs of the situation deteriorating.

Activity

> What are advisers in your organisation asked to do if a situation becomes particularly difficult?

In some situations, such as where the customer has become abusive, advisers are required to warn the customer and then terminate the call. This gives both parties a chance to regain their composure and the call can be continued at another time.

16.3.4 Closing the conversation

If the conversation has gone well, the customer should feel that they have been listened to and that their complaint will be dealt with. The adviser should have enough information to investigate the complaint and give a response to the customer in the correct timescale. The customer should be advised what will happen next and when this will happen. As mentioned at the beginning of this topic, if the complaint is handled well then it can help to strengthen the relationship and help retain the customer for the future.

Review questions

The following review questions are designed so that you can check your understanding of this topic.

The answers are provided at the end of these learning materials.

1. What are the benefits of retaining customers?

2. What is 'churn'?

3. What can advisers do personally to help retain customers?

4. Why do customers switch?

5. How might dealing with a complaint help customer retention?

6. Why do people complain?

7. During a conversation with a customer about a complaint, what do you, as an adviser, have to focus on?

Topic 17
The sales process

Learning objective

After studying this topic, students should be able to demonstrate a knowledge and understanding of the sales process in retail banking.

Introduction

Sales are the responsibility of every member of staff who comes into contact either directly or indirectly with the customer. Although not all members of staff are classed as sales personnel, they have an important role to play. Frontline staff can gather important information through well-defined conversations with their customers. Discussions about the weather seldom generate sales, but the discovery that Mrs Smith's husband is about to buy a new car could prompt the adviser to sell a loan that might otherwise have gone to a competitor company.

In this topic, we will consider how advisers obtain the information they need from their customers, as well as considering how they assess and structure that information to determine the most suitable products and services to recommend.

In recent years, there have been radical changes in the ways in which banks and building societies conduct business. More and more personal accounts held with banks are now sold and accessed either by telephone or through the Internet. Most cash transactions are done anonymously via ATMs in supermarkets, shopping centres and petrol stations, which can be accessed 24 hours a day, 365 days a year. Customers are more likely to visit their bank branch to organise a mortgage, life insurance or investments than they are to make a withdrawal from their bank account.

Competition between and among financial organisations to sell products with similar features is fierce. Providers of customer advice and cross selling of products require sophisticated client-communication skills. There is a need for qualifications for those selling financial services products, particularly qualifications recognised by the regulator, the Financial Services Authority (FSA).

17.1 The role and importance of needs-based sales in financial services

In earlier topics we discussed the need to 'know your customer': partly because of regulatory requirements relating to the prevention of money laundering but also in order to ensure that customers have the product or service most suitable to their needs. We looked at customer needs and wants in section 2.3 and defined needs as those things without which we would not survive. We saw that people also have 'wants', which are not necessarily essential items but are important to them. People buy products to satisfy both needs and wants. Financial services are an enabler for people achieving their life choices, which will be a combination of wants and needs. Sometimes, advisers will identify a need but the customer, for whatever reason, does not want to buy a product that will address that need. In this situation the adviser needs to highlight that the need has been identified and that the customer has refused the product.

The requirement for needs-based selling is to ensure that products are not mis-sold or misrepresented in any way and that customers fully understand what the product will (or will not) do for them. It is the most ethical way to sell and, in the long run, the most successful, as customers will recognise that they have been sold products on the basis of what is right for them rather than what would make the most commission for the adviser. Building relationships and trust are important factors in the sales process, and selling to needs is one of the best ways for an adviser to gain this with customers.

17.1.1 Retail Distribution Review

The status of financial advisers is likely to change as a result of the FSA's Retail Distribution Review (RDR). This review, published in 2008 and intended to be implemented by the end of 2012, outlines proposals for increasing consumer confidence in the retail investment market. The main aims of the proposed changes are as follows:

◆ To provide **greater clarity** for consumers about the advice being offered, by making a distinction between independent advice and sales advice:

  — **Independent advice**: the adviser provides recommendations that are 'unrestricted and unbiased', in other words, the adviser considers all investments and providers from across the whole market. These advisers will be required to adhere to significantly higher professional standards.

  — **Sales advice**: the adviser recommends the products of one or a limited range of providers, and this must be made clear to clients.

◆ To raise **professional standards** of all advisers by setting minimum qualifications for different types of advice, and by setting up a Professional Standards Board.

◆ To modernise the way in which advice is paid for, by requiring independent advisers to agree the **cost of advice** with clients up front, removing the potential for commission bias.

At the same time, the FSA in conjunction with the Treasury is piloting a free, impartial scheme known as Money Guidance. This scheme is designed to provide general advice on investment and other money issues such as debt and retirement planning, particularly to people who are the most vulnerable to making poor financial decisions. Guidance is delivered by telephone, face-to-face and on the Internet by a range of independent advice organisations, including Citizens Advice. It is not intended to replace regulated financial advice but is there to help people feel confident, informed and able to make the financial decisions that are appropriate for them.

17.2 Assessing customer needs

Assessing customer needs is a major part of the sales process and this will be done through verbal and non-verbal communication. The key skills required are:

◆ listening;

◆ non-verbal communication;

◆ empathy;

◆ rapport; and

◆ questioning skills.

We will now go on to consider each of these.

17.2.1 Listening

Listening is a key skill in many situations. Effective listening will enable the listener to gain an **understanding** of what the speaker is really saying, and will encourage the speaker by showing interest and indicating that you have heard what was said.

We get very frustrated when we tell a colleague or friend something and their actions or words indicate quite clearly that they have not taken in what we said. They have not '**actively**' listened; the same applies to customers. Signs of not listening include asking for information already given and recounting information given earlier but getting it wrong.

Activity

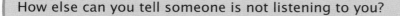

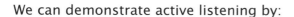
How else can you tell someone is not listening to you?

We can demonstrate active listening by:

◆ saying 'yes' and 'mmm' regularly, but not so often as to be annoying;

◆ summarising what the customer has said at regular intervals, perhaps by saying, 'can I just sum up...', 'can I just check my understanding...', or 'as you just said...';

◆ echoing words and phrases that the customer has used (but not sounding like a parrot!);

◆ using expressions such as 'as you said earlier';

◆ asking follow-up questions relating to what was said.

17.2.2 Non-verbal communication

Albert Mehrabian (1971) researched human communication and discovered some interesting facts:

◆ 55 per cent of meaning is communicated in facial expressions;

◆ 38 per cent of meaning is communicated in the way, or tone, in which something is said;

◆ 7 per cent of meaning is communicated by what is said, the words.

Other researchers claim that up to 80 per cent of communication is non-verbal, with only 20 per cent depending on the words used.

It is important to ensure that your **words and body language match**, or else the customer will detect a problem, even if only on a subconscious level. For example, if you are unsure of your product knowledge, your words may not give this away but your body language might, through your posture or facial expression.

When we use the telephone, we are denied visual communication with the other person, which can make it trickier to manage difficult people. Body language remains important, however, because how you are feeling is exhibited in your body language and ultimately affects how your voice sounds.

When using the telephone, general tips to manage the sound of your voice include:

◆ maintain a relaxed and open posture:

◆ arms unfolded;

◆ shoulders back;

◆ sit upright so that your voice sounds clear;

◆ relax the facial muscles – smile (although it seems odd, people will pick up on the fact that you are smiling, even if they are 100 miles away);

◆ breathe slowly:

◆ ensure your breathing is slow and calm, because fast breathing may indicate you are nervous and lacking the confidence to deal with the situation;

◆ stand up – some people find it easier to deal with difficult people over the telephone by standing up. It can give them confidence and make them feel in control of the situation because they are elevated above the other person (who is probably sitting). Your voice can also sound clearer if you stand upright.

Activity

How do you alter your communication style when you are on the phone?

How do you find it easiest to communicate – face to face or on the phone with customers?

17.2.3 Empathy

Empathic listening is about listening for what is *not* being said as well as what is being said, and demonstrating your understanding to the other person. Empathic listening is more than hearing the words: it is truly understanding and accepting the person's message and their situation and feelings.

According to definitions from Collins Dictionary, **empathy** can be defined as:

'The ability to sense and understand someone else's feelings as if they were one's own.'

Sympathy can be defined as:

'Agreement with someone's feelings or interests.'

When dealing with customers, empathy is a skill that we can use to improve the relationship. Remember that only 7 per cent of the impact of our communication comes from the words we use.

To empathise, therefore, is to put yourself in the other person's shoes, without necessarily agreeing with their point of view. This is in contrast with sympathy, where you would agree with the other person. Building empathy with the customer is a vital element in creating a positive and co-operative relationship that will allow any problems to be solved to mutual satisfaction. Empathy is vital because:

◆ it shows the other person that you care and you understand;

◆ you will learn more about the speaker's issues and concerns;

◆ it shows the speaker that you (the listener) are allowing them to vent their emotions and feelings;

◆ it can help in defusing a situation, because you invite the speaker to express their feelings;

◆ it underpins a good relationship.

Building empathy with a customer can be done in the following ways:

◆ **Taking their needs and concerns seriously**: if another person has taken the time and effort to express how they are feeling about a particular circumstance or situation, take a step back and consider how the other person is feeling, even if you are unable to identify with their specific needs and concerns. What is it that they are concerned about? What do they need from you?

◆ **Placing value on feelings and attitudes**: demonstrate that you value the other person's feelings and attitudes even if they differ from your own. You can do this by allowing them simply to express their feelings openly and honestly, without criticism or judgement from you. Accept that another person may see the world differently from you or express different attitudes from your own. There is nothing to say that the other person's opinions are of any less value than your own.

◆ **Respect experience, beliefs and values**: we all have different experiences that go towards shaping our beliefs and values. In being empathic to another person, we should put aside our own experience, beliefs and values. This does not mean that we have to agree with what the other person is saying but that we must accept that their perspective may differ from our own.

◆ **Reserve judgement**: when we are listening to another person, we link what is being said to us with what we already know. By doing this, we inevitably begin to judge the other person. You can avoid making judgements by focusing on what the other person is saying: pay close attention to their tone of voice – does the pitch become higher when speaking about emotions?

◆ **Show interest in what is being communicated**: it is easy to lose concentration when we are listening to another person. If you make a conscious decision to focus on exactly what a person is saying, it will be easy to demonstrate your interest.

There are, however, behaviours that *prevent* us from building empathy and therefore from truly listening to what the customer has to say:

◆ **Comparing**: sometimes when we listen to someone else, we find ourselves comparing them with what we would have said or done. We can be thinking things such as 'I wouldn't have done/said that', 'I've had worse happen to me', and so on. We are so busy judging the other person that we are not able to take in what is really being said. The problem can be compounded if we say or do something that shows that we are judging or comparing.

◆ **Rehearsing**: on occasion, we don't think about what is being said but think instead about how we will respond; in face-to-face conversations, this can be compounded by body language that shows we are not listening or are waiting to have our say. This might mean vital information is missed and may upset the other person.

◆ **Deleting**: 'deleting' occurs when you listen to some things and not others. This happens when you feel that the speaker's mood, emotions and what is being said does not directly impact on you. Once you have determined this, you will start to think of other things and delete things you do not want to hear – perhaps those things that are threatening, negative, critical or unpleasant. You will have no memory of the words that have been said to help you later in the conversation.

◆ **Prejudging**: as we talk to people on the telephone, we often build up a mental picture of what they are like – perhaps they may seem lacking in intelligence or less 'worthy' than ourselves. This can lead us to dismiss what they say or to pay less attention to it. When building empathy, we should reserve judgement until after we have listened to, and evaluated, what is being said.

◆ **Preoccupation**: sometimes, when we listen to someone else, what they say triggers thoughts of our own and our minds then begin to wander. If we are preoccupied with other thoughts it can appear to show that we do not value or appreciate what the other person has to say.

Activity

Which of the above 'preventors' do you find yourself doing without even intending to?

In your next few interactions with customers make a note **not** to do them.

How does this affect the response from the customer?

17.2.4 Rapport

Rapport can be defined as a 'sympathetic relationship or understanding' (Collins Dictionary). People are more likely to be able to **trust** those who appear to think and speak in the same way as they do. Most people see building rapport as finding common interests or things to talk about; it is actually much deeper than that and requires a degree of deeper thinking. Most people build rapport without consciously realising what they are doing and it is a natural development of empathy.

Activity

> How do you think you build rapport with friends and colleagues?

The following techniques can help to build rapport:

◆ **Matching**: you have probably heard that it is possible to build rapport by subtly matching someone's body language. You may not be aware that you can achieve similar results in a telephone conversation by matching the customer's language, tone and pace.

◆ **Language**: the words that the customer uses will give clues to the way they see the world and take in information. If you can match their language, the customer will see you as sympathetic and someone to work with. Language may be used in different ways, with the following characteristics:

  – **Visual**: the visual thinker uses words such as 'see'; 'look; 'picture'; 'view',and so on. Try to use visual words in your responses: 'I see what you mean'; 'Let's look at the situation'; 'What's your view?'

  – **Auditory**: the auditory thinker uses 'hearing' words such as 'hear', 'listen', 'sound', etc. Try to use hearing words in your responses: 'I hear what you're saying'; 'How does that sound?'; 'Shall we talk through the problem?'

  – **Kinaesthetic**: the kinaesthetic thinker uses 'feeling' words such as 'touch'; 'feel': 'grasp'. Try to use kinaesthetic words in your responses: 'I think I've grasped the problem'; 'Let's touch on the next point'; 'How does that feel to you?'

  – **Logical/theoretical**: the logical thinker uses 'reason' words such as 'think'; 'reckon'; 'know' and so on. Try to use logical words in your response: 'What do you think?'

◆ **Pace**: it is also important to match the pace of the other person. In addition to building rapport, pacing will also allow you to control the conversation once matching has been successful. If the customer speaks quickly, speak more quickly to match; if the customer speaks slowly, slow down to match. After a while, once you are in harmony, you will find that you can start to control the pace of the customer to an extent. If you start to slow down as you speak, a fast talker will also slow down to match you.

◆ **Volume and tone**: you should also try to match the volume and tone of the customer. Speak quietly to a quiet customer and more loudly to the louder customer. When speaking to an angry, loud customer, it is important not to use angry or threatening words in response, although you may raise the volume of your voice in order to match their own. Adopt a similar tone, at least to start with.

◆ **Control**: once harmony has been established, you will be able to use pace, tone and volume to control the conversation to an extent. You will be able to enthuse by increasing pace and adopting a lighter tone; you will be able to emphasise points by adopting a slower pace and a more serious tone.

Warning! Matching should be very subtle. If the customer thinks you are mimicking them, they will react negatively.

17.2.5 Questioning skills

When interviewing a customer or dealing with a complaint, you may be required to find out a great deal of information to help you to deal with it efficiently. The way in which you structure questions is an important part of the **investigation** process, because poor questioning will lead to poor information. Questioning skills are a major subject in themselves and we can do little more than look at the basics in this study text.

Broadly there are two types of question: closed and open.

17.2.5.1 Closed questions

Closed questions are those that can be answered by 'yes' or 'no', or by giving a fact. The question itself limits the response. For example:

◆ 'Are you hungry?'

◆ 'Do you like chocolate?'

◆ 'Can I take it that you are satisfied?'

Closed questions are very good for collecting **factual** information. They state clearly what information is required and leave little room for confusion.

Closed questions can also be effective to **summarise** a conversation or to 'close' the customer. 'Closing' in this context, means to **gain agreement** to a solution or course of action.

Examples of summarising questions would be:

◆ 'So, what you told me was . . .?'

◆ 'So, when you rang the firm, you were told . . .?'

◆ 'Your total income from all sources is . . .?'

You will notice that all of these questions require the customer to confirm a piece of information. In many cases, the 'question' may be a statement that clearly requires a yes/no response.

Closing questions are likely to begin with (or feature) 'can', 'may', 'do', 'does', 'are' or 'would'.

Examples of 'closing' questions would be:

◆ 'So, are you ready to sign the form?'

◆ 'So, if I can arrange that, would you be happy?'

◆ 'Would that solve the problem for you?'

While closed questions are very useful for gaining factual information, they are not good for finding out feelings, opinions and other less specific information. In addition, over-use of closed questions will make the conversation feel like an interrogation, which is something to be avoided at all times.

17.2.5.2 Open questions

Open questions are those that cannot usually be answered with a fact or a simple 'yes' or 'no'. They do not limit the response. Generally they start with:

◆ how;

◆ what;

◆ why;

◆ when;

◆ where;

◆ who;

◆ which.

This does not mean that every question that starts with one of these words will be an open question; some starting with 'who', 'when', 'which' and 'where' might be answered with a fact. The point is that open questions encourage a **longer response** and allow the questioner to **explore** the subject. For example, 'What made you decide on a career in financial services?' is unlikely to be answered 'yes' or 'no', or with a short factual statement. It is exploring the individual's ambitions, feelings and motives, helping the questioner to build a deeper picture than that based purely on fact.

Another example of the effective use of open questions may include: 'What do you think would be a good solution to the problem?' This question will help the questioner to discover the customer's **expectations**, allowing him or her to manage unrealistic expectations from the start, rather than risking alienation later on.

Other examples include:

◆ 'How would you feel if . . .?'

◆ 'What would that mean to you . . .?'

◆ 'Why do you see that as a problem?'

'Why' is a very powerful question. In most cases, the answer to a 'why' question will start with 'because', which usually means that the answer is based on a **belief** or an opinion, based on the customer's previous experience; it might not represent the true facts. It is a very good way to identify beliefs but should be used with caution; if you want to find out the 'truth', it might be better to use alternatives.

A good example of this can be seen in the question: 'Why do you think that?' The question is clearly asking for an answer based on opinion and belief. The answer is likely to relate to a previous experience that has shaped the respondent's feelings on the subject. The questioner should not rely on the answer to represent fact – other questions should be asked to clarify the facts.

In addition:

◆ 'how' and 'what' can be used to seek clarification;

◆ 'when', 'who' and 'where' can be used to seek extra information;

◆ 'which' can be used to confirm a choice.

When **building rapport**, the majority of questions are likely to be of an open nature — you want the customer to talk and build up trust before going into factual detail.

There are, however, some potential problems when asking questions.

◆ **Impatience**: one of the most common faults is to fail to allow enough time for a response. We do not generally enjoy silence during a conversation; it sometimes feels threatening, so we like to fill in the space by asking another question or making another statement. The respondent needs time to answer; they are likely to be thinking their response through, and interrupting is likely to upset their train of thought. When asking a closing question, silence is vital: you are asking for a decision and should not interrupt. It might also be the case that the question asks the customer to face a reality they have managed to avoid so far; silence increases the pressure while they consider all the options before accepting the inevitable. Interrupting will release the pressure and allow them to avoid the reality.

◆ **Multiple questions**: another common mistake is to ask multiple questions. You can often see television interviewers do this, asking a question such as: 'How did you feel about the performance? I mean, were you excited? What was it like playing in front of such a big crowd?' The interviewer has sought to clarify the original question by adding supplementary detail but, in so doing, has confused the issue. Which question do they want the interviewee to answer? Can the interviewee remember the first two questions? What does the interviewer want to know — how the interviewee felt, or if they were excited, or what the experience was like?

◆ **Long questions**: the longer the question, the more chance of the interviewee becoming confused. It is far more effective to ask a series of short, linked questions than a single long one.

Activity

> When watching an interview on TV or listening to one on the radio, pick out the types of question used by the interviewer.
>
> How does the interviewer use the questions to control the conversation?
>
> How might they improve their technique?

17.3   The sales process

We now consider the steps that are involved in the selling process. These are listed as:

◆ identifying leads;

◆ gathering information about the customer;

◆ identifying customer needs;

◆ recommending solutions;

◆ obtaining commitment to buy.

The process we are going to consider is one that relates to non-regulated sales as undertaken by most customer advisers. Regulated advisers follow a similar but slightly lengthier process that involves a detailed factfind and the production of specific documentation.

17.3.1 Identifying leads

A key part of the sales process is to identify the **opportunities** for a sale. This means that there has to be some mechanism for identifying and locating prospects and matching up the likely needs with what the organisation has to offer.

Many financial services providers now offer annual financial reviews, particularly at times when it becomes apparent that a customer's situation has changed. This is an ideal opportunity for the adviser to create a sales opening, initiate good customer relations and at the very least keep the database record current.

Table 17.1 covers the main sources of leads; however, the most obvious source of sales is the existing customer. Provided they are happy with services from their provider, they are more likely to continue to buy from them and recommend them to others. This emphasises the importance of regular customer reviews and feedback, as this data can provide opportunities for cross sales.

Table 17.1   Sources of leads

Company inspired	Adviser inspired
Sales records	Scanning directories
Advertising responses	Referrals – direct or via sales support staff
Exhibitions and trade show lists	Observation of new economic trends
General enquiries	Watching the media
Purchased lists	Networking events, eg CBI, chambers of commerce or Rotary Clubs
Existing customers	

A sales adviser is in a key position to identify and qualify (assess the likelihood of a sale) leads for their mortgage and financial planning advisers during their conversations with customers. They do need, however, to ensure that they gather enough information to identify real needs, while not being seen to be giving advice.

Activity

Where do most of your sales leads come from?

17.3.2 Gathering information

Regulations that were first introduced by the Financial Services Act 1986, and which now continue to operate under the Financial Services and Markets Act 2000, oblige advisers to 'know your customer'. Advisers must be able to identify the customer's needs, which are a key feature of the sales process.

It is an adviser's responsibility to **define** the customer's needs and objectives quickly and accurately. Knowing the customer makes it necessary to ask questions in respect of all of the following:

◆ the customer's existing and future needs;

◆ their ability to provide for them;

◆ their attitude towards providing for them;

◆ the customer's objectives.

This means, in practice, that any factfind or interview should look at the following.

◆ **Customer's circumstances**: this will include personal and family details if these have changed since the records were last updated, including details of any dependents.

◆ **Financial situation**: including employment details, income and expenditure, a customer's assets and their liabilities. They should also be asked about details of any existing insurance policies that they have. Customers are often unaware of the details of any arrangements that they have. It is an adviser's responsibility to try to obtain this information and customers should be asked, wherever possible, to bring all relevant details with them.

◆ **Plans and objectives**: these details tend to be more intangible in nature: here the aim is to find out 'why?', 'how?' or 'do you feel that?' – in other words, to discover the customer's feelings about what they have, what they want and where they want to go from a financial point of view.

   – The personal and family details and the financial situation are concerned with the gathering of **hard facts**, ie about tangible items and people.

   – The intangible nature of plans, objectives and attitudes means they are known as **soft facts**.

Activity

> How much time do you spend gathering hard facts, compared with time spent gathering soft facts? How do you think this affects the quality of the conversation with the customer?

◆ **Attitude to risk/debt**: as well as the soft facts, additional information is needed to ascertain correctly the customer's attitude to risk, or **risk profile**. It is essential to take full account of this attitude when giving recommendations to a customer, and attitude to risk will differ from customer to customer. The customer must understand what the risk is, which may mean providing explanations – for example, to distinguish between the degrees of risk. There is, for example, risk to the capital that is invested: the value of an investment may fall as well as rise; the amount of income or capital growth may not be guaranteed. The customer's attitude towards this must be explored. Historically, many so-called low-risk investments, such as bank or building society accounts, have provided a safe haven and a relatively stable level of income, although inflation will cause the value of the investment to fall. When considering borrowing applications the customer's attitude to debt must also be ascertained. Some customers, for example, are happy to rely on the performance of an investment vehicle to repay their mortgage at the end of its term, whereas other customers want to ensure that there is certainty of repayment and will choose a capital and interest repayment mortgage instead.

◆ **Customer preferences**: it is important to take note of a customer's stated preferences, but advisers should also be aware of their own duty of care: this means recognising that, while customers may have a clear view on what they want to do, their appreciation of what they ought to do can be less than clear. This means that advisers may have an 'educational' role in helping customers to explore their own financial circumstances and to make the right choices.

17.3.3 Identifying customer needs

The adviser's role is to define the customer's needs and objectives accurately, to enable them to see the **key issues** facing them and to **recommend and discuss an order of priority** in which to tackle them.

We can categorise an individual's financial needs and objectives into the following five areas:

◆ **protecting dependants** from the financial effects of either a **loss of income** or a need to meet extra outgoings in the event of premature death;

◆ **protecting oneself and dependants** from the financial effects of **losing the ability to earn income** in the long term;

◆ **providing an income in retirement** sufficient to maintain a reasonable standard of living;

◆ **wanting to increase and/or to protect the value of money saved or invested**, wanting to increase income from existing savings or investments or wanting to build up some savings in the first place;

◆ **minimising tax liabilities**.

In seeking to assess any of these areas, an adviser should look for examples of typical things that customers either do wrong or fail to do at all. This might include:

◆ a young family, with little or no savings, relying solely on mortgage protection cover for life assurance – such cover would repay the mortgage but is not designed to meet the ongoing costs of running the house and bringing up the family;

◆ unnecessarily large amounts being held on deposit in bank and building society accounts over the long term and so not gaining access to better returns available elsewhere;

◆ a non-taxpayer holding investments where tax on interest received cannot be reclaimed;

◆ no pension contributions being paid, or very small pension contributions as a percentage of total earnings, which will mean being dependent upon state benefits unless action is taken;

◆ people who have not made a valid will, whose assets on death may therefore not be distributed as desired.

Activity

> Which needs are most often **not** addressed by your customers?

17.3.4 Recommending solutions

Once an adviser has gathered all of the necessary information about the customer's circumstances and preferences, has a clear appreciation of their ability to pay, and has obtained agreement on priorities, then the process of **matching solutions to requirements** can begin.

When suggesting solutions to the customer, the adviser should be able to turn the **features** of the product into **benefits** to the customer.

Example

Product feature	**Benefits to customer**
Repayment terms of a loan	Ability to spread the cost over 24 months, thus reducing outlay

---

The difference between benefits and features is not a question of semantics. If people buy services for **what they will do for them**, ie the benefits of using the services, then the adviser has to emphasise those benefits during the sales process. Every service has its features, such as interest rates, free travel cover or tiered savings bands within an account. Many advisers fall into the trap of talking to customers about these features rather than what the features mean to the customer.

A simple formula to ensure a customer-oriented approach is always to use the phrase '**which means that**' to link a feature to the benefits it brings, such as: 'We can supply travellers' cheques in US dollars, which means that travel in the US will be easy because hotels, restaurants and even petrol stations will accept your travellers' cheques without any problem'.

Activity

Demonstrate your understanding of the above by transferring the following features to benefits.

Features	Benefits
Loan – base-rate-related interest rate	
Mortgage – capped interest rate	
Insurance – life policy to cover the amount of the mortgage loan	
Credit card – with a new current account	
Home insurance – building and contents cover	

The best way to proceed is to go step by step through each product, at the customer's pace. As each feature and its benefits are covered, the adviser should check that the customer understands the benefits, perhaps by asking a few simple questions.

There are a number of steps that should always be included when presenting recommendations:

◆ the purpose of the product and the customer's needs that the product will address;

◆ the benefits that the customer will enjoy;

◆ the risks and limitations inherent to the product;

◆ any options that exist within the product that may be appropriate to the customer;

◆ a summary of reasons why the product is being recommended.

17.3.5 Obtaining a commitment to buy

Obtaining a commitment from the customer in the form of a completed application form will depend on how effectively all of the earlier stages of the sales process have been carried out. Attempting to close a sale too early is clearly not sensible, and deciding when to close a sale is determined by two factors: the reaction of the customer and their understanding of the proposal.

Advisers should listen and look out for **signals** from the customer that they are ready to buy. Comments such as 'that sounds good to me' or 'how do I go ahead?' are clear indications that the customer is ready to buy.

Activity

> What else might the customer say or do to indicate that they are ready to buy?

Closing the sale simply involves asking the customer if they are happy to go ahead and complete the application. Sometimes the customer may expect the adviser to complete the form on their behalf. It is permissible to do this but only with the customer's permission. If the adviser does complete any forms, the customer must read it through thoroughly, checking what has been written before they sign it.

In particular, the customer must be made aware of the consequences of **non-disclosure**. If the contract is later made void because of something that the customer failed to disclose on the application form, then the whole process will have been a waste of time.

17.4   Handling customer objections

It is indeed a rare and skilful sales adviser who can complete an entire sales presentation without the customer coming out with words to the effect of 'that's all very well, but...'. At any stage in the selling process that involves the customer, objections can and probably will be made. These may arise for various reasons:

◆ lack of understanding;

◆ lack of interest;

◆ misinformation;

◆ a need for reassurance, or genuine concern.

The sales adviser must be prepared to overcome objections where possible, as otherwise the sale is likely to be lost completely. If the customer is concerned enough to raise an objection, then the adviser must have the courtesy to answer it in some way. Many experienced sales advisers argue that the real selling does not begin until the customer raises an objection. Whenever a customer raises an objection, the adviser should always base their response on facts.

The list below summarises typical objections that occur time after time, regardless of the specific selling situation:

◆ I am not interested in the product.

◆ I am not happy with your service.

◆ The price is too high.

◆ The product isn't competitive.

◆ You can't sort it out for me quickly enough.

◆ I can't afford it.

◆ I don't need it.

Activity

> Which objections do you most commonly encounter from customers?

Some objections are so predictable that it should be possible to anticipate them and answer them even before the customer gets around to raising them. It is important to develop counter-arguments. For example, many customers raise an objection to the effect that the product or service is too expensive. Whether this is a real concern or a first-ditch attempt to provoke the adviser into price concessions is irrelevant. The adviser must have an answer — perhaps to discuss the other benefits and the savings that can be made through them, for example with a packaged current account.

Organisations that do not subscribe to the formula approach to selling often train their sales staff to handle specific objections that commonly arise in their field in a set way. The following is a selection of objection-handling techniques that can be used in personal selling. Each is appropriate for a different kind of objection.

17.4.1 Qualify the objection

The first point in handling an objection is to 'qualify' it. This means finding out whether it is a **real or a false objection** and how important it is. This can be done by trying to understand the objection as specifically as possible, ie by clarifying exactly what the customer means. A good way of doing this is by paraphrasing what the customer has said: 'So what you're saying is . . .?'

Once the nature of the objection and its importance is clear, then an attempt can be made to solve the problem. If the problem lies in the customer's understanding or interpretation of what they have heard, then it should be straightforward to solve. If the problem lies in something specific and the customer is not willing to move, then the obstacle should be put into perspective and other compensating factors stressed.

The handling of objections or queries is another step in helping the customer to buy something for which they have seen a clear need and of which they can now see the full benefit.

17.4.2 Ask the objection back

If the customer says something vague, then it is appropriate for the adviser to ask for further elaboration, either to **define the objection better**, or to **find out whether the objection is real or a stalling excuse**. Exploring the objection also allows the adviser and the customer to define whether the objection is fundamental or peripheral.

If a buyer says 'I think your product is not as good as product X', the sales adviser should explore what is meant by the use of the word 'good'. This could cover a whole range of different areas in the competitive offering. The representative's response may therefore be designed to explore in more detail the underlying problem by asking 'In what way is it not as good?'

17.4.3 Agree and counter

Agreeing with the objection and countering it is often called the 'yes, but' technique. When the objection is based on fact, all the representative can legitimately do is **agree** with the substance, then **find a compensating factor** to outweigh it. Thus if the customer argues that the product being sold is more expensive than the competition's, the representative will reply with 'Yes, I agree that value for money is important. Although our product is expensive initially, you will find that the day-to-day running costs and the annual maintenance add up to a lot less.' Such a technique avoids creating excessive tension and argument because the customer feels that their objection has been acknowledged and satisfactorily answered.

Activity

> What techniques are used by advisers in your organisation to handle objections?

Handling objections requires a very careful response from advisers. They must *not* react by saying whatever is necessary to overcome the objection and clinch the sale, since doing so will only lead to legal or relationship problems later. The adviser must assess the situation, the type of objection, the mood of the customer and then choose the most appropriate style of response, without overstepping any ethical boundaries in terms of content. It is critical that winning the argument used to overcome the objection does not lead to a lost sale. Objections may interrupt the flow of the sales process either temporarily or permanently, and unless they are overcome, the final stages of the selling process cannot be achieved. Remember a 'no' now can be a 'yes' later.

17.5 After-sales care

Providing a professional service means more than selling a product to meet needs: it means ensuring that proper after-sales care is given and that reviews are carried out.

This will include ensuring that, where the acceptance procedure involves any delay, the customer is kept fully informed. It will also mean dealing with other related matters such as direct debits, delivery of documents, cancellation notices, standard reviews and any requests to alter the agreement.

After these general areas, customer servicing falls into two categories: proactive and reactive servicing.

17.5.1 Proactive servicing

Proactive servicing involves **instigating action** by contacting the customer to discuss future needs. This might relate to matters previously discussed, such as a salary review or job change, or to the customer now finding themselves in a position to address previously identified needs.

Even where there is no known future event or requirement, it is a good idea to agree a time to review the customer's situation. At a review, an adviser can find out if there have been any changes to the customer's circumstances and can update the records. By doing this, an adviser is in a strong position to identify opportunities to recommend new products appropriate to the customer's needs, or to recommend changes to existing products.

17.5.2 Reactive servicing

Reactive servicing happens as the result of a **request from the customer**, such as a request to discuss the recommendation after comments made in the media or by competitors. The customer's circumstances might change unexpectedly, resulting in a request for advice.

The request may not be received directly from the customer: it might be notification of non-payment of premiums or notification of death of a customer by the next of kin. In order to be fully prepared for all eventualities, clear and concise records must be maintained.

The keeping of all appropriate records will not only comply with the requirements of the Financial Services and Markets Act 2000, but it can also lead to more business through the collection of up-to-date information that could lead to a cross sale.

17.6 Cross sales

Unfortunately, cross selling can have a bad name – for example, when you go to buy a television or a washing machine the salesperson is always very keen to offer the extended warranty guarantee and expends a lot of effort doing this. This is because they get commission on the guarantee and not on the goods. It appears to be a hard sell and, often, people do not like it.

Unsurprisingly cross selling is one of the activities that many financial services providers find hard to do. It is, however, one of the best ways of growing the business, satisfying customers and improving your own personal skills. If done well, it will also improve and strengthen your relationships with your customers.

It can be good practice for all advisers to cross sell under the FSA rules because it ensures that all a customer's needs are covered and solutions offered. This leads to good customer care. It helps customer retention by improving the service and ensuring that the customer has more products with the provider, so making it more difficult for them to switch.

However, it is not a case of tagging some closed questions on to the end of an interview or exchange over the phone. It can be done well as:

◆ a natural part of conversation;

◆ a development of rapport and the relationship;

◆ a result of listening well to a customer. Even a throwaway line could be picked up by the adviser and returned to later in the conversation – 'You mentioned you were going away on holiday earlier; what travel insurance do you have in place for that?'

The key is to identify and strongly pursue those good opportunities that arise in sales contacts and dealings with customers.

Review questions

The following review questions are designed so that you can check your understanding of this topic.

The answers are provided at the end of these learning materials.

1. Why are 'needs'-based sales important?

2. How can you show you are listening actively?

3. What is empathy? Why is it a useful communication skill?

4. What can stop people from building empathy with others?

5. How can you build rapport with a customer?

6. In what situations can closed questions be useful?

7. What are the potential problems when asking questions?

8. What are the steps in the sales process?

9. Why is it important for an adviser to gather information about a customer's attitude to risk?

10. What are the five areas for a customer's financial needs and objectives?

11. Why is it important to talk to customers about 'benefits' rather than just the 'features' of a product or service?

12. What might be the reasons behind a customer objection?

13. What techniques can be used to handle objections? When would each be appropriate?

14. How can after-sales care be undertaken?

15. Why are cross sales important to the organisation?

Appendix A
Answers to review questions

Topic 1 Common types of retail customer

1. Customers prefer to have bank accounts rather than deal in cash because they:

    ◆ need to be able to receive their income in a form other than cash (cheque or direct credit);

    ◆ want access to different payment systems (cash, bank account systems, electronic or payment card);

    ◆ may like to be in control and have records of their transactions;

    ◆ want the convenience of using automatic payments (standing orders and direct debits) to manage their money;

    ◆ want to use credit available through a bank or building society, or to take finance from another provider and make repayment from the bank account;

    ◆ want access to plastic cards linked to their bank account;

    ◆ want the convenience of managing their money using telephone banking;

    ◆ want access to their money using the Internet via their computer.

2. Financial services organisations segment or divide their customer base further into groups of individuals with similar attributes to allow them to deliver

services particular to that segment. This enables the provider to target the customers with a range of products that are most likely to be suitable.

3. The account holders are jointly and severally liable for any debts incurred on the account. This means that if one of the account holders incurs a debt on the account, the other account holders will also be liable to repay it.

4. A 'minor' is a person under the age of 18, ie who has not achieved the 'age of majority' (power to vote in an election and be legally viewed as an adult). The prime consideration is the minor's ability to enter into a contract that may lead to their account being overdrawn. While minors are allowed to borrow for the purchase of 'necessities' (such as food or clothing, although not for luxury items such as an iPod), banks generally avoid making it possible for a minor to take an account overdrawn, as in the majority of cases the debt would be unenforceable. The lender would have to check what the borrowing was for and in many cases this is not practical. A way round this is to take a guarantee from the minor's family; however, if this is not taken correctly this form of security can be difficult to enforce, adding a further complication for the lender.

5. The main facilities required from a business account are:

    ◆ money transmission services;

    ◆ working capital;

    ◆ capital investement;

    ◆ protection from risk;

    ◆ foreign business services;

    ◆ treasury services;

    ◆ business advice.

6. The purpose of forming a limited liability partnership is that if the business should collapse, the partners' liability is limited to the amount that they have invested in the partnership, together with any personal guarantees they have given, for example to a bank that has made a loan to the business.

7. A **private limited company** (Ltd) has shares that are not easily transferable, as they are not listed on the stock exchange. This means the values may be difficult to assess, because if the holder wanted to sell them they would not have access to a ready market for them. Traditionally, many of these types of business have been owned by several members of a family, who would not be attracted to selling the shares.

    A **public limited company** (plc) can sell its shares to members of the public via the Alternative Investment Market (AIM) or via the London Stock Exchange. This means that plcs have ready access to investor funding in a way that private limited companies do not. The owners of the company will not necessarily be the individuals who are responsible for running the organisation, which is often the case with a private limited company.

    A plc obtains a trading certificate, rather than the certificate of incorporation required for a private limited company.

8. The holder of a large financial asset may decide to put it into trust to allow other individuals (often relatives) or organisations to benefit from it without having control over it. For example, a parent may decide to place a portfolio

of stocks and shares into trust for the benefit of their children, so that the children can use the income from dividends but not use the capital. There used to be tax advantages in doing this, although the law in this area has recently been tightened. A trust can also be created under the terms of a will.

9. The dangers of not making a will are that the deceased does not give any direction as to how their estate should be divided between their remaining relatives, which could cause considerable family tension at a time when it would be least welcome. Dying without making a will is called dying 'intestate' and if this occurs the estate is dealt with according to the laws of intestacy, which surviving relatives may feel is unfair.

10. The banking facilities required by a large charity with a chain of retail outlets would be:

    ◆   the ability to pay in cash and cheques at locations near shop premises, possibly with night safe facilities, and card payment services for those customers wishing to pay by card;

    ◆   money transmission services to pay for the costs of running the shops and for the salaries or wages of those people who are employed by the charity;

    ◆   protection from risk in the form of insurance for the premises, and public liability insurance should a member of the public have an accident in one of the shops;

    ◆   some working capital requirements in the form of overdraft facilities to cover the day-to-day running expenses.

Topic 2   The range of customer backgrounds, needs, wants and aspirations

1. Financial capability means being able to manage your money, keep track of your finances, plan ahead, make informed decisions about financial products and stay up to date about financial matters. Financial capability is a broad concept, encompassing people's knowledge and skills to understand their own financial circumstances, along with the motivation to take action. Financially capable consumers plan ahead, find and use information, know when to seek advice and can understand and act on this advice.

2. It is necessary to improve levels of financial capability because people are increasingly being asked to take responsibility for managing their money and making decisions that will affect their long-term financial health. It makes consumers more knowledgeable about what is available and leads to their demanding better products and services from providers. The complexity and number of options for the consumer has increased, and better financial capability enables them to understand this and make better choices as a result.

3. The life-cycle events that tend to be fixed for most people are growing up and getting old.

4. The life cycle is important to the marketing of products and services because consumers can be put into life-cycle categories to facilitate accurate targeting of marketing and advertising. Examples of these categories are: trendy singles, nest invaders, double income no kids (dinkies), new parents and empty nesters.

5. The lifestyle choice of 'consume now, pay later' means that someone will buy an item now that they cannot actually afford. They make the purchase by taking out a loan for the funds, so anticipating their future income, paying back the loan over the coming months or years. However, they need to be aware of what will happen if they cannot afford the repayments at some future time. The inability to pay off debts will leave the individual in a position of over-indebtedness and financial hardship, which could potentially have greater consequences, such as losing their home.

    The lifestyle choice 'saving now, buy later' means that someone will save money to finance a purchase; they will wait until they have enough saved before they buy. This works well in the short term for expenditure such as a holiday; however, someone may never save enough to buy a house and the cost of renting a house to live in may mean that they cannot save enough to purchase one of their own.

    Both attitudes rely on future income to fund purchases but the former is riskier than the latter if the source of the income dries up. 'Consume now, pay later' people need to know the level of debt that they can actually afford and consider the impact of an increase in interest rates on the repayments they are making. 'Save now, buy later' people need to accept that unless they do borrow there are some purchases, such as a house, they will never be able to afford.

    These attitudes stem from people's life experiences, how they were brought up, their schooling, their life-cycle stage, the influences of their peer group and society in general. For example, in the UK homeownership is much more widely accepted than in the rest of Europe. Many European families rent a property for all their lives, so never have a mortgage debt.

6. **Needs** are defined as those things without which we would not survive. People also have **wants**, which are not necessarily essential items but those that satisfy the ego in some way, such as a top-of-the-range car, when the basic model would be equally good at transporting someone to work every day. People will buy products to satisfy both needs and wants.

7. Being 'risk averse' means that people do not want to take too many risks, or risks that could potentially have serious consequences. In terms of financial services, one drawback may be that they do not have the opportunity to benefit from some of the rewards that taking a risk could bring, such as the income from an investment. It may also mean that an individual does not enjoy a holiday abroad, or own a car that could open up better job prospects by making them more mobile, because they are averse to taking out a loan for these items of expenditure.

8. The impact of cases like that of Barclays is that consumers' confidence in financial services institutions, the organisations that regulate them, such as the FSA, and the government is diminished. This may mean the consumers look for alternative ways of investing their money, for example in property or business ventures that they perceive carry less risk and over which they have more personal control.

9. People would be reluctant to take out financial services in a language that was not their own because they would be worried that they could not understand what was being said to them and also that they were not making themselves understood. This could lead to money being paid away in error and taking products and services that are not suitable for their needs.

10. It is appropriate to consider an individual's religious beliefs when offering banking services in order to provide services that are compliant with those

beliefs. For example, Islamic banking, in which the payment of interest is prohibited, is a very different model from that on which UK banking is based.

Topic 3   Consumer sources of guidance and information

1. The FSA's view of consumer responsibility stems from the Financial Service and Markets Act, which states that that it must note the 'general principle that consumers should take responsibility for their decisions'. In other words, the FSA can require that consumers are provided with appropriate advice and information within an effectively regulated industry, but consumers have a responsibility to ensure that they understand the information they are given and make financial decisions accordingly.

2. Consumers require protection because there is often an imbalance between the resources and knowledge of financial services providers and the individual consumers. All consumers do not have the same level of understanding of financial matters and some products and services are extremely complex.

3. The limits of compensation under the Financial Services Compensation Scheme are as follows:

    ◆ **Default of an insurance company**: compensation is 90 per cent of the balance, with no upper limit. If the insurance is compulsory (such as employer's liability cover or some types of motor insurance), the figure is 100 per cent of the whole amount.

    ◆ **Loss due to insolvency** of a firm carrying out investment business regulated under FSMA 2000: 100 per cent of the claim, up to a maximum of £50,000.

    ◆ **Loss of deposited funds due to the default of a bank or building society**: 100 per cent of the first £85,000. The majority of cases are paid within seven days, with more complex cases taking up to 20 days.

    ◆ **Claims against firms involved in mortgage advice and arranging**: 100 per cent of the claim, up to a maximum of £50,000.

    ◆ **Claims against insurance intermediaries**: the amount that can be claimed will depend on the nature of the circumstances.

4. Before a customer can present their complaint to the Financial Ombudsman Service they must have first complained to the provider itself. The FOS will become involved only when a provider's internal complaints procedures have been exhausted without the customer obtaining satisfaction. Complaints to the FOS must be made within six years of the event that gives rise to the complaint, or within three years of the time when the complainant should have become aware that they had cause for complaint, whichever is the later. The FOS will not usually consider any complaint that is the subject of a court case.

5. The Lending Code covers all unsecured lending to retail customers – overdrafts, loans and credit cards. Secured lending to small businesses is also covered.

6. The main functions of the ICO are to:

- ◆ **educate and influence** by promoting good practice and give information and advice;

- ◆ **resolve problems** by dealing with eligible complaints from people who think their rights have been breached;

- ◆ **enforce** by using legal sanctions against those who ignore or refuse to accept their obligations.

7. The 'Common Financial Statement' (CFS) sets out the income and **essential expenditure** of a person in debt and how much money is available to repay creditors. These factors have always been a key tool in the money advice process. Creditors need to know that when reduced debt repayments are offered, these are fair and reasonable. Money advisers need to know that their clients will receive consistent treatment from the people to whom they owe money. Historically, a lack of agreement among money advisers regarding a common format for financial statements has led to a lack of consistency and, in some instances, this has led to creditors being reluctant to accept offers of payment.

8. The CAB adviser:

- ◆ helps to empower the client to deal with the problem themselves;

- ◆ gains the client's trust to talk about their financial situation;

- ◆ establishes the extent of the debt problem;

- ◆ checks whether the client is legally liable to pay all their debts;

- ◆ identifies ways in which the client could increase their income, including by claiming benefits and tax credits, getting benefits claims backdated, claiming on payment protection insurances and applying for charitable grants;

- ◆ helps the client to draw up a budget and advises them on reducing expenditure;

- ◆ identifies the debtor's most important debts – those for which, if acceptable payment arrangements are not made, the debtor could lose their home, their liberty, fuel supply, or essential household goods on hire purchase;

- ◆ helps the client to decide a suitable strategy for dealing with their debt problem, including making arrangements with creditors, bankruptcy or individual voluntary arrangements;

- ◆ works out and negotiates fair and sustainable repayments to all the client's creditors, and if possible, arranges for the client to pay these via a payment distribution system;

- ◆ advises the client on court procedures for debt recovery, and if possible, represents them at any debt-related hearings.

9. The CCCS provides access to trained advisers by telephone and to its anonymous assessment process, CCCS Debt Remedy, via the Internet.

10. These methods could be helpful to consumers because they can access both from the comfort and convenience of their own home without having to go to a face-to-face appointment, which they could find embarrassing or stressful.

Topic 4   The financial services environment and regulation

1. The characteristics of money are that it must be:

    ◆ sufficient in quanity;

    ◆ generally acceptable to all parties in transactions;

    ◆ divisible into small units, so that transaction of all sizes can be precisely carried out; and

    ◆ portable.

2. Intermediation is undertaken by any organisation that acts as a middleman to a transaction. A financial intermediary is an institution that borrows money from the surplus sector of the economy and lends it to the deficit sector. A lower rate of interest is paid to the person with the surplus and a higher rate of interest is charged to the person with the deficit. An intermediary's profit margin is the difference between the two interest rates. Banks and building societies are the best-known examples of a financial intermediary who undertakes this function.

3. The functions of the Bank of England are to:

    ◆ issue bank notes;

    ◆ act as banker to the government;

    ◆ act as banker to the banks;

    ◆ advise the government on the economy and set interest rates through the Monetary Policy Committee;

    ◆ manage the UK's official reserves of gold and foreign currencies on behalf of the Treasury;

    ◆ act as lender of last resort to the banks

4. A building society is owned by its customers, who are classed as 'members', and it is therefore termed a 'mutual' organisation. This type of organisation is one that is not constituted as a company and does not, therefore, have shareholders. The most common types of mutual organisation are building societies, co-operatives, friendly societies and credit unions and a small proportion of life assurance companies. This is in contrast to a bank, which is owned by shareholders and aims to make a profit that it can pay out to them as a dividend.

5. A credit union is another example of a mutual organisation. Credit unions are financial co-operatives run for the benefit of their members, who are all linked in a particular way, for instance by living in the same area or belonging to the same club, church, employer or other association. A co-operative is an autonomous (self-governing) group of people who have come together to meet common economic, cultural and social needs by forming a jointly owned, democratic organisation. In order to join a credit union, the member (customer) must meet the membership requirements, pay any required entrance fee and buy at least one £1 share in the union. All members are equal, regardless of the size of their shareholding. This is in contrast to banks, which are owned by their shareholders, who can buy as many shares as they choose to invest.

6. Legislation has increased in the financial services industry:

    ◆ in response to scandals or crises such as the collapse of Baring Bank and the problems that hit Equitable Life;

    ◆ as a result of greater consumer awareness and a demand for a more customer-focused business approach;

    ◆ in response to changes in lifestyle, with more relaxed attitudes to marriage and divorce and the strengthening of the rights of civil partners;

    ◆ as a result of changes in business methods and, in particular, technology, creating a need to regulate the way providers operate;

    ◆ in response to innovation in product design, leading to a need to provide consumers with appropriate information about the features and benefits of the products they are buying;

    ◆ due to the increase and complexity of financial products, again leading to the need for more information and advice.

7. The financial marketplace changed rapidly following deregulation, increasing in size and complexity. This quickly revealed the inadequate protection afforded to customers by existing legislation. Many existing laws were quite inadequate to deal with what was now a much more sophisticated and competitive industry.

8. The statutory objectives of the FSA are to:

    ◆ maintain confidence in the UK financial system;

    ◆ promote financial stability – contributing to the protection and enhancement of the stability of the UK financial system;

    ◆ secure an appropriate level of protection for consumers;

    ◆ reduce the scope for financial crime.

9. The powers of enforcement held by the FSA are to:

    ◆ withdraw a firm's authorisation;

    ◆ prohibit an individual from operating in financial services;

    ◆ prevent an individual from undertaking specific regulated activities;

    ◆ censure firms and individuals through public statements;

    ◆ impose financial penalties;

    ◆ seek injunctions;

    ◆ apply to court to freeze assets;

    ◆ seek restitution orders; and

    ◆ prosecute firms and individuals who undertake regulated activities without authorisation.

10. The OFT regulates the financial services industry via the following Acts:

    ◆ Consumer Protection from Unfair Trading Regulations;

    ◆ Consumer Credit Acts 1974 and 2006;

◆ Unfair Terms in Consumer Contracts Regulations 1999;

◆ Enterprise Act 2002.

It also achieves its aims through others so will work with sector regulators, government, the courts, the Competition Commission, the European Commission, local authority trading standards services, and businesses, consumers and their representatives.

Topic 5   Fundamental regulatory themes

1. It is important to manage financial services providers prudently in order to protect the firms themselves, their customers and the economy, by establishing rules and principles that should ensure the continuation of a safe and efficient market, able to withstand any foreseeable problems.

    One of the key areas of prudential control for financial institutions relates to their capital adequacy. Simply put, capital adequacy is the requirement for firms conducting investment business to have sufficient funds. There are different rules for deposit-takers (banks and building societies), investment firms and life assurance companies.

2. Liquidity risk (as defined by the FSA) is the risk that a firm, though solvent, does not have sufficient financial resources available to enable it to meet its obligations as they fall due. In assessing liquidity risks, banks need to consider the timing of both their assets and their liabilities and endeavour to match them as far as possible.

3. The purpose of 'Treating Customers Fairly' is to develop a more ethical frame of mind within the industry, leading to more ethical behaviour at every stage of firms' and individuals' relationships with their customers.

4. A financial promotion is defined as an 'invitation or inducement to engage in investment activity'. This includes:

    ◆ advertisements in all forms of media;

    ◆ telephone calls;

    ◆ marketing during personal visits to clients;

    ◆ presentations to groups.

    Financial promotions can be 'communicated' only if they have been prepared, or approved, by an authorised person.

    There is a distinction between:

    ◆ **non-written financial promotions**, such as personal visits and telephone conversations; and

    ◆ **written financial promotions**, such as newspaper advertisements and those on Internet sites.

5. The rules regarding unsolicited promotions (cold calls) are as follows:

    ◆ They are permitted only in relation to certain investments, including packaged products, such as life assurance policies and unit trusts. They are not permitted in relation to higher volatility funds (which use gearing) or life policies with links to such funds, due to the increased investment risk involved. Cold calls are not permitted in relation to mortgage contracts.

◆ Unsolicited telephone calls or visits must not be made during unsocial hours, generally taken to mean between 9.00pm and 9.00am Monday to Saturday, and not on a Sunday.

◆ The caller must check that the recipient is happy to proceed with the call.

6. 'Know Your Customer' relates to the need to obtain evidence of identification when entering a new business relationship in order to prevent money laundering and the need for financial advisers to take reasonable steps to find out and record all the details of the customer in relation to the services they are offering. The information must be collected before any recommendation is made.

7. Under the Proceeds of Crime Act 2002 the three principal money laundering offences are as follows:

◆ **Concealing criminal property**: criminal property is property that a person knows, or suspects, to be the proceeds of any criminal activity; it is a criminal offence to conceal, disguise, convert or transfer criminal property – clearly, money laundering is included in those definitions.

◆ **Arranging**: this happens when a person becomes involved in a process that they know or suspect will enable someone else to acquire, retain, use or control criminal property (where that other person also knew or suspected that the property derived from criminal activity).

◆ **Acquiring, using or possessing**: it is a criminal offence for a person to acquire, use or possess any property when that person knows or suspects that the property is the proceeds of criminal activity.

8. A hard complaint is one where there is an allegation that the complainant has suffered financial loss, material distress or material inconvenience. Soft complaints are any other complaints and are, for the most part, subject to the same rules as hard complaints – the only differences are that they are not subject to the usual deadlines and they do not have to be reported to the FSA.

9. BCOBS was introduced because the FSA felt:

◆ that it was irregular to have a situation whereby it would regulate payment services and not the consumer's core retail relationship;

◆ that this irregularity would potentially affect the FSA's regulatory effectiveness because it would be unable to look comprehensively across all risks affecting firms' retail market activities within its scope; and

◆ this could be to the consumers' detriment.

In addition, the Banking Code Standards Board did not have a strong media profile nor did it have the power to fine organisations.

10. Under the Payment Services Directive changes will occur in relation to payment services made in euro or sterling, so primarily to sterling and euro denominated accounts. The FSA will take over regulation of the following:

◆ a shift to statutory obligations for 'payment services business';

◆ some detailed changes on information provision before the opening of a 'payment account', and subsequently amending its terms, and in respect of individual transactions;

◆ specific requirements on the 'value dating' and availability of funds to customers (for example, funds to be available to the payee immediately after funds have been credited to a payment account);

◆ the content of the terms and conditions of the account (a 'framework contract');

◆ provisions on post-sale information;

◆ requirements on the operation of accounts (including interest rate changes) and termination; and

◆ requirements on changes to information already provided, for example, two months' notice of changes to framework contracts.

Topic 6   Legal concepts relating to banking – general

1. The Banking Conduct of Business Sourcebook defines a banking customer as:

    ◆ a consumer;

    ◆ a micro enterprise that employs fewer than 10 people with a turnover of less than €2m;

    ◆ a charity that has an annual income of less than £1m;

    ◆ a trustee of a trust that has a net asset value of less than £1m.

2. Banks can make reasonable adjustments to their services to meet the needs of disabled people by:

    ◆ providing ramps and wider doorways for wheelchair users;

    ◆ installing an induction loop for people who are hearing impaired;

    ◆ giving the option to make enquiries by email as well as by phone;

    ◆ providing disability awareness training for staff who have contact with the public;

    ◆ providing larger, well-defined signage for people with impaired vision.

3. The purpose of the fair trading laws is to *prevent false claims* being made about products and services and to ensure a *fair environment* for commerce. The main areas covered by fair trading laws are:

    ◆ safety;

    ◆ pricing;

    ◆ weights and measures;

    ◆ descriptions of products and services;

    ◆ the contract between a buyer and seller;

    ◆ competition between businesses;

    ◆ intellectual property and counterfeiting;

4. The UTCCRs aim to protect consumers from terms that have not been individually negotiated and impose unfair burdens on them, or which reduce their statutory or common law rights. The Office of Fair Trading (OFT) deals with complaints under these regulations.

   Where a term is 'unfair' as defined under the regulations, it is not binding on the consumer. However, if the remainder of the contract is capable of continuing despite the removal of that unfair term, then it will do so.

   Terms that have not been individually negotiated include any standard contract terms such as those in account-opening forms, or personal loan, investment or insurance agreements. These are examples of where the terms have been drafted in advance. Even if some terms of a contract have been individually negotiated, the regulations will apply to the rest, if overall the contract's terms are standardised. The onus is on the supplier to prove that a term was individually negotiated. If this is in dispute, then this is a good reason to ensure that providers keep detailed notes when negotiating terms with prospective customers.

5. Sensitive personal data is data that can only be processed if the individual has given explicit consent (in other words, it is not sufficient to claim that the individual has never specifically withheld their consent). Sensitive data includes information about an individual's:

   ◆ racial origin;

   ◆ religious beliefs;

   ◆ political persuasion;

   ◆ physical health;

   ◆ mental health;

   ◆ criminal (but not civil) proceedings.

6. Customers can obtain information an organisation holds about them by making a written request to the data controller and paying a fee of £10. The organisation then has 40 days to respond to this request.

7. The enforcement powers of the Information Commissioner include the power to prosecute a data controller that fails to comply with an information notice or enforcement notice. This is a criminal offence and there are two further criminal offences under the Act.

   ◆ It is an offence to fail to make a proper notification to the Information Commissioner. Notification is the way in which a data controller effectively registers with the Office of the Information Commissioner, by acknowledging that personal data is being held and by specifying the purpose(s) for which the data is being held.

   ◆ It is also an offence to process data without authorisation from the Commissioner.

   The maximum penalty for these offences is £500,000, unless the case goes to the Crown Court, in which case there is no limit on the possible fine.

8. Regulations for organisations that deal with their customers at a distance are the:

◆ Consumer Protection (Distance Selling) Regulations 2000;

◆ Electronic Commerce Regulations;

◆ Privacy and Electronic Communication Regulations.

Financial services providers need to comply with the Financial Services (Distance Marketing) Regulations 2004.

9. Financial services sold at a distance should be followed up by a communication on paper or other durable medium (such as email).

10. The Advertising Standards Authority has jurisdiction over:

◆ commercial mail, sent through the post, by email or text message;

◆ advertisements and sales promotions on TV or radio, and also on the Internet, whether these are paid-for ads or not.

Topic 7   Legal concepts relating to banking – specific

1. Business standards required by the FSA are described in the Prudential sourcebooks, Conduct of Business sourcebooks, Market Conduct sourcebook and the Training and Competence sourcebook.

2. The Mortgage Conduct of Business Rules covers lending, administering, advising on and arranging regulated mortgage contracts.

3. The Banking Conduct of Business Sourcebook covers:

   1. application – accepting deposits from customers from premises based in the UK;

   2. communications with banking customers and financial promotions;

   3. distance communications and e-commerce;

   4. information to be communicated to banking customers and statements of account;

   5. post-sale requirements – the service must be prompt, efficient and fair. This includes service to customers in financial difficulty, those who wish to move bank accounts, and lost and dormant accounts;

   6. cancellation – this includes rights to cancel and when these are applicable.

4. Once a decision has been made by the Financial Ombudsman Service (FOS), it is binding on the financial services provider; the customer, however, can choose to take the matter to court if they wish. If the customer decides to accept the FOS's decision then both the customer and the provider are bound by the decision.

5. The Consumer Credit Act 1974 was designed to regulate, supervise and control certain types of lending to individuals and to provide borrowers with protection from unscrupulous lenders.

6. The Office of Fair Trading regulates the relationship between consumers and providers under the Consumer Credit Acts. Part of this activity is the issuing of licences to providers without which they cannot provider credit to consumers.

7. Insolvencies increased from 2003 onwards, due to a change in legislation which made it easier for people to start afresh, having made arrangements with their creditors. The social stigma relating to insolvency has decreased, making it a more attractive solution for people with mounting debts who have no means to pay them off. A further reason is the worsening economic climate which has meant people have lost their jobs through redundancy as businesses fail, thus losing their income, which they had been using to repay their debt.

8. A debt relief order (DRO) is:

   ◆ applicable for people who do not own their own home, have little surplus income (less than £50 per month) or assets and owe less than £15,000;

   ◆ run by the Insolvency Service in partnership with skilled debt advisers called approved intermediaries, and requires approval of the court.

   An Individual Voluntary Arrangement (IVA) is a formal version of a DRO in which the individual is helped by an insolvency practitioner:

   ◆ The individual may own their own home and there are no limits on the amounts owed. It gives them some control of how their assets are dealt with, but, again, with the approval of the court.

   ◆ It may be applicable if the individual has some surplus income to pay regular sums to creditors.

   ◆ It carries none of the restrictions applicable to bankruptcy and is a cheaper option than bankruptcy as far as the insolvency practitioner's fees are concerned.

   Bankruptcy involves the court making a bankruptcy order after a bankruptcy petition has been presented by either the debtor or one or more creditors who are owed at least £750:

   ◆ There is no upper limit to the amount that can be owed.

   ◆ An official receiver or an insolvency practitioner can be appointed to take responsibility for administering the bankruptcy process and protecting the bankrupt's assets from the date of the bankruptcy order.

   ◆ There are restrictions that do not apply to a DRO or IVA. These are that it is a criminal offence for an undischarged bankrupt to:

     – obtain credit of more than £500 without disclosing their bankruptcy;

     – carry on a business in a different name from that in which they were made bankrupt;

     – be involved with a limited company or act as a director without the court's permission.

9. The UK Payments Administration (UKPA) is a trade association for payments and for those institutions that deliver payment services to customers. It provides a forum for its members to come together on non-competitive issues relating to the payments industry. It also co-ordinates a range of activities to tackle payment-related fraud. The UKPA sets guidelines for the industry relating to plastic cards, CHAPS and cheques.

10. The Finance and Leasing Association Lending Code of Practice covers three types of provider that the customer took the loan from. This could be:

◆ direct from the finance company;

◆ through a supplier of goods and services, for example in a shop or motor dealership;

◆ through a credit broker (a third party who arranges finance).

Topic 8   Key retail financial products and services

1. The basic features of a bank account is that it:

    ◆ gives the ability to hold credit balances with a bank or building society and, sometimes, receive a small amount of interest on credit balances over a certain amount;

    ◆ provides regular statements showing transactions in and out of the account;

    ◆ provides a means of making payments to third parties – all of the banks and building societies provide a chequebook and/or a debit card, plus the ability to set up standing orders and direct debits;

    ◆ provides a debit card, which enables account holders to draw cash from cash machines around the country in a variety of locations outside normal banking hours, and also overseas;

    ◆ may allow overdrafts up to a pre-set agreed overdraft limit (although this might only be offered to customers with a good track record with the provider);

    ◆ attracts certain charges – for example, in relation to overdrafts or for duplicate statements, and interest will be charged on overdrawn balances;

    ◆ can generally be accessed via online or telephone banking.

2. Banks segment their customers in order to cross sell more financial services to groups of customers with similar attributes.

3. The 'basic' bank account is a simplified current account, designed for people who might not otherwise open a current account, or want anything more sophisticated. They are particularly appropriate for people receiving state benefits or pensions who have been used to collecting their payments in cash at the post office.

    Basic bank accounts are able to receive money by a wide variety of methods, but the methods of withdrawing money are limited. Cash can be obtained with a card from ATMs and also from post offices. Payments can be made by direct debit, but no chequebooks are issued on these accounts, and there is no overdraft facility. The simplicity of operation is to ensure that customers with less financial capability feel comfortable using them and in control.

4. A customer may choose a fixed-term deposit account because they will know exactly when they will be able to access their funds. They could choose to make this date up to five years into the future, so obtaining a better rate of interest. This is in contrast to a notice account where the customer has to give a specified amount of time as notice to withdraw the funds. Typically this is up to twelve months and no longer, so potentially affecting the rate they will obtain.

5. Borrowing money on an overdraft means that:

    ◆ no set amount has to be repaid each month;

    ◆ the interest rate charged may be lower than interest rates charged on credit cards (although the interest rate on an unauthorised overdraft will be higher than that on a credit card);

    ◆ the facility will be set for a fixed period, at the end of which it will need to be repaid or renegotiated.

    Borrowing money on a credit card means that:

    ◆ a minimum amount has to be repaid each month;

    ◆ interest rates are typically higher than overdraft rates;

    ◆ customers who repay their credit card balances in full at the end of each month do not pay any interest, unless it is for a cash advance;

    ◆ it is possible to swap between providers that offer interest-free periods for card balances obtained from a competitor;

    ◆ the card limit remains in place with no fixed expiry date. It may, however, be adjusted by the provider depending on card usage.

6. A customer may be attracted to borrowing money on a credit card because it is simple to arrange and manage. There is no set repayment plan so they can repay as much or as little as they can afford each month.

7. A prepaid card is a useful solution for:

    ◆ giving someone a gift;

    ◆ travelling abroad;

    ◆ helping younger family members to learn about managing their money;

    ◆ managing money by separating it into different places for different purposes;

    ◆ someone who is having difficulty opening a bank account and needs to have benefits or wages paid electronically to the card.

8. For a lender, the main risk with an unsecured loan is non-repayment: the lender relies purely on the borrower's personal promise to repay. There are further risks relating to errors in the documentation that could lead to the contract being avoided by the borrower. Errors in the assessment method might result in the lender taking on borrowing that is too high a risk, leading to problems later.

9. The main benefit to a customer of taking a personal loan for a holiday is that they can repay the debt before the next holiday is due. They will have a structured repayment plan which they can afford and can budget for. It is quick and easy to arrange with monthly payments being made from their current account.

10. The potential disadvantage of borrowing on a personal loan rather than overdraft, where the customer has credit balances for part of the month, is that interest is not being charged while the current account is in credit. This means that the personal loan would be a more expensive way of borrowing in terms of total interest paid (assuming the interest rates were similar).

Topic 9   Key retail financial products, services and the methods of service delivery

1. The mortgagor is the person who owns the property and the mortgagee is the lender.

2. The rights of a borrower when they give a legal charge over their property are as follows:

   ◆ They have the legal right to repay the loan at any time, although this may be subject to an early repayment penalty if the borrower has chosen a fixed-rate, capped-rate, or discounted mortgage rate deal. (The lender will have obtained matched funds to create these sorts of deals so will incur costs in releasing the customer from the agreement.)

   ◆ Borrowers whose properties have been taken into possession by a lender are still entitled to repay the loan right up to the time when the property is sold.

   ◆ The borrower is entitled to the remainder of the sale price after a loan has been repaid, so if the lender sells the property to repay the loan, any surplus remaining after the first and any subsequent charges have been met must be paid over to the borrower. In many cases the property is sold at auction and the price obtained is relatively low to reflect the quick sale. This means there may well be little or no surplus to return to the customer.

3. Affordability is one of the main factors that affects the borrower's likelihood of repaying the debt. It is based on the borrower's surplus income after other monthly bills and outgoings have been met.

4. A further advance is a way of releasing equity in a borrower's property. The borrower takes another loan from the same lender secured by a charge over their property.

   A second mortgage is one that is created when the borrower offers the property as security for more borrowing with a new lender while the first lender still has a mortgage loan on the property. The new lender takes a second charge on the property and ranks behind the first lender for any share in the proceeds in the event of a forced sale.

5. Saving should be considered to be a relatively short-term deposit of funds that can be easily accessed, perhaps for an emergency or 'rainy day' money. Investment, however, is for funds that are surplus to these deposits, which the customer is happy to tie up for a longer period (say, for a minimum of five years) with the expectation of a better rate of return. Investments often carry a higher risk to the capital deposited depending on the type of 'asset class' to which they belong. The customer may have to accept a higher degree of risk for investing in some of these asset classes (such as stocks and shares) in return for the potential for a higher reward.

6. The benefit of a pooled investment is that the customer puts their money with that of other investors into a fund to be invested into a variety of assets (such as shares, bonds or property). This creates a larger 'pool' of money than a single investor would have been able to accumulate on their own and so enables the fund managers to spread the risk of loss between the investors and to save on costs. Open-ended investment funds, investment trusts and life assurance bonds are the most common pooled investments.

7. Pensions are tax efficient because the government will refund any income tax paid on the value of the contributions made by individuals to their pension. The retirement benefits are also tax free.

8. A customer might be attracted to a SIPP because they can invest in other types of asset, notably commercial property, which they might prefer to the usual stock-market-based assets in which personal and stakeholder pensions are normally invested. A further benefit is that a SIPP fund can lend money to any unconnected third party, either an individual or company (but not a family member or the business of a family member) and so be another way of investing for a pension fund.

9. Term assurance is where the sum assured is payable only if the life assured dies before the end of a specified term. If the life assured survives the term, the cover ceases and no payment or refund of premiums is made. Similarly, if the policy is cancelled part way through the term, it has no cash surrender value. The term can be from one month to 30 years or more.

    Level term assurance is where the amount of insurance remains at the same level throughout the term of the policy. Decreasing term assurance is where the amount reduces throughout the term. Both of these types of policy can be used to cover mortgage loans. Level term assurance is used to cover interest-only mortgages, as no capital is repaid during the term, and decreasing term assurance is used for capital and repayment mortgages, where the capital amount outstanding reduces over the time of the loan.

10. Branch banking features and benefits:

    ◆ The ability to hold face-to-face meetings with an adviser, which gives customers peace of mind when dealing with complex situations such as taking out a mortgage.

    ◆ A counter service to pay in cash or cheques, which gives the convenience of being able to deal with income in this format.

    ◆ Staff available to help customers with queries and to cross sell appropriate products, thereby ensuring that customers needs are met.

    Telephone banking features and benefits:

    ◆ The facility to speak to an adviser out of normal office hours, which makes banking easier and more convenient.

    ◆ Simple transactions can be carried out from the comfort of the customer's own home; again, this is more convenient than going to a branch.

    ◆ A range of products and services for which the customer can apply at a time that is convenient for them.

    Internet banking features and benefits:

    ◆ The ability to self-serve at any time and from any location that suits the customer. This makes Internet banking highly convenient for the customer and gives them full control of their finances.

    ◆ The ability to apply online for a number of products/services, which reduces the time required for decisions to be made.

- Brochureware is available for existing and potential customers to browse through at their convenience, so allowing them to make comparisons and informed choices about products.

- Price comparison websites provide a wide range of information on competitors' products, again making it easier for the customer to make an informed choice.

Topic 10   The opening and running of accounts

1. The various different entities that may open a bank account are:

   - a sole personal customer;

   - a joint personal customer;

   - a sole proprietor;

   - a number of people trading as a partnership;

   - a number of people trading as a limited liability partnership;

   - a private limited company;

   - a public limited company;

   - trustees;

   - executors or administrators of a deceased person;

   - clubs, societies or associations;

   - charities.

2. The principle of joint and several liability means that each party to an account (most commonly personal joint accounts and partnerships) is liable for any debts created on the account in two ways. They are 'jointly liable' – as a group, for the whole amount of the debt created on the account, and can be sued as a whole unit. They are also 'severally liable' – each individual is liable in their personal capacity for all of the debt. So, joint and several liability means that a debt can be recovered from an individual, or the group. Either a part of the debt or all of the debt can be recovered from an individual.

3. A mandate may be terminated by:

   - notice;

   - death;

   - mental illness;

   - bankruptcy;

   - resolution of a limited company;

   - winding up of a company;

   - liquidation of the provider.

4. If a sole customer dies leaving an account overdrawn then the personal representatives of the deceased will have to account to the provider for repayment out of the deceased's estate when it is wound up. If there are no funds in the estate to make the payment then the debt will have to be written off.

   In the case of a joint personal account the bank has to approach the surviving party regarding the repayment of the funds.

5. A bank can exercise its right of set-off when a customer has more than one account in the same name. The bank can set-off (or combine) the customer's account that is in credit with the one that is in debit.

6. *Clayton's Case* is likely to come into effect at the end of a banking relationship, particularly on the death of a partner, but also on the winding up of companies, or where security for a debt has been taken. It relates to current accounts and mainly where the account is in debit (overdrawn).

7. The factors affecting the price of a loan are the:

   ◆ lost opportunity of the depositor for investing the money elsewhere;

   ◆ amount;

   ◆ term;

   ◆ risk;

   ◆ term and risk relationship and any security provided.

8. A secured loan is cheaper than an unsecured loan because the customer is giving the lender a secondary source of repayment (an asset given as security) should they be unable to keep up the loan repayments. The lender relies purely on the borrower's personal promise to repay on an unsecured loan.

9. The frequency with which interest is applied to an account affects the total amount of interest paid to (or received from) the customer. For deposit accounts this means that the customer will receive more interest during a twelve-month period if the interest is applied quarterly rather than, say, annually. For customers with a loan account this means that if interest is applied quarterly they will, overall, pay more interest than if interest is applied annually. This assumes that in both cases interest rates remain unchanged.

10. Annual percentage rate (APR) is used to describe the true cost of money borrowed on mortgages, loans and credit cards. The calculation for APR takes into account the basic interest rate, the frequencywith which it is charged, all initial fees and any other costs the customer has to pay.

    Equivalent annual rate (EAR) is used to illustrate the full percentage cost of overdrafts and any type of account that that can be in credit and also go overdrawn. The calculation shows the true cost if the overdraft facility is used. In the same way as APR calculations, EAR takes account of the basic rate of interest and when the interest is charged, plus any additional charges.

    In most respects EAR and APR achieve the same thing; however, APR applies to pure lending products only whereas EAR applies to a service such as a bank current account that can be in credit or overdrawn.

Topic 11   Payments and payment systems

1. The effect of endorsing a cheque (signing it on the back) is that the holder (who does not have to be the original payee) now has title (legal ownership) of it. The new holder becomes the 'holder in due course' and can sue the original drawer for the amount of the cheque should it be unpaid.

2. The purpose of crossing a cheque is to reduce the risk of the cheque being misappropriated and funds going to the wrong person. This is especially useful where cheques are sent through the post. If the drawee acts contrary to the mandate given in the crossing it is liable to the drawer for breach of contract and cannot debit the drawer's account.

3. The effect of the 'not negotiable' crossing is that it restricts the negotiability of the cheque but not its transferability. It means that the cheque is no longer a bill of exchange: a person who takes the cheque cannot obtain a better title (legal ownership) than that of the transferor and can, in turn, only confer a limited title to a subsequent transferee. Consequently, although a transferee can be a 'holder for value', they cannot be a 'holder in due course'. A third party taking a cheque crossed in this manner therefore takes the risk that the person from whom they have taken it has no title to it in the first place and therefore cannot pass on a valid title.

4. A bank may be guilty of conversion where it has not conformed to the terms of the instructions given to it by its customer – a written cheque is an instruction to make a payment. If a bank makes payment contrary to that instruction, it cannot debit the customer's account. This could be, for example, where the customer's signature has been forged, there has been an unauthorised alteration to the cheque, or where a cheque has been stopped but paid by the bank.

5. Banks and building societies that do not have their own clearing service have to establish an agency arrangement with one of the clearing banks, which undertakes the payments on their behalf.

6. The checks that a bank will make to a cheque that is presented for payment before a customer's account is debited include the following.

    ◆ Are there sufficient funds to pay the cheque? Are the funds all cleared?

    ◆ Is the cheque signed in accordance with the mandate? The signature on the cheque should conform to the specimen held by the bank and the appropriate person(s) should have signed the cheque in accordance with the mandate held.

    ◆ Is the cheque post-dated?

    ◆ Is the cheque in date? Cheques that are over six months old are considered to be out of date.

    ◆ Do the words and figures on the cheque differ?

    ◆ Is the cheque mutilated?

    ◆ Are there any other alterations on the cheque? If an alteration has been made on a cheque, it needs to have been confirmed by the drawer adding their signature.

    ◆ Has the cheque been stopped by the drawer?

7. The purpose of truncation is to reduce the volumes of paper moving around the clearing system, thereby reducing cost and time.

8. The three types of payment made by the Bacs system are:

   ◆ standing order;

   ◆ direct debits;

   ◆ customer credits.

9. If a direct debit has been incorrectly taken from a customer's account the provider must refund the customer and then claim the funds from the originator of the direct debit.

10. 'Float' is where paying customers are debited on day 1 but the beneficiary is not credited with the payment until day 3; providers thereby earn two days' interest on the payment. Float is a legacy of the older BACS payment systems for interbank payments and is now prohibited under the Payment Services Regulations.

Topic 12   Dealing with debt

1. It is important to complete credit agreements in a timely and accurate manner because the document is legally binding and governed by the Consumer Credit Acts. Under the Acts the credit agreement must contain the prescribed terms that clearly define all the conditions of the loan and to which the lender and borrower must adhere. If a dispute arises later on and the customer has difficulties repaying the debt, both parties must understand what their rights and responsibilities are.

2. A connected lender is a credit card company that lends money on credit cards it has issued to customers.

3. If a customer has used their credit card to purchase goods that subsequently turn out to be faulty they can approach the supplier or the credit card issuer for a refund.

4. The FSA's stance on customers in arrears is that they should be treated sympathetically and positively.

5. The main reasons for customers getting into debt are:

   ◆ redundancy or loss of job;

   ◆ ill health;

   ◆ mental incapacity;

   ◆ relationship breakdown – divorce or separation;

   ◆ death of a relative on whom the customer depends financially;

   ◆ bankruptcy and individual voluntary arrangements arising from insolvency of the customer.

6. A lasting power of attorney enables a third party to act on behalf of a customer and deal with their financial affairs. It can give the third party the authority to operate a bank account on the customer's behalf. This power can be used where someone is deemed incapable of making decisions as a result of a mental impairment.

7. 'Hardcore' debt describes overdraft or credit card balances that do not return to credit after salary or wages payments have been received each month. It can also be known as 'structural' debt.

8. A dormant account that suddenly becomes active and is overdrawn might indicate a customer is in financial difficulty. It could suggest that the customer is searching for any available credit facilities to make ends meet.

Topic 13   Lending products

1. A lender relies solely on the borrower's intention and ability to repay when making unsecured lending facilities available.

2. The features of an overdraft are:

    ◆ available for short-term needs of a temporary nature;

    ◆ repayable on demand, so the lender does not need to give any notice to request repayment;

    ◆ the amount lent is usually equivalent to one month's salary;

    ◆ it is a form of revolving credit, which is a line of credit that is restored as the borrower pays off an amount each month;

    ◆ interest is charged on overdrawn balances and an arrangement fee may be charged;

    ◆ the interest charged is higher on unauthorised overdrafts than on authorised overdrafts;

    ◆ the interest rate is usually a variable rate linked to the movements in Bank of England base rate.

3. A customer who has become over-borrowed may find that their overdraft facility is in permanent use and they may be unable to repay the debt. In such cases, the lender may agree to consolidate the borrowing onto a loan account to provide a structured repayment plan and may also include borrowing with other providers.

4. Credit cards are unsuitable for purchases over the longer term because the interest tends to be higher than on an unsecured personal loan, thus making it a relatively expensive way to borrow. Also, to ensure that repayment remains within the customer's control, the discipline of a personal loan with monthly repayments will allow them to budget an amount to reduce the loan each month.

5. The features of a personal loan are that:

    ◆ it is for a fixed amount;

    ◆ it has a fixed rate of interest;

    ◆ the repayments are usually of a fixed amount and consist of both interest and a portion of the capital each month;

    ◆ it has a predetermined repayment date;

- the term of the loan should be linked to the lifetime of the asset, so, for example, a car loan should be for, say, 5–7 years;

- it should generally be used for a specific purpose and sometimes for rescheduling or consolidation of debt.

6. The benefit to a lender of taking security from a customer is that the lender has a secondary source of repayment. Should the borrower default on the borrowing the lender can then claim legal rights to the asset or rights to enforce recovery, thereby limiting its loss. An example is where a mortgage loan is secured by a legal charge over the customer's house. Should the customer default on the loan repayments then the lender may decide, when all other avenues have failed, to take possession of the house and sell it in order to repay the debt.

7. A repayment mortgage is least risky for a customer because they know that at the end of the mortgage term there will be nothing left to pay, as all of the debt will have been paid off. An interest-only mortgage, by contrast, relies on an investment vehicle to pay off the capital outstanding at the end of the mortgage term; the customer is therefore solely dependent on the performance of the investment. If the investment does not perform well they will have to find other means of repaying the debt. Conversely, if the investment does well they may have a surplus, although this is in no way guaranteed, which is where the risk lies.

8. A capped and collared mortgage is a variable-rate mortgage with an upper limit, or cap, above which the rate cannot go, and a lower limit, or collar, below which the rate cannot fall. This arrangement protects the customer against very high interest rates and the lender against making a loss when rates are very low. It also makes budgeting easier: the customer knows that payments may vary but the range over which they may vary is restricted.

9. The factors affecting the margin applied to assets held as security are:

- fluctuations in the asset's price, which could affect the future value of the asset;

- expenses incurred in realising the asset if required;

- time taken to realise an asset, as the longer it takes to sell means the longer it takes to reduce the debt.

10. A lender would be most likely take security in the following circumstances:

- Where the loan is to buy a specific asset, that asset itself may be used as security for the loan. An example is a mortgage loan to fund a property purchase.

- Where loan repayment is intended from the proceeds of a specific asset, that asset may be used as security for the loan. An example is where a bank lends money to a client against the security of an investment that will mature in the future, so that the eventual proceeds of the investment will repay the loan.

- Risks and consequences of the expected source of repayment failing are such that it is necessary to have a clearly defined alternative source, for example where parents are asked to guarantee a loan taken by one of their children because the child's income is only just sufficient to cover the loan repayments.

Topic 14   Making credit decisions

1. Credit risk is the risk to the lender of not being repaid. The skill of the lender is to get money repaid safely, along with an appropriate reward for the risk involved, ie a profitable interest charge. The risk must be managed well across the whole customer portfolio and for the different types of lending product.

2. CAMPARI stands for:

   ◆ Character;

   ◆ Ability;

   ◆ Margin;

   ◆ Purpose;

   ◆ Amount;

   ◆ Repayment;

   ◆ Insurance.

3. Credit scoring has become a popular way of assessing lending propositions because it:

   ◆ removes the subjective human element of the assessment process;

   ◆ enables the lender to process applications faster through the use of technology;

   ◆ reduces costs through automation;

   ◆ enables lending organisations to apply and change a standard set of lending criteria across their branch and other delivery networks through the centralised computer programme;

   ◆ enables the ongoing improvement of the model through the data collected, enhancing the robustness of the assessment of potential borrowers.

4. Behavioural scoring uses information on live, operational accounts to support risk management decisions on these existing accounts. In effect it assesses the customer's track record. Credit scoring is different in that it can be used for assessing applicant risk before business is taken on. While it can be used for existing customers, it can also be used for potential customers who have no track record with the organisation.

5. Credit bureaux collect their information from:

   ◆ information in the public domain:

       – electoral rolls,

       – county court judgment records (CCJs);

   ◆ information supplied by lenders;

   ◆ searches made by other potential lenders in the past six months that could suggest debt elsewhere;

♦ shared industry information databases covering material such as fraud and 'goneaways';

♦ databases supplying geodemographic information.

6. Adverse credit is where an applicant for credit has a poor credit history owing, for example, to late mortgage, rent or credit payments, CCJs (which are records of unpaid debts), individual voluntary arrangements (IVAs) or bankruptcy. It does not necessarily mean that an individual will be unable to borrow, but they will be regarded with great care and avoided by some lenders.

7. A budget is a plan that predicts the income on which the customer might be able to rely in the future and where it might be spent. This is also known as 'cash flow analysis', because it looks at what cash is coming in, what is going out and the net effect.

   If a budget has more income than expenditure, it is in surplus — that is, extra money. If there is no surplus and the customer is just making ends meet, the budget is balanced. If the customer is spending more than they have coming in, then they are either using savings or using debt. Either way, the budget is running a deficit.

   The budget is important to both the customer and the lender as it will indicate if there is sufficient surplus to meet the monthly commitment of a new loan or not. It will also show, for example, how well the customer may be able to afford an increase in repayments if interest rates should rise. If affordability is a problem then lenders will be reluctant to lend.

8. In a situation where a customer has not responded to a request to contact their lender to discuss an unauthorised overdraft, the lender could then consider tougher action such as:

   ♦ returning cheques, if they have not already done so;

   ♦ cancelling standing order and direct debit mandates;

   ♦ cancelling any unadvised internal limits on the account;

   ♦ requesting the return of the customer's cheque book and cheque/debit card;

   ♦ cancelling debit cards so the customer is unable to use them at retail outlets or in ATMs;

   ♦ searching with a credit reference agency in case there are problems elsewhere.

9. A collections team will handle a delinquent debt by:

   ♦ undertaking a full reappraisal of the creditworthiness of the borrower and their prospects of repaying the loan;

   ♦ examining any security held promptly to ensure that there are no deficiencies in the way it has been taken, and that it has not deteriorated in value.

   Assessing the current and likely future position will lead to the agreement of an action plan, which is likely to include encouraging the borrower to 'manage for cash'. This means taking actions that will improve their cash flow generally and hence their ability to service the debt. The action plan may also include a recommendation to the credit committee that the loan be repriced, either upwards (to reflect the increasing risk) or outwards (spread over a longer period so as to reduce monthly payments to a more manageable level). It might also include a recommendation for a refinancing package. This referral to the credit committee may not be practical for high volumes of lending where individual discretion may be allowed up to certain limits.

Refinancing takes the form of a consolidation loan to pay off the existing loan with the provider and any other loans that the borrower has outstanding, so as to bring all the borrowings under one roof. The team will make a direct payment to the other lenders so as to minimise the danger of funds being diverted for other uses. The borrower then has the advantage of a single consolidated loan to one lender, with whom they can work out a single, realistic repayment package. The team has the certainty of some control over the situation and (provided the borrower does not immediately go out and arrange further borrowings with new lenders) knows the borrower's overall status. This arrangement can also protect the long-term relationship with the borrower, who may grow into a valuable customer over time and with the benefit of a fresh start.

Where no refinancing package can be arranged, and the borrower's prospects of repaying the loan appear limited, the team may recommend removing the loan from the lender's portfolio. This can mean that the lender encourages a borrower whose account is not yet seriously delinquent, but who is exhibiting warning signs (late payments, cross-firing), to take their borrowings to another lender. This assumes that the story is not yet so bad that no other borrower would take the customer on. Alternatively, the next stage is action for recovery, and prompt action is required.

10. The recoveries team take over from the collections team once it is apparent that an ongoing solution cannot be achieved and that the customer is not going to be profitable in the long term. They aim to recover as much as is possible and thereafter to sever the relationship. This is the stage of the process where a default notice is served on the customer and the need for legal action arises. The recoveries process frequently involves the need to trace absconded debtors, recover cards and maybe outsource to a debt recovery agency.

Topic 15   Customer service

1. One of the main problems associated with defining a 'good' level of service is that customer expectations are all different, depending on their prior experiences and personal values. Also, services are intangible, inseparable, heterogeneous and perishable and so individual customer experiences may differ when the service is delivered, depending on who is involved and when and where it is happening.

2. The benefits of online service delivery are:

   ◆ reduced time dependence – 24/7 access;

   ◆ consistent service delivery;

   ◆ consistent imagery and branding;

   ◆ customer-led customisation – the customer can choose where they go on the website;

◆ consumer empowerment – the range of choice is available across the Internet without having to visit many different providers' physical premises;

◆ effective separation of production and consumption – the producer of the service can make their information available on their website, which can be used by consumers at a later time and date.

3. Organisations can improve their service quality by having:

    ◆ the commitment of top management to service quality;

    ◆ documented service standards;

    ◆ training and coaching for staff, with the standards required reflected in the appraisal system;

    ◆ a complaint-handling system that encourages the logging of complaints and enables employees to take primary responsibility for handling those complaints;

    ◆ internal satisfaction surveys to ensure that all back-office functions support the frontline employees in delivering service quality;

    ◆ a customer satisfaction reporting system that collects regular data on which action can be taken and training put in place for employees;

    ◆ a commitment to celebrating the success of employees for delivering sales and service quality.

4. Unethical sales activities in financial services are those that pressurise people into making a purchase, or use aggressive sales tactics. Also, tactics that breach codes of ethics should not be allowed.

5. The FORGE guidelines suggest that the four greatest areas of impact for CSR issues in the financial services industry are the community, marketplace, workplace and environment.

6. An organisation might research its service quality with customers by:

    ◆ regular customer surveys;

    ◆ customer panel events;

    ◆ transaction analysis with post-sales questionnaires;

    ◆ mystery shopper activity.

7. An organisation will benchmark its customer satisfaction performance against that of competitors to give an indication of its service quality and its impact on attracting and retaining customers. Benchmarking done by third parties such as *Which?* will be considered quite influential in helping customers to decide the right provider for them.

8. The process for dealing with complaints is as follows:

    ◆ receipt;

    ◆ log and acknowledge;

    ◆ gather data;

    ◆ review and investigate;

◆ decide and calculate;

◆ inform.

9. The organisation must acknowledge the complaint promptly. Under normal circumstances, it has a total of eight weeks within which to resolve it.

10. If an organisation decides to find in favour of a customer following a complaint where a financial loss has been incurred, the customer should be put back into the position in which they would have been had the advice not been given, or had the appropriate advice been given or the incident had not occurred.

Topic 16   Customer retention

1. The benefits of retaining customers are that it increases the profitability of individual customers, positively affects the brand image, removes the cost and effort of replacing lost customers and adds to the overall profitability of the organisation.

2. Churn is the term used when an organisation loses existing customers and replaces them with new customers. 'Churn rate' is a measure of customer attrition. It is defined as the number of customers who discontinue a service during a specified time period, divided by the average total number of customers over that same time period.

3. Advisers can help to retain customers by:

◆ displaying good interpersonal skills;

◆ keeping promises;

◆ being willing to help, so making it easy for customers to do business with them;

◆ inspiring confidence;

◆ treating customers as individuals;

◆ ensuring the physical aspects of the product or service (such as the office, its contents, documentation and staff uniforms) give a favourable impression.

4. Customers switch for eight main reasons (Keaveney, 1995):

◆ pricing;

◆ inconvenience;

◆ core service failures;

◆ service encounter failures;

◆ employee responses to service failures;

◆ attraction by competitors;

◆ ethical problems;

◆ involuntary switching and seldom-mentioned incidents.

5. Dealing with a complaint might help customer retention because complaints that are dealt with to a customer's satisfaction will help to strengthen the relationship rather than weaken it. Often, customers will judge the way the complaint is dealt with in terms of how the adviser deals with them, and if this is done well then they will be more inclined to stay with the provider.

6. People complain for a variety of reasons:

   ◆ they have not received the service or goods they expected;

   ◆ something has gone wrong;

   ◆ they feel that the organisation has let them down;

   ◆ they perceive an injustice has occurred.

7. During a conversation with a customer about a complaint, advisers have to focus on:

   ◆ gathering as much information as possible so that the real problem can be analysed;

   ◆ identifying how aggressive the customer is being;

   ◆ making the customer feel part of the solution;

   ◆ adopting positive words and a constructive approach;

   ◆ respecting the rights of others and compromising if necessary.

Topic 17   The sales process

1. Needs-based sales are important because it is important to ensure that products are not mis-sold or misrepresented in any way and that customers fully understand what the product will (or will not) do for them. It is the most ethical way to sell and, in the long run, the most successful, as customers will recognise that products have been sold to them on a basis of what is right for them rather than what would make the most commission for the adviser.

2. You can show you are listening actively by:

   ◆ saying 'yes' and 'mmm' regularly, but not so often as to be annoying;

   ◆ summarising what the customer has said at regular intervals, perhaps by saying, 'can I just sum up . . . ', 'can I just check my understanding . . .', or 'as you just said . . .';

   ◆ echoing words and phrases that the customer has used (but not sounding like a parrot!);

   ◆ using expressions such as 'as you said earlier';

   ◆ asking follow-up questions relating to what was said.

3. Empathy is defined by Collins Dictionary as:

   'The ability to sense and understand someone else's feelings as if they were one's own.'

Empathic listening is about listening for what is not being said as well as what is being said, and demonstrating your understanding to the other person. Empathic listening is more than hearing the words: it is truly understanding and accepting the person's message and their situation and feelings.

It is a useful communication skill because it:

◆ shows the other person that you care and understand;

◆ helps you learn more about the speaker's issues and concerns;

◆ shows the speaker that you (the listener) are allowing them to vent their emotions and feelings;

◆ can help in defusing a situation, because you invite the speaker to express their feelings;

◆ underpins a good relationship.

4. Behaviours that prevent people from building empathy with others are:

◆ comparing;

◆ rehearsing;

◆ deleting;

◆ prejudging;

◆ preoccupation.

5. Techniques for building rapport with a customer are:

◆ matching your body language with the customer's;

◆ language – using similar words and phrases that match the way the customer sees the world;

◆ pace – matching the pace of the conversation with that of the customer;

◆ volume and tone – again matching with that of the customer;

◆ control – once harmony has been established you can use pace, tone and volume to control the conversation.

6. Closed questions are useful when collecting factual information (for a yes or no response), for summarising or closing a conversation where it is necessary to gain agreement.

7. The potential problems when asking questions are:

◆ impatience on the part of the adviser in not allowing enough time for a response;

◆ multiple questions, ie adding supplementary questions to the original question without allowing the customer time to respond to the first question;

◆ long questions that confuse the customer.

8. The steps in the sales process are:

◆ identifying leads;

◆ gathering information about the customer;

◆ identifying customer needs;

◆ recommending solutions;

◆ obtaining commitment to buy.

9. It important for an adviser to gather information about a customer's attitude to risk as it is essential to take full account of this attitude when giving recommendations to a customer, and attitude to risk will differ from customer to customer. The customer must understand what the risk is, which may mean providing explanations, for example, to distinguish between the degrees of risk.

10. The five areas for a customer's financial needs and objectives are:

◆ protecting dependants from the financial effects of either a loss of income or a need to meet extra outgoings in the event of premature death;

◆ protecting oneself and dependants from the financial effects of losing the ability to earn income in the long term;

◆ providing an income in retirement sufficient to maintain a reasonable standard of living;

◆ wanting to increase and/or to protect the value of money saved or invested, wanting to increase income from existing savings or investments or wanting to build up some savings in the first place;

◆ minimising tax liabilities.

11. It is important to talk to customers about 'benefits' rather than just the 'features' of a product or service because customers should know what the product or service will do for them and how it relates to their needs.

12. The reasons behind a customer objection could be any one of the following:

◆ lack of understanding about the product or service;

◆ lack of interest;

◆ misinformation;

◆ a need for reassurance;

◆ genuine concern.

13. The following techniques can be used to handle objections:

◆ Qualify the objection – this should be used in the first instance to find out whether it is a real objection or a false objection and how important it is.

◆ Ask the objection back – used when the customer says something vague; the adviser should try to define the objection more clearly or find out whether the customer is stalling.

◆ Agree and counter – when an objection is based on fact, all the adviser can do is to agree with the substance of the objection and find a compensating factor to outweigh it.

14. After-sales care be undertaken by keeping the customer informed about any documentation that is going out to them, dealing with related matters such as direct debits or standing orders, any cancellation notices and any request to

alter the agreement. It will also be useful to agree and keep to any reviews that should be undertaken following the sale.

15. Cross sales are important to the organisation because they are one of the best ways of growing the business, improving customer satisfaction and honing adviser skills. Cross selling helps to strengthen relationships with customers, improving customer retention and thereby increasing profits. Customers may also be more reluctant to switch provider if it means having to move several products, so this is another way in which cross selling can aid customer retention. Cross selling can help a provider to fulfil the FSA's requirements, by helping to ensure that all a customer's needs are covered and solutions offered.

Index

e-commerce   104
enforcement   66, 69
Financial Services and Markets Act (FSMA)
   2000   110
Financial Services Authority   63, 109
FSA Handbook   110
insurance   110
Know Your Customer   80
liquidity   75
mortgages   110–111, 213
Office of Fair Trading   68
payment services   32, 87, 112
products   76
Treating Customers Fairly   77
Regulations   96
Repayment mortgages   212
Research, customer   254
Resolution, company   171
Responsibility, consumer   37
Retail banks   56, 61
   conduct of business   86, 112
   service quality   238
Retention   251
Retirement   30
Retirement benefits   153
Revolving credit   207–208
Reward   29
Riba   33
Risk   19, 29
   and interest rates   176
   attitudes to   220, 272
   credit   220, 222
   credit cards   209
   lending   216
   liquidity   75
   personal loans   210
   regulation   74
   secured lending   211
   unsecured lending   206
Risk transformation   56

s
Sales   261, 270, 279
   after-sales care   278
   closing the sale   275
   customer objections   276
   techniques   276
Sales tactics   240
Satisfaction, customer   233, 238, 252
   and complaints   247
   index   245
Savings   27, 29
   accounts   138
   children's accounts   137
   credit unions   60
Second mortgages   150
Secured loans   144, 211

Security   147, 211, 214
Segmentation   4, 26, 136
Self-invested personal pension (SIPP)   153
Self-service banking   158, 161, 234, 237
Serious Organised Crime Squad   82
Service sector   234
   characteristics   234
Service standards   242, 245, 252
Servicing   278–279
Set-off   172
Settlement process   187
Settlors   13
Shareholders   58
Shares   10, 12, 151
Shari'a banking   33
Simple interest   174
Small-to-medium sized enterprises (SMEs)   7
Societies   16
Sole accounts   5
Sole proprietors   8
Sole traders   8
Solvency ratio   75
Stakeholder pension schemes   9, 153
Standard variable rate   213
Standing orders   191
Stopped cheques   189
Structured deposits   139
Supermarket banking   191
Supply of Goods and Services Act   98
Surplus sector   55
Surveys   243
Switching   253
Sympathy   265

t
Tax   10, 152
Tax wrappers   151–152
Technology   64, 162, 236
   credit scoring   223
Telephone banking   3, 159, 161–162, 236, 261
Telesales   105
Term assurance   155
Term loans   210
Text-messaging (SMS)   161, 163
Trade Descriptions Act   96
Trading certificate   12
Training and Competence Sourcebook   111
Training, staff   261
Transaction analysis   244
Treasury services   7
Treating Customers Fairly   77, 198
Truncation, cheques   190
Trustees   13
Trusts   13, 151

u
UK Payments Administration (UKPA)   130, 187

'Unbanked', the   2
'Underground' economy   2
Underwriters   220
Unemployment   199
Unfair Contract Terms Act   99
Unfair Relationship Test   122
Unfair Terms in Consumer Contracts Regulations
   69, 99
Unit trusts   151
Unlimited liability   9
Unsecured loans   144, 205
Unsolicited promotions   80

v
Value   54
Value proposition, customer   233
Verbal communication   264

w
Wants, customer   22, 28, 262
Wealth management   56
Whole-of-life assurance   155
Wholesale banks   61
Wills   14
Winding-up order   171
Working capital   6